THE EARLY CHRISTIAN
ATTITUDE TO WAR

THE EARLY CHRISTIAN ATTITUDE TO WAR

A CONTRIBUTION TO THE HISTORY OF CHRISTIAN ETHICS

C. JOHN CADOUX

A Vineyard Book

THE SEABURY PRESS · NEW YORK

1982
The Seabury Press
815 Second Avenue
New York, N.Y. 10017

First edition published by Headley Bros. Publishers,
London, in 1919. This Seabury U.S. edition published
by arrangement with George Allen & Unwin Publishers,
London.

Printed in the United States of America

Library of Congress Cataloging in Publication Data

Cadoux, Cecil John, 1883-1947.
   The early Christian attitude to war.

   "A Vineyard book."
   Reprint. Originally published: London:
Headly Bros., 1919 (Christian revolution
series)
   Includes bibliographical references and
index.
   1. Christianity and war—History of
doctrines—Early church, ca. 30-600. I. Title.
II. Series: Christian revolution series.
BT736.2.C24   1982   261.8'73'09015   82-3325
ISBN 0-8164-2416-0   AACR2

TABLE OF CONTENTS

Contents

Contents

CHRONOLOGICAL TABLE

Names of Emperors are printed in Capitals.

Many of the dates given are conjectural or approximate. Where two figures are given, they indicate either the limits of a reign or the probable termini between which the date of an event or a composition falls.

In the case of martyrdoms, it is to be noted that the written Acta do not always date from immediately after the events they narrate. The Acta quoted however usually contain for the most part early and reliable material.

A.D.

  14 Death of AUGUSTUS.

14–37 TIBERIUS.

  29 Crucifixion of Jesus.

37–41 GAIUS (CALIGULA).

 ?40 Conversion of the centurion Cornelius.

41–54 CLAUDIUS.

  41 Martyrdom of James, the son of Zebedee.

  47 Paul preaches to Sergius Paulus, proconsul of Cyprus.

  49 Conversion of the gaoler of Philippi.

50–61 The extant Epistles of Paul.

54–68 NERO.

 ?62 The Epistle of James.

  64 Fire at Rome ; Nero persecutes the Christians.

      The Martyrdom of Peter and Paul at Rome.

64–70 The Gospel of Mark.

      The Pastoral Epistles (? of Paul), i.e. 1 and 2 Tim. and Tit.

      The Epistle to the Hebrews.

      The (First) Epistle of Peter.

68–69 GALBA : OTHO : VITELLIUS.

69–79 VESPASIANUS.

  66 Outbreak of Jewish War against Rome.

 ?67 Christians of Jerusalem withdraw to Pella.

  70 Jerusalem captured by the Romans.

A.D.

70–80 The Gospel of ' Matthew.'

The Gospel and Acts of Luke.

? 75 The Epistle of ' Barnabas ' (Egypt).

79–81 TITUS.

80–90 The Didakhe (Syria).

81–96 DOMITIANUS.

93 The *Apocalypse* of John (Asia Minor).

? 94 The (First) Epistle of Clemens of Rome to the Corinthians.

96–98 NERVA.

98–117 TRAJANUS.

100 *The Vision of Isaiah* (= *Ascension of Isaiah* vi–xi. 40)

100–110 The Fourth Gospel (Asia Minor).

The Johannine Epistles (Asia Minor).

? 110 The *Epistles* (Asia Minor) and martyrdom (Rome) of Ignatius of Antioch.

? 110 The *Epistle* of Polukarpos of Smyrna to the Philippians.

112 The Correspondence between Plinius and Trajanus about the Christians of Bithynia.

117–138 HADRIANUS.

110–130 The apocryphal *Gospel of Peter*.

? 130–150 The ' Elders ' cited by Eirenaios.

138–161 ANTONINUS PIUS.

140 The *Shepherd* of Hermas (Italy).

140–141 The *Apology* of Aristeides (Athens).

144–154 Markion flourished (Italy).

? 150 The so-called Second Epistle of Clemens of Rome.

The so-called Second Epistle of Peter.

The *Epistle to Diognetos*.

153 The *Apology* of Justinus (usually reckoned as two) (Rome).

? 154 (before 165) Tatianus' *Address to the Greeks* (Rome).

155 The martyrdom of Polukarpos at Smyrna.

155–160 Justinus' *Dialogue with Truphon the Jew*.

? Justinus' *On the Resurrection*.

? 160 The apocryphal *Acts of John*.

161–180 MARCUS AURELIUS.

160–170 The apocryphal *Acts of Paul*.

161–169 The martyrdom of Karpos, Papulos, and Agathonike at Pergamus.

163–167 The martyrdom of Justinus and his companions at Rome.

? 170 The *Excerpta ex Theodoto*.

173 or 174 The incident of the so-called ' Thundering Legion.'

177–180 Athenagoras' *Legatio pro Christianis* (? Athens) and *De Resurrectione*.

Celsus' *True Discourse*.

A.D.

177–178 Persecution at Lugdunum (Lyons) in Gaul.
180–192 COMMODUS.
180 (July) Martyrdom of the Scillitans.
? 181 Theophilos of Antioch's *Ad Autolycum.*
180–185 Martyrdom of the Senator Apollonius (Rome).
181–189 Eirenaios' *Adversus Haereses* (Lyons).
    Clemens of Alexandria's *Logos Protrepticus.*
? 190 Eirenaios' *Proof of the Apostolic Preaching* (quoted in footnotes
    as *Demonstr*) (Lyons).
170–200 Pseudo-Justinus' *Oration to the Greeks.*
  193 PERTINAX, etc.
193–211 SEPTIMIUS SEVERUS.
  195 Julius Africanus serves under Severus in an expedition to
    Osrhoene.
  197 Tertullianus' *Ad Martyres.*
     ,,   *Ad Nationes.*
     ,,   *Apologeticus.*
198–203 ,,   *De Spectaculis.*
     ,,   *De Cultu Feminarum.*
     ,,   *De Baptismo.*
     ,,   *De Paenitentia.*
     ,,   *De Patientia.*
     ,,   *De Oratione.*
     ,,   *De Idololatria.*
     ,,   *De Praescriptione Haereticorum.*
     ,,   *Adversus Judaeos.*
190–210 Clemens' *Stromateis.*
190–200 ,, *Paedagogus.*
? 200 Pseudo-Justinus' *Cohortatio ad Gentiles.*
  200 Hippolutos' *De Antichristo.*
200–210 ,, treatise *against Noetos.*
  203 ,, *Commentary on Daniel.*
  203 Martyrdom of Perpetua, etc., at Carthago.
? 205 Clemens' *Quis Dives Salvetur?*
204–206 Tertullianus' *De Exhortatione Castitatis.*
  207 Tertullianus becomes a Montanist.
200–220 The apocryphal *Acts of Peter.*
208–213 Tertullianus' *Adversus Marcionem.*
     ,,   *De Anima.*
  210 ,,   *De Pallio.*
211–217 CARACALLA and (211–212) GETA.
  211 Tertullianus' *De Resurrectione Carnis.*
     ,,   *De Corona Militis.*

A.D.

Trial of Achatius at Antioch in Pisidia.

251 Cyprianus' *De Lapsis*.

251–253 GALLUS and VOLUSIANUS.

252 Cyprianus' *Ad Demetrianum*.

,,   *De Dominica Oratione*.

253–260 VALERIANUS.

253–254 Cyprianus' *De Mortalitate*.

254 Gregorios Thaumatourgos' *Canonical Epistle* (Pontus).

? 255 Novatianus' (?) *De Spectaculis*.

Pseudo-Cyprianus' *Quod Idola Dii non sint*.

256   ,,   ,,   *De Rebaptismate*.

Cyprianus' *De Bono Patientiae*.

,,   *De Zelo et Livore*.

257   ,,   *Ad Fortunatum de exhortatione martyrii*.

258 Martyrdom of Cyprianus (Carthago).

259 (Jan.) Martyrdom of Fructuosus (Spain).

(May)   ,,   ,, Montanus and Lucius (Carthago).

,,   ,,   ,, Marianus and Jacobus (Numidia).

,,   ,, Codratius.

? 259 { Pontius' *Life of Cyprianus*.

Pseudo-Cyprianus' *Adversus Judaeos*.

260–268 GALLIENUS. Edict of Toleration.

260 Martyrdom of the soldier Marinus at Caesarea.

265 The *Periodoi Petrou*, which are lost, but of which the *Clementine Homilies* and the *Clementine Recognitions* are later abridgements, and to which the so-called *Epistles of Clemens and Peter to James* were originally prefixed.

268–270 CLAUDIUS II.

270–275 AURELIANUS.

272 Paulus of Samosata ejected from the see of Antioch by the secular power.

275–284 TACITUS, etc., etc.

284–305 DIOCLETIANUS and (286–305) MAXIMIANUS.

270–300 Methodios' *Symposium* (Olympus in Lycia).

Writings of Victorinus, bishop of Petavium (Petau).

293 Constantius Chlorus and Galerius made Caesars.

295 Martyrdom of Maximilianus at Teveste in Numidia for refusing to be a soldier.

298 Martyrdom of Marcellus and Cassianus at Tingi in Mauretania.

? 300 The Synod of Illiberis (Elvira in Spain).

Galerius tries to purge the army of Christians.

303 Outbreak of the Great Persecution.

? Martyrdom of the veteran Julius in Moesia.

A.D.

304 (April) Martyrdom of Pollio in Pannonia.
(Oct.)   ,,   ,, Tarakhos, etc., in Cilicia.
305 Diocletianus and Maximianus resign, leaving GALERIUS and
CONSTANTIUS as Augusti, and Maximinus Daza and
Severus as Caesars.
305 or later (Jan.) Martyrdom of Typasius in Mauretania.
305 Lactantius' *De Opificio Dei.*
,,   *Divinae Institutiones.*
,,   *De Ira Dei.*
306 Constantius dies at York : Constantinus becomes Caesar in the
West.   Maxentius supplants Severus in Italy.
304–310 Arnobius' *Adversus Nationes.*
300–313 'Adamantios'' *Dialogus de Recta Fidei.*
Eusebios' *Praeparatio Evangelica.*
307 LICINIUS made Augustus by Galerius.
CONSTANTINUS assumes the title of Augustus.
309 (Jan.) Martyrdom of Quirinus in Pannonia.
310 MAXIMINUS DAZA becomes Augustus.
311 Death of Galerius.
312 (Jan.) Martyrdom of Lucianus at Nicomedia.
300–325 ? The Egyptian Church-Order.
312 Constantinus adopts the sign of the cross in his campaign against
Maxentius.
Maxentius defeated at the Milvian Bridge, and slain.
313 (Jan.) Constantinus and Licinius issue the Edict of Milan.
Licinius defeats Maximinus Daza in Thrace and publishes
the Edict of Milan at Nicomedia.   Suicide of Daza at
Tarsus.
312–314 Eusebios completes his *Church History* (including *The Martyrs
of Palestine*).
Lactantius inserts the panegyrical addresses to Constantinus in
his *Divinae Institutiones* (I i. 13–16, VII xxvi. 11–17, and
four brief apostrophes in II i. 2, IV i. 1, V i. 1, VI
iii. 1).
314 Lactantius' *De Morte Persecutorum.*
Synod of Arelate (Arles) in Gaul.
320 f. Licinius persecutes the Christians.
Martyrdom of Theogenes and Marcellinus, and of the Forty
Martyrs of Sebaste.
323 Licinius defeated by Constantinus, captured, and shortly afterwards slain.
CONSTANTINUS sole Emperor.
325 Council of Nicaea.

A.D.

330–340 *Acta Disputationis Archelai.*

   336 St. Martinus of Tours leaves the army.

337–340 CONSTANTINUS II. ⎫

337–350 CONSTANS.   ⎬

337–361 CONSTANTIUS.   ⎭

337–339 Eusebios' *Life of Constantinus.*

? 350 Letter of Athanasios to Ammonios (Amun) pronouncing slaughter in warfare legal (Migne *PG* xxvi. 1169 f, 1173).

361–363 JULIANUS, the last pagan Emperor.

  363 ff JOVIANUS, etc., etc., etc.

   363 Gregorios of Nazianzus complains of the character of soldiers.

350–375 The *Testament of Our Lord* (Syria or S.E. Asia Minor).

   ? St. Victricius (later archbishop of Rouen) leaves the army.

   374 Basilios the Great recommends that soldiers who have shed blood should abstain from communion for three years.

375–400 The *Apostolic Constitutions.*

386–387 Ambrosius of Milan declares the rightfulness of military service.

   390 Johannes Khrusostomos (Chrysostom) complains of the character of soldiers.

   400 Paulinus of Nola persuades a friend to leave the army.

       Augustinus argues for the legitimacy of military service for Christians in *Contra Faustum Manichaeum.*

   412 and in a letter *to Marcellinus.*

   416 Non-Christians forbidden by law to serve in the army.

   418 Augustinus' letter *to Bonifacius.*

LIST OF ABBREVIATIONS AND EXPLANATIONS

Ac	The Book of the Acts of the Apostles (70–80 A.D.).
Acta Disput Achat	The *Acta Disputationis Achatii* (250 A.D.) (in Gebhardt, q.v.).
Acts of Apollonius	(180–185 A.D.) (in Conybeare and Gebhardt).
Acts of John (? 160 A.D.)	The section is given, and then, in brackets, the vol. and p. in
Acts of Peter (200–220 A.D.)	Lipsius and Bonnet (q.v.) and
Acts of Thomas (230–250 A.D.)	the page in Pick (q.v.)
Adamant	The anonymous *Dialogus de Recta Fidei* (300–313 A.D.), in which the chief speaker is Adamantios (? = Origenes).
Anal Bolland	*Analecta Bollandiana* (a selection of martyr-acts). Paris and Brussels, 1882 ff.
ANCL	*The Ante-Nicene Christian Library: translations of the writings of the Fathers down to A.D. 325.* Edited by Roberts and Donaldson. Edinburgh, 1867–1872.
Ap	The Apocalypse of John (about 93 A.D.).
Arist	Aristeides' Apology (about 140 A.D.). The section is given, and, in brackets, the page in *Texts and Studies* I 1.
Arnob	Arnobius' *Adversus Nationes* (304–310 A.D.).
Athenag *Legat*	Athenagoras' *Legatio pro Christianis* (177–180 A.D.). The section is given, and, in brackets, the column in Migne *PG* vi.
Athenag *Res*	„ *De Resurrectione*
Barn	The (so-called) Epistle of Barnabas (? 75 A.D.).
B.-Baker *ICW*	*The Influence of Christianity on War*, by J. F. Bethune-Baker. Cambridge, 1888.
Bestmann	*Geschichte der christlichen Sitte*, by H. J. Bestmann. 2 vols. Nördlingen, 1880, 1885.

xix

Bigelmair	*Die Beteiligung der Christen am öffentlichen Leben in vorkonstantinischer Zeit*, by Andreas Bigelmair. Munich, 1902.
Blunt	*The Apologies of Justin Martyr*, by A. W. F. Blunt (Cambridge Patristic Texts). Cambridge, 1911.
Can Arel	*Canons of the Synod of Arelate* (Arles) (314 A.D.) (in Hefele, q.v.).
Can Illib	*Canons of the Synod of Illiberis* (Elvira) (? 300 A.D.) (in Hefele and Dale, q.v.).
1 Clem	The (so-called) first Epistle of Clemens of Rome to the Corinthians (about 94 A.D.).
2 Clem	The (so-called second) Epistle of Clemens of Rome (about 150 A.D.).
Clem Ep Jas	The so-called Epistle of Clemens to James, prefixed to the *Clementine Homilies* (265 A.D.).
Clem Hom	*The Clementine Homilies* (see 265 A.D. in the Chronological Table).
Clem *Paed*	Clemens of Alexandria's *Paedagogus* (190-200 A.D.).
Clem *Protr*	Clemens of Alexandria's *Logos Protrepticus* (180-190 A.D.).
Clem *Quis Dives*	Clemens of Alexandria's *Quis Dives Salvetur?* (circ. 205 A.D.).
Clem Recog	*The Clementine Recognitions* (see 265 A.D. in the Chronological Table).
Clem *Strom*	Clemens of Alexandria's *Stromateis* (190-210 A.D.).
Col	Paul's Epistle to the Colossians.
Commod *Carm*	Commodianus' *Carmen Apologeticum* ⎫
Commod *Instr*	,, *Instructiones* ⎬ (250 A.D.).
Conybeare	*The Apology and Acts of Apollonius, and other Monuments of Early Christianity*, by F. C. Conybeare. London, 1894.
Cooper and Maclean	*The Testament of our Lord: translated into English from the Syriac*, by Jas. Cooper and A. J. Maclean. Edinburgh, 1902.
1 Cor, 2 Cor	Paul's First and Second Epistles to the Corinthians.
Cunningham	*Christianity and Politics*, by Rev. W. Cunningham, Archdeacon of Ely. London, 1916.
Cypr *Bon Pat*	Cyprianus' *De Bono Patientiae* (256 A.D.).
Cypr *Demetr*	,, *Ad Demetrianum* (252 A.D).
Cypr *Dom Orat*	,, *De Dominica Oratione* (252 A.D.).

Cypr *Donat*	Cyprianus' *Ad Donatum* (247 A.D.).
Cypr *Ep*	,, *Epistles* (250–258 A.D.). The first no. is that of the Epistle in Hartel's edition, the second (in brackets) that of the same Epistle in *ANCL* viii, the third that of the paragraph.
Cypr *Fort*	Cyprianus' *Ad Fortunatum de exhortatione martyrii* (257 A.D.).
Cypr *Hab Virg*	,, *De Habitu Virginum* (249 A.D.).
Cypr *Laps*	,, *De Lapsis* (251 A.D.).
Cypr *Laud*	,, *De Laude Martyrii* (250 A.D.).
Cypr *Mort*	,, *De Mortalitate* (253–254 A.D.).
Cypr *Test*	,, *Testimonia adversus Judaeos (ad Quirinum)* (247 A.D.).
Cypr *Zel Liv*	,, *De Zelo et Livore* (256 A.D.).
Dale	*The Synod of Elvira, and Christian Life in the fourth century: a historical essay,* by A. W. W. Dale. London, 1882.
DCA	*A Dictionary of Christian Antiquities,* edited by W. Smith and S. Cheetham. 2 vols. London, 1875, 1880.
DCB	*A Dictionary of Christian Biography, Literature, Sects, and Doctrines,* edited by W. Smith and H. Wace. 4 vols. London, 1877–1887.
De Jong	*Dienstweigering bij de oude Christenen* (Refusal of [military] service among the early Christians), by K. H. E. De Jong. Leiden, 1905.
Didask	Didaskalia (in Funk's *Didascalia et Constitutiones Apostolorum,* vol. i, Paderborn, 1905) (circ. 250 A.D.).
Diog	The Epistle to Diognetos (? 150 A.D.).
Dion Alex	Dionusios of Alexandria (bishop, 247-265 A.D.).
Eiren	Eirenaios' (Irenaeus') *Adversus Haereses* (181–189 A.D.). The bk. and ch. according to Massuet's edition are given, and then, in brackets, the vol. and p. in Harvey's (Cambridge, 1857).
Eiren *Demonstr*	Eirenaios' work *on the Demonstration of the Apostolic Preaching* (about 190 A.D.). I quote the section (and page) in the German version made from the Armenian by Ter-Mekerttschian and Ter-Minassiantz and edited by Harnack (*Des heiligen Irenäus Schrift zum Erweise der apostolischen Verkündigung,* Leipzig, 1908, 2nd edn.).

Eiren *frag* — The fragments of Eirenaios (no. and p. in Harvey).

Eph — Paul's 'Epistle to the Ephesians.'

Eus *HE* — Eusebios' *Historia Ecclesiastica* (finished about 314 A.D.).

Eus *Mart* — Eusebios' *Martyrs of Palestine* (at end of *HE* VIII).

Eus *PE* — Eusebios' *Praeparatio Evangelica* (300–313 A.D.) (sections given as per Gifford's edition, Oxford, 1903).

Eus *Vit Const* — Eusebios' *Life of Constantinus* (337–340 A.D.).

Excerp Theod — *Excerpta ex Theodoto* (? 170 A.D.) found with the 8th bk. of Clem *Strom*.

Feltoe — *The letters and other remains of Dionysius of Alexandria*, by C. L. Feltoe (Cambridge Patristic Texts). Cambridge, 1904.

Gal — The Epistle of Paul to the Galatians.

Gebhardt — *Acta Martyrum Selecta. Ausgewählte Märtyreracten und andere Urkunden aus der Verfolgungszeit der christlichen Kirche*, edited by O. von Gebhardt. Berlin, 1902.

Greg Thaum *Paneg* — Gregorios Thaumatourgos' *Panegyric on Origenes* (241 A.D.).

Greg Thaum *Ep Can* — Gregorios Thaumatourgos' *Epistola Canonica* (254 A.D.).

Guignebert — *Tertullien : étude sur ses sentiments à l'égard de l'empire et de la société civile*, by C. Guignebert. Paris, 1901.

Harnack *C* — *Die Chronologie der altchristlichen Litteratur bis Eusebius*, by A. Harnack. 2 vols. Leipzig, 1897, 1904.

Harnack *MC* — *Militia Christi : die christliche Religion und der Soldatenstand in den ersten drei Jahrhunderten*, by A. Harnack. Tübingen, 1905.

Harnack *ME* — *The Mission and Expansion of Christianity in the first three centuries*, by A. Harnack. London, 1908. ET from 3rd German edition of 1906.

HDB — *A Dictionary of the Bible*, edited by J. Hastings. 5 vols. Edinburgh, 1898–1909.

Heb — The Epistle to the Hebrews.

Hefele — *A History of the Christian Councils from the original documents to the close of the Council of Nicaea A.D. 325*, by C. J. Hefele. Edinburgh, 1872. ET from the German.

Herm *M*	*Mandata* ⎫ parts of the *Shepherd* of Hermas
Herm *S*	*Similitudines* ⎬ (140 A.D.).
Herm *Vis*	*Visiones* ⎭
Hipp *Ant*	Hippolutos' *De Antichristo* (200 A.D.).
Hipp *Dan*	,, *Commentary on Daniel* (203 A.D.).
Hipp *Noet*	,, treatise *against Noetos* (200–210 A.D.)
Horner	*The Statutes of the Apostles or Canones Ecclesiastici*, by G. Horner. London, 1904.
Ig *E*	Ignatius' Epistle to the Ephesians ⎫
Ig *M*	,, ,, ,, Magnesians ⎪
Ig *P*	,, ,, to Polukarpos ⎬ (? 110
Ig *Ph*	,, ,, to the Philadelphians ⎪ A.D.)
Ig *R*	,, ,, ,, Romans ⎪
Ig *S*	,, ,, ,, Smyrnaeans ⎪
Ig *T*	,, ,, ,, Trallians ⎭
Jas	The Epistle of James
Just 1 *Ap*	The first *Apology* of Justinus ⎫ (153 A.D.).
Just 2 *Ap*	,, second ,, ,, ,, ⎭
Just *Dial*	Justinus' *Dialogue with Truphon* ⎫ The col. in
	the Jew (155–160 A.D.). ⎪ Migne *PG*
Just *Res*	Justinus' fragment *De Resurrectione* ⎬ vi is added in brackets.
Karp	*Acta Carpi, Papyli, et Agathonices* (161–169 A.D.) (in Gebhardt).
Krüger	*History of early Christian Literature in the first three centuries*, by G. Krüger. New York, 1897. ET from the German.
Lact *Inst*	Lactantius' *Divinae Institutiones* ⎫ (circ. 305 A.D.)
Lact *Ira Dei*	,, *De Ira Dei* ⎭
Lact *Mort Pers*	,, *De Morte Persecutorum* (314 A.D.).
Lact *Opif Dei*	,, *De Opificio Dei* (circ. 305 A.D.).
Lecky	*History of European Morals from Augustus to Charlemagne*, by W. E. H. Lecky. London (1869), 1913.
Lightfoot *AF*	*The Apostolic Fathers*, edited by J. B. Lightfoot. 5 vols. London (1885), 1889, 1890.
Lipsius and Bonnet	*Acta Apostolorum Apocrypha*. 3 vols. Leipzig, 1891–1903.
Maclean	*The Ancient Church Orders*, by A. J. Maclean. Cambridge, 1910.
Method *Symp*	Methodios' *Symposium* (270–300 A.D.).
Migne *PG, PL*	*Patrologia Graeca, Patrologia Latina*, edited by J.-P. Migne.
Minuc	Minucius Felix' *Octavius* (238–248 A.D.).

M Lugd	The Epistle of the Church of Lugdunum (Lyons), describing the persecution of 177–178 A.D. (in Eus *HE* V i–iii).
Moffatt *INT*	*Introduction to the Literature of the New Testament*, by J. Moffatt. Edinburgh, 1912 (2nd edn.).
M Paul	*The Martyrdom of Paul*, being part of the apocryphal *Acts of Paul* (160–170 A.D.) (in Lipsius and Bonnet).
M Petr	*The Martyrdom of Peter*, being part of the apocryphal *Acts of Peter* (200–220 A.D.) (in Lipsius and Bonnet).
M Pionii	*The Martyrdom of Pionios* (250 A.D.) (in Gebhardt).
M Pol	*The Martyrdom of Polukarpos* (155 A.D.) (in Gebhardt and the Apostolic Fathers).
Neumann	*Der römische Staat und die allgemeine Kirche bis auf Diocletian*, by K. J. Neumann. Leipzig, 1890.
Novat *Spect*	Novatianus' (?) *De Spectaculis* (255 A.D.).
Orig *Cels*	Origenes' *Contra Celsum* (248 A.D.).
Orig *Comm, Hom*, etc.	Origenes' Commentaries and Homilies. The vol. and column in Migne *PG* are added to each reference.
Orig *Mart*	Origenes' *De Exhortatione Martyrii* (235 A.D.).
Orig *Orat*	,, *De Oratione* (233 A.D.).
Orig *Princ*	,, *De Principiis* (228–230 A.D.).
Perpet	*Passio Sanctae Perpetuae* (203 A.D.) (in *Texts and Studies* I 2).
Phil	Paul's Epistle to the Philippians.
Pick	*The Apocryphal Acts of Paul, Peter, John, Andrew, and Thomas*, by B. Pick. Chicago, 1909.
Pol	The Epistle of Polukarpos to the Philippians (circ. 110 A.D.).
Pont *Vit Cypr*	Pontius' *Life of Cyprianus* (259 A.D.).
P Scill	*Passio Sanctorum Scillitanorum* (180 A.D.). The no. is that of the page in *Texts and Studies* I 2.
Ps-Cypr *Jud*	Pseudo-Cyprianus' *Adversus Judaeos* (? 259 A.D.).
Ps-Cypr *Pasch*	,, ,, *De Pascha Computus* (243 A.D.)
Ps-Cypr *Quod Idola*	,, ,, *Quod Idola Dii non sint* (? 255 A.D.).

For notation see above, under *Acts of John*, etc.

Ps-Cypr *Rebapt*	Pseudo-Cyprianus' *De Rebaptismate* (256 A.D.).
Ps-Just *Cohort*	Pseudo-Justinus' *Cohortatio ad Gentiles* (? 200 A.D.)
Ps-Just *Orat*	,, ,, *Oratio ad Gentiles* (170–200 A.D.)
Ps-Mel	Pseudo-Meliton's *Apology* (in Syriac) (215 A.D.). The nos. are those of the section in Otto's version, and the p. in *ANCL* xxiib.
Robinson and James	*The Gospel according to Peter, and the Revelation of Peter*, etc. By J. A. Robinson and M. R. James. London, 1892.
Routh	*Reliquiae Sacrae*, edited by M. J. Routh. 5 vols. Oxford, 1846–1848 (2nd edn.).
Ruinart	*Acta Martyrum P. Theodorici Ruinart opera ac studio collecta selecta atque illustrata* (Paris, 1689). Ratisbon, 1859.
Scullard	*Early Christian Ethics in the West*, by H. H. Scullard. London, 1907.
Tat	Tatianus' *Oratio ad Graecos* (? 154–165 A.D.). The column in Migne *PG* vi is added in brackets.
Tert *Anim*	Tertullianus' *De Anima* (208–213 A.D.)
Tert *Apol*	,, *Apologeticus* (197 A.D.).
Tert *Bapt*	,, *De Baptismo* (198–203 A.D.).
Tert *Cor*	,, *De Corona Militis* (211 A.D.).
Tert *Cul*	,, *De Cultu Feminarum* (198–203 A.D.).
Tert *Cast*	,, *De exhortatione Castitatis* (204–206 A.D.).
Tert *Fug*	,, *De Fuga* (211–212 A.D.).
Tert *Idol*	,, *De Idololatria* (198–203 A.D.).
Tert *Jejun*	,, *De Jejunio* (218 A.D.).
Tert *Jud*	,, *Adversus Judaeos* (198–203 A.D.).
Tert *Marc*	,, *Adversus Marcionem* 208–213 A.D.).
Tert *Mart*	,, *Ad Martyres* (197 A.D.).
Tert *Monog*	,, *De Monogamia* (218 A.D.).
Tert *Nat*	,, *Ad Nationes* (197 A.D.).
Tert *Orat*	,, *De Oratione* (198–203 A.D.).
Tert *Paen*	,, *De Paenitentia* (198–203 A.D.).
Tert *Pall*	,, *De Pallio* (210 A.D.).

The vol. and col. in Migne *PL* are added in brackets to each reference.

Tert *Pat*	Tertullianus' *De Patientia* (198–203 A.D.).	
Tert *Praescr*	,, *De Praescriptione Hereticorum* (198–203 A.D.).	The vol. and col. in Migne *PL* are added in brackets to each reference.
Tert *Pudic*	,, *De Pudicitia* (220 A.D.).	
Tert *Res*	,, *De Resurrectione Carnis* (211 A.D.).	
Tert *Scap*	,, *Ad Scapulam* (212 A.D.).	
Tert *Scorp*	,, *Scorpiace* (213 A.D.).	
Tert *Spect*	,, *De Spectaculis* (198–203 A.D.).	
Tert *Virg*	,, *De Virginibus velandis* (204–206 A.D.).	

1 Th, 2 Th	Paul's first and second letters to the Thessalonians.
Theoph	Theophilos of Antioch's *Ad Autolycum* (181 A.D.)
Troeltsch	*Die Soziallehren der christlichen Kirchen und Gruppen. Erste Hälfte*, by Ernst Troeltsch. Tübingen, 1912.
Weinel	*Die Stellung des Urchristentums zum Staat*, by H. Weinel. Tübingen, 1908.

ET	= English Translation.
f (ff)	= 'and the following page(s)', 'verse(s)', etc.
frag	= fragment.
n	= footnote.

Roman and arabic numerals generally refer respectively to book (sometimes chapter) and section in the case of an ancient work, and to volume and page in the case of a modern work.

Bracketed words in passages translated from other languages are those inserted in order to bring out the sense or make good English.

The Early Christian Attitude to War

INTRODUCTION

WHILE ethics, in the usual sense of the word, do not exhaust the content of Christianity, they form one of its largest and most important phases. And inasmuch as ethics are concerned with the practical duties of human life, it is not unnatural that Christian thought should have included among its various activities many investigations into the rules and principles of personal conduct, and should have carried these investigations to an advanced degree of speciality and detail. The quest however has only too often been marred by errors, oversights, and misunderstandings, with the result that 'casuistry' has fallen into bad odour and has become suggestive of unreality and pedantry—if not of positive hypocrisy. But a moment's thought will show us that every sincere and practical Christian must, however he may dislike the word, be a casuist at least for himself; he must think out the practical bearing of his principles, weigh up pros and cons, balance one principle against another whenever (as is continually happening in the complexities of actual life) they come into conflict, and so work out some sort of a code of laws for his daily guidance. Further than that, Christianity imposes upon

1

its adherents the duty of explaining, defending, inculcating, and propagating the Christian virtues, as well as that of living them out : and this duty is not completely met even by the strong witness of a good example, nor is it cancelled by the important modifications introduced by the subjective differences between oneself and one's neighbour. Casuistry therefore, when properly understood, must always remain an important branch of Christian study, as the science which is concerned with the determination, within duly recognized limits, of the practical duties of the Christian life.

Of this science the history of Christian ethics will necessarily be a very important part. The example of our Christian forefathers indeed can never be of itself a sufficient basis for the settlement of our own conduct to-day: the very variations of that example would make such dependence impossible. At the same time the solution of our own ethical problems will involve a study of the mind of Christendom on the same or similar questions during bygone generations : and, for this purpose, perhaps no period of Christian history is so important as that of the first three centuries. It is true that during that period the Christian mind was relatively immature : it was still in the simplicity of its childhood ; it was largely obsessed and deluded by mistaken eschatological hopes ; it was not faced with many of the urgent problems that have since challenged the Church and are challenging it to-day ; it seems to us to have been strangely blind and backward even on some matters that did face it, e.g. the existence of slavery, and of various other social anomalies. But over against all this we have to set the facts that the first three centuries were the period in which the work of the Church in morally and spiritually regenerating human life was done with an energy and a success that have never since been equalled, when the power springing from her Founder's personal life pulsated with more vigour and intensity than was possible at a greater distance, when incipient decay was held in check by repeated purification in the fires of persecution, and when the Church's vision had not been distorted or her conscience dulled by compromises with the world.

Among the many problems of Christian ethics, the most urgent and challenging at the present day is undoubtedly that of the Christian attitude to war. Christian thought in the past has frequently occupied itself with this problem ; but there has never been a time when the weight of it pressed more heavily upon the minds of Christian people than it does to-day. The events of the past few years have forced upon every thoughtful person throughout practically the whole civilized world the necessity of arriving at some sort of a decision on this complicated and critical question— in countless cases a decision in which health, wealth, security, reputation, and even life itself have been in- volved. Nor—if we look only at the broad facts of the situation—would there seem to be much doubt as to the solution of the problem. Everywhere by over- whelming majorities Christian people have pronounced in word and act the same decision, viz. that to fight, to shed blood, to kill—provided it be done in the defence of one's country or of the weak, for the sanctity of treaties or for the maintenance of international righteousness—is at once the Christian's duty and his privilege. But only by an act of self-deception could anyone persuade himself that this is the last word the Christian conscience has to say on the matter. The power with which the decision of the majority has been—and is still being—delivered owes a large share of its greatness (I say it in no uncharitable spirit) to other factors than the calm, impartial, and considered judgment of the Christian intellect and heart. In the tense excitement and ever-increasing flood of passion called forth by a state of war, an atmosphere is generated in which the truth and reasonableness of the vox populi is not only taken for granted, but elevated into a sort of sacrosanctity, and dissent from it or disobedience to it appears to merit not toleration or even argument, but contempt, censure, and punishment. But however the state of public feeling or the watchfulness of a government at grips with the enemy may check or silence the expression of dissent, however the exigencies of an acute international crisis may lead many to regard the problem of Christianity and war as (for the time being at least) a closed question, it cannot but be clear to those who will look beneath the surface that forces are at work, within as well as without the organized Church, which will not allow Christian feeling to remain where it is on the matter, and which clearly show that the growing generation of Christians is not going to rest satisfied with the variegated and facile answers that have been given to its doubts and queries in this particular emergency, notwithstanding the enormous weight of extra-Christian sentiment with which those answers have been reinforced.

The purpose of the following pages is not to force or pervert the history of the past in the interests of a present-day controversy, but plainly and impartially to present the facts as to the early Christian attitude to war—with just so much discussion as will suffice to make this attitude in its various manifestations clear and intelligible—and to do this by way of a contribution towards the settlement of the whole complicated problem as it challenges the Christian mind to-day.[1] Having recently had occasion for another purpose to work through virtually the whole of pre-Constantinian Christian literature, the present writer has taken the opportunity to collect practically all the available material in the original authorities. His work will thus consist largely of quotations from Christian authors, translated into English for the convenience of the reader, and arranged on a systematic plan. The translations are as literal as is consistent with intelligible English [2]; but the original Latin or Greek has as a rule been dispensed with : full references are given in the footnotes for those who wish to turn them up, and a chronological table is provided as a key to the historical development.

Few fields of knowledge have been so thoroughly worked and amply written upon as the New Testament and the Early Church ; and, inasmuch as no work on Church History, or Christian ethics, or even Christian teaching in the wider sense, could altogether ignore the subject before us, it has been out of the question to make an exhaustive consultation of the writings of modern scholars upon it. I have, however, endeavoured

---

[1] I am sorry to see that Dr. P. T. Forsyth, in his *Christian Ethic of War* (1916), hardly touches (68) on the early Christians' views on the subject (see below, pp. 115, 191), except in connection with the exegesis of the N.T.

[2] See the last observation on p. xxxii.

to get hold of the principal modern works either wholly devoted to the treatment of this particular subject or containing important references or contributions to it. The following list, therefore, is not an exhaustive bibliography, but merely an enumeration with brief comments of such works as have come under my notice.

What may be called the modern interest in the early Christian attitude to war, begins with the great work of Hugo Grotius, *De Jure Belli ac Pacis*, published in 1625. In lib. i, cap. ii, of that work, Grotius quotes some of the New Testament and patristic passages bearing on the subject, and controverts the conclusion that might be drawn from them as to the illegitimacy of all warfare for Christians. In 1678 Robert Barclay published *An Apology for the True Christian Divinity, as the same is Held Forth, and Preached, by the People called, in Scorn, Quakers*: the work had already appeared in Latin two years earlier. Towards the end of it he argued for the Quaker position in regard to war, quoting passages of scripture, and giving a number of references to the early Fathers to whose judgment he appealed in support of his thesis. In 1728 there was published at Amsterdam a book entitled *Traité de la Morale des Pères de l'Eglise*, by Jean Barbèyrac. It was written in reply to a Roman Catholic monk, R. Ceillier, who had attacked Barbèyrac for some strictures he had passed on the ethics of the Fathers. He takes up one Father after another, and thus has occasion to criticize the attitude which certain of them took up towards military service.[1] In 1745 there appeared at Magdeburg a small quarto pamphlet of thirty pages by Johannes Gottlieb Calov, entitled *Examen Sententiae Veterum Christianorum de*

---

[1] See pp. xix f, xxiv, 85 f, 104 f n 1, 141 f, 154 ff.

Militia. It argued that those Christian authors who regarded military service as forbidden to Christians were mistaken. In 1776 Edward Gibbon brought out the first volume of his *Decline and Fall of the Roman Empire.* Chapters 15 and 16 of that famous work deal with the status of Christians in the pre-Constantinian Empire, and contain brief but critical paragraphs on the Christian attitude to military service.[1] The passages are interesting on account of the eminence and learning of the author and his frank avowal of the early Christian aversion to all bloodshed, rather than for their fulness or for the justice of the criticisms they contain.

In 1817 Thomas Clarkson, the great anti-slavery agitator, published the second edition [2] of his *Essay on the Doctrines and Practice of the Early Christians as they relate to War* (twenty-four pages). It was a brief and popular, and perhaps somewhat onesided, treatment of the subject. It has often been republished, e.g. in 1823, 1839, 1850. A Spanish translation of it appeared in 1821. In 1828 were published Jonathan Dymond's three *Essays on the Principles of Morality and on the private and political Rights and Obligations of Mankind.* The last chapter (xix) of the third Essay is on War. The author, a member of the Society of Friends, defends the position of that Society that all war is unlawful from the Christian point of view, and attempts to justify it from the practice and the words of the early Christians, quoting a few examples.[3] In 1846

[1] See vol ii, pp. 38 f, 120 f, in Bury's edition (1897).
[2] I have not succeeded in discovering the date of the first edition.
[3] The third edition of Dymond's Essays was published in 1836, the eighth in 1886. The chapter on war has been published separately, first in 1823, then in 1889 with an introduction by John Bright, and again in 1915 with a Foreword by the Rt. Hon. Thomas Burt, M.P.

there appeared at Philadelphia, U.S.A., a small book on *Christian Non-resistance*, by Adin Ballou. He treats briefly of the early Christian practice, quoting a few passages from the Fathers and from Gibbon.[1] A few pages are devoted to the subject in C. Schmidt's *Social Results of Early Christianity* (published in French, 1853 ; English Translation, 1885),[2] Le Blant's *Inscriptions chrétiennes de la Gaule* (Paris, two vols, 1856, 1865),[3] W. E. H. Lecky's *History of European Morals* (first edition, 1869 : several new editions and reprints),[4] Loring Brace's *Gesta Christi* (1882),[5] and Canon W. H. Fremantle's *Pleading against War from the pulpit of Canterbury Cathedral* (1885).[6] P. Onslow's article on 'Military Service,' and J. Bass Mullinger's on 'War,' in the second volume of Smith and Cheetham's *Dictionary of Christian Antiquities* (1880), contain a good deal of useful information. In 1881 John Gibb wrote an article for *The British Quarterly Review* on *The Christian Church and War*,[7] suggested by the political situation of the time, and dealing mainly with the post-Augustinian age, but also touching briefly on the earlier period. In 1884 appeared a volume on *Early Church History*, which has a special interest in this connection, in that it was the work of two Quakers, Edward Backhouse and Charles Tylor, and as such naturally laid stress on the early Christian attitude to war : the topic was faithfully, though not exhaustively, handled.[8]

Hitherto, however, contributions to the study of the

[1] pp. 61-64.   [2] pp. 282-289.   A new edition appeared in 1907.
[3] vol i, pp. 81-87.
[4] See vol ii, pp. 248 ff of the 1911 impression.
[5] See pp. 88-92 (several quotations from Dymond).   [6] pp. 51 f.
[7] *Brit. Quarterly Review*, vol lxxiii (Jan and April, 1881), pp. 80-99.
[8] See pp. 126-130, 313-317 of Backhouse and Tylor's third edition 1892).

subject had been for the most part very brief and fragmentary. A more thorough treatment of it was attempted by Mr. (now Professor) J. F. Bethune-Baker, of Cambridge, in his *Influence of Christianity on War*, published in 1888. This scholar gave a larger selection of passages from ancient authors and a fuller discussion of them than had hitherto appeared, besides pursuing his subject far beyond the limits of the early Church : but he unfortunately allowed his prepossessions in favour of a particular theory to mislead him in his presentation of the facts and in the inferences he drew from them. I shall have occasion in the following pages to criticize some of his statements in detail. The misconceptions that unfortunately mar his work are the more to be regretted in that it has been taken as an authority by a more recent writer, Rev. William Cunningham, Archdeacon of Ely (*Christianity and Politics*, 1916),[1] who has thus prolonged the life of a number of serious inaccuracies.

In 1890 appeared the first of an important series of works by Continental scholars—K. J. Neumann's *Der römische Staat und die allgemeine Kirche bis auf Diocletian* (The Roman State and the general Church down to Diocletianus), vol i (Leipzig). The book was a new and scholarly investigation of the historical problems connected with the relations between Church and State, and contained a number of paragraphs and shorter passages on the Christian view of war.[2] In 1901 Charles Guignebert brought out at Paris a large work entitled *Tertullien : étude sur ses sentiments à l'égard de l'empire et de la société civile.* He handles the views of many people

---

[1] See the Appendix to Cunningham's book, pp. 249 ff, 251 n 3.
[2] See, e.g., pp. 37, 115, 126–128, 182 ff, 197, 240 f.

besides Tertullianus; and his chapter on 'Le service militaire, le service civil et l'impôt'[1] contains much useful information on the whole subject. The following year, there appeared at Munich Andreas Bigelmair's *Die Beteiligung der Christen am öffentlichen Leben in vorkonstantinischer Zeit* (Participation of the Christians in public life in the period before Constantinus). The book is in two parts: the concluding chapter (4) of the first of these deals with the Christian attitude to military service.[2] The work is on the whole thorough and scholarly, but the author's leanings as a Roman Catholic here and there unduly influence his judgment. In 1902 also came the first edition of Adolf Harnack's monumental work, *Die Mission und Ausbreitung des Christentums in den drei ersten Jahrhunderten* (The mission and expansion of Christianity in the first three centuries) (Leipzig). An English translation was published in 1904–5, while in 1906 appeared a new edition of the original, which was followed in 1908 by a revised English translation. The work is an encyclopædia of information on all aspects of the growth of early Christianity, and contains a full summary of the available evidence on the subject before us, with many quotations from the original authorities.[3] In 1905 Harnack brought out a monograph specially devoted to the early Christian view of war, and amplifying the material he had collected in his *Mission und Ausbreitung*. It was entitled *Militia Christi. Die christliche Religion und der Soldatenstand in den ersten drei Jahrhunderten* (The soldiery of Christ. The Christian religion and the military profession in the first three centuries) (Tübingen). It is without doubt the most

[1] pp. 189–210.   [2] pp. 164–201.   [3] vol. ii, pp. 52–64 (ET).

thorough and scholarly work on the subject that has yet been produced. It has, unfortunately, not been translated into English : and, despite the author's thoroughness, the extent of his learning, and his general saneness and impartiality of judgment, the arrangement of the material, and, in some cases, the conclusions arrived at, leave something to be desired. The same year (1905) appeared at Leiden a small book by a Dutch scholar, Dr. K. H. E. de Jong: *Dienstweigering bij de oude Christenen* (Refusal of [military] service among the early Christians). No translation of this book into English has appeared ; but my friend, Mr. Cornelis Boeke, late of Birmingham, has very kindly placed an English rendering at my disposal. The book does not aspire to that phenomenal level of scholarship that characterizes all Harnack's work, but it contains a large amount of useful material, including some passages from ancient authors which I have not seen quoted elsewhere ; and its generalizations seem to me to be nearer the truth than those of Bigelmair and in some cases even of Harnack.

In 1906 Mr. F. W. Hirst's *The Arbiter in Council* appeared anonymously. It is a record of discussions, held on seven consecutive days, on various aspects of war. The subject of the seventh day's discussion was 'Christianity and War,' and a considerable section of it [1] consists of a freshly written study of the New Testament and early Christian teaching on the subject. The same year was published the first volume of Edward Westermarck's *The Origin and Development of the Moral Ideas*. This comprehensive work contains several chapters (xiv–xxi) on homicide, the second of which

[1] pp. 516–534.

opens with a brief sketch of the early Christian view of war.[1]   Heinrich Weinel's brief monograph, *Die Stellung des Urchristentums zum Staat* (The Attitude of Primitive Christianity to the State) (Tübingen, 1908), touches only briefly on the particular subject we are to study,[2] but is useful and important for the courageous and sympathetic emphasis that it lays on an aspect of early Christian thought which has since been largely snowed under and is often belittled and disregarded by modern students.   The first volume of Ernst Troeltsch's great work, *Die Soziallehren der christlichen Kirchen und Gruppen* (The social teaching of the Christian churches and sects) (Tübingen, 1912), has some interesting references to the early Christian attitude to war,[3] but does not deal with the topic as a complete or connected whole.   More in line with *The Arbiter in Council* and less technical than Westermarck's book and the recent works of German scholars are Rev. W. L. Grane's *The Passing of War* (London, 1912, two editions), which however makes only a few random allusions to the early Christian attitude,[4] and Mr. W. E. Wilson's *Christ and War*, published for the Society of Friends in 1913. The latter was written as a study-circle text-book, and has had a wide circulation among the younger generation of Christians.   The first two chapters of it deal with the teaching of Jesus on the subject, the third with the rest of the New Testament and the Early Church down to the time of Constantinus.   The material is judiciously selected, and the comments are accurate and suggestive.   Other comparatively recent utterances by

[1] pp. 345 ff.   [2] pp. 25 ff.
[3] e.g. pp. 40, 70, 111, 123 ff, 153.
[4] pp. 31, 151, 161 f (second edition).

members of the Society of Friends are an undated pamphlet of sixteen pages by Mr. J. Bevan Braithwaite of London, and Mr. J. W. Graham's *War from a Quaker point of view* (London, 1915).[1]   A brief sketch and discussion of the available evidence was attempted by the present writer in chap. ii of *The Ministry of Reconciliation* (London, 1916).   Archdeacon Cunningham's *Christianity and Politics*—published the same year—has already been alluded to.

The question may quite properly be asked why, if so much valuable work on the subject has already appeared before the public, it is necessary to add yet another book to the list.   The answer is that, notwithstanding all that has been produced, we are still without an English book dealing solely and thoroughly with this important topic.   The problem of Christianity and war is one that claims serious attention even at ordinary times ; and recent events have immeasurably magnified that claim.   It is submitted that, for the adequate discussion and settlement of it, a full and accurate presentation of the early Christian view is indispensable.   Harnack's *Militia Christi* is the only book that comes anywhere near meeting the case : and this, not being translated, is of no use to those who cannot read German, and furthermore is for the present practically unobtainable in this country.   But in any case the subject is such as to lend itself to more than one method of treatment ; and I venture to think that it is possible to present the material more proportionately and com-

---

[1] See pp. 14 f, 23-32. I might also mention a briefer pamphlet issued by the Peace Society, and the Rectorial Address delivered by Andrew Carnegie at the University of St. Andrews, entitled, *A League of Peace* (Boston, 1906, pp. 6 f).

prehensibly—and even, on a few points—more accurately than has been done by Harnack.

No writer on the subject—least of all in these days—can be without his own convictions on the main question ; and a Christian will naturally expect to find support for his convictions, whatever they happen to be, in the words and example of our Lord and his early followers. It has unfortunately happened only too frequently that writers have allowed their own opinions—perhaps unconsciously—to distort their view of historical facts. But a strong personal conviction, even coupled with the belief that it has support in history, does not necessarily conflict with an honest and thorough treatment of that history. While I have not refrained from interpreting the early Christian teaching in the sense which I believe to be true, I trust I have succeeded in preventing the spirit of controversy from introducing into this treatise anything inconsistent with the rigid demands of truth, the dignity of scholarship, and the charitableness of Christianity.

Before we plunge into an examination of the ancient records themselves, something must be said on one or two matters which will need to be kept constantly before our minds if the documents we are about to study are to be rightly understood and interpreted. The first of these is the distinction between what a man holds to be right for himself, and for others also in the sense of his being ready to exhort them to follow it as he does, and, on the other hand, what a man may recognize to be *relatively* right for his neighbour in view of the fact that his neighbour's mind, views, abilities, etc., are different from his own.

The moral standards by which A feels it right to live and to recommend others also to live, he may quite fully realize that B, in his present state of mind, education, feeling, intellect, etc., cannot in the nature of things for the time being adopt ; and he may frankly say so, without prejudice to his own consistency. This simple fact, which I would call the, *relative justification* of other moral standards than our own, and which rests upon our subjective differences from one another, is daily illustrated in the judgments, opinions, and thoughts which we have of others : and yet it is surprising how easily it is overlooked, and how ready scholars have been, whenever they find it, to assume inconsistency and to make it a ground for disbelieving or ignoring whichever of the two complementary moral judgments conflicts most with their own sense of what is proper. We shall have throughout our study frequent occasion to notice mistaken inferences of the kind here described.

Not unconnected with this distinction is another, namely that between a writer's personal convictions as to what is morally right or wrong, on the one hand, and on the other hand statements and allusions which he may make by way of illustrating something else, or of supporting an argument with one who differs from him, when he speaks, as we say, ad hominem, and is not for the moment necessarily voicing his own view. In order to make this distinction quite lucid, examples would be necessary, and these are for the present postponed ; but it is well at the outset to be on our guard against inferring too much from statements and allusions of this character.

Lastly, a word must be said on the conditions of

military service in the early Roman Empire ; for these naturally determined very largely the form which the early Christian attitude to war took.   We must remember in the first place that the Roman soldier was also the Emperor's policeman.   Police duties throughout the Empire were performed by the military.   That fact naturally affected Christian thought in regard to the military calling.   Whatever be the similarity or connection between the offices of the soldier and those of the policeman, there are yet important distinctions between them ; and objections or scruples felt in regard to the former of them might not hold good against the latter. The natural result is that Christian utterances against military service are often less downright and uncompromising than they would have been if the soldier's calling had been in those days as distinct from that of the policeman as it is in ours.   Secondly, it goes without saying that practical ethical questions are not discussed and adjudicated upon before they arise, i.e., before circumstances make the settlement of them an urgent matter of practical importance.   Now the state of things in the Empire was such as to defer for a long time the realization by Christian people of the fact that the question whether a Christian might be a soldier or not was an acute and important one.   It was contrary to law to enrol a slave as a soldier, and Jews were legally exempt from military service on account of their national peculiarities : and when we consider what a large proportion of the early Christian communities consisted of slaves, Jews, and women, we shall realize that the percentage of members eligible for service must have been small.   Further than that, while the Emperor was entitled by law to levy conscripts, in actual practice he hardly ever found it necessary to have recourse to this expedient : the population was so large in comparison with the armies, that the Emperor could get all the soldiers he needed by voluntary enlistment. This meant that any attempt to force a man into the ranks against his will was a very rare occurrence, and rarer still in the case of a Christian.[1] Now no Christian ever thought of enlisting in the army after his conversion until the reign of Marcus Aurelius (161–180 A.D.) at earliest (our oldest direct evidence dates from about 200 A.D.[2]), while cases of men being converted when already engaged in the military profession (such as Cornelius the centurion of Caesarea, and the gaoler of Philippi) were during the same early period few and far between. There was thus very little to bring the practical question before the minds of Christian teachers, not only during this early period, but in many cases even subsequently ; and this fact must be allowed for in studying statements made by them under such conditions. If it be our object to discover the real views of a writer or of a body of early Christians, we shall only land ourselves in error if we treat their words and acts as conveying their considered judgment on problems which—we have reason to believe—were never consciously before their minds at all.

[1] Neumann 127 f; Harnack *ME* ii. 57 n 1, *MC* 48 f ; Bigelmair 25, 175–177, De Jong 2 f.
[2] See below, pp. 113 ; 235 f.

PART I

THE TEACHING OF JESUS

THE RANGE OF JESUS' TEACHING ON THE SUBJECT OF WAR.—There is a sense in which it is true to say that Jesus gave his disciples no explicit teaching on the subject of war. The application of his ethical principles to the concrete affairs of life was not something which could be seen and taught in its entirety from the very first, but was bound to involve a long series of more or less complex problems; and the short lapse and other special conditions of his earthly life rendered it impossible for him to pronounce decisions on more than a very few of these. Upon large tracts of human conduct he rarely or never had occasion to enter, and hence little or no specific teaching of his is recorded concerning them. A familiar instance of this silence of Jesus on a matter on which we none the less have little doubt as to the import of his teaching, is the absence from the Gospels of any explicit prohibition of slavery. And what is true of slavery is also true—though to a much more limited extent—of war. Whatever be the bearing of his precepts and his example on the subject, the fact remains that, as far as we know, no occasion presented itself to him for any explicit pronouncement on the question as to whether or not his disciples might serve as soldiers. It does not however follow that no definite conclusion on the point is to be derived from the Gospels. The circumstances of the time suffice to explain why an absolutely definite ruling was not given. Jesus was living and working among Palestinian Jews, among whom the proportion of soldiers and policemen to civilians must have been infinitesimal. No Jew could be compelled to serve in the Roman legions; and there was scarcely the remotest likelihood that any disciple of Jesus would be pressed into the army of Herodes Antipas or his brother Philippos or into the small body of Temple police at Jerusalem. But further, not only can the silence of Jesus on the concrete question be accounted for, without supposing that he had an open mind in regard to it, but a large and important phase of his teaching and practical life cannot be accounted for without the supposition that he regarded acts of war as entirely impermissible to himself and his disciples. The evidence for this last statement is cumulative, and can be adequately appreciated only by a careful examination of the sayings in which Jesus utters general principles that seem to have a more or less direct bearing on war and those in which he explicitly alludes to it, and by an earnest endeavour to arrive at the meaning that is latent in them.

STATEMENTS OF JESUS INCONSISTENT WITH THE LAWFULNESS OF WAR FOR CHRISTIANS.—I. The first precept of which account has to be taken is Jesus' reiteration of the Mosaic commandment, *Thou shalt not kill.* This commandment appears in the Sermon on the Mount as the first of a series of Mosaic ordinances which, so far from being narrowed down

as too exacting, are either reinforced or else replaced
by stricter limitations in the same direction.[1] It is
included in the list of commandments which Jesus
enjoined upon the ruler who asked him what he
would have to do in order to inherit eternal life.[2]
'Acts of homicide' (φόνοι) are mentioned by him
among the evil things that issue from the heart of
man.[3] It is commonly argued that this commandment of Jesus refers only to acts of private murder,
and does not apply to the taking of life in war
or in the administration of public justice. It is true
that the Hebrew word used in the Mosaic commandment has almost exclusively the meaning of murder
proper, and is not used of manslaughter in war, and that
the Mosaic Law in general certainly did not prohibit
either this latter act or capital punishment. On the
other hand, it has to be noted (1) that the Hebrew
word for 'murder' is used two or three times of a
judicial execution,[4] (2) that the Greek word which
appears in the Gospel passages quoted has the more
general sense of 'killing,' and is used of slaughter in
war both in classical Greek [5] and in the Septuagint,[6] and
(3) that, while there is undoubtedly an ethical distinction between murder or assassination on the one hand
and slaughter in war on the other, there is also an
ethical similarity between them, and the extension of
the Mosaic prohibition to cases to which it was not

---

[1] Mt v. 21 ff, cf 27 f, 31–48.   [2] Mt xix. 16–19 ||s.
[3] Mt xv. 18–20 ; Mk vii. 20–23.
[4] Numb xxxv. 27, of the avenger of blood slaying a murderer ; ibid. 30,
of the officers of justice doing so ; 1 Kings xxi. 19, of Naboth's execution.
[5] Herodot i. 211 ; Aiskhulos *Theb* 340 : cf the Homeric use of
φόνος.
[6] Exod xvii. 13 ; Levit xxvi. 7 ; Numb xxi. 24 ; Deut xiii. 15, xx. 13 ;
Josh x. 28, 30, 32, 35 ; Isa xxi. 15.

commonly thought to apply, but with which it was not wholly unconnected, was just such a treatment as we know Jesus imposed upon other enactments of the Jewish Law.[1]

II. Still more explicit is the well-known *non-resistance teaching* in the Sermon on the Mount. I quote from the version of that Sermon in Mt v: (38) " Ye have heard that it was said : ' Eye for eye ' and ' tooth for tooth.' (39) But I tell you not to withstand him who is evil : but whoever strikes thee on thy right cheek, turn to him the other also : (40) and if anyone wishes to go to law with thee and take away thy tunic, let him have thy cloak also : (41) and whoever ' impresses ' thee (to go) one mile, go two with him. (42) Give to him that asks of thee, and from him who wishes to borrow of thee, turn not away. (43) Ye have heard that it was said : ' Thou shalt love thy neighbour, and hate thine enemy.' (44) But I say to you, Love your enemies and pray for those who persecute you, (45) in order that ye may become sons of your Father who is in heaven, for He raises His sun on evil and good (alike) and rains upon righteous and unrighteous. (46) For if ye love (only) those who love you, what reward

---

[1] B.-Baker parries the force of this argument by an appeal to the well-known distinction between letter and spirit. He says (*ICW* 11–13): " Thus it is that Christ never seems to wish so much to assert a new truth, or a new law, as to impress upon His hearers the spiritual significance of some old truth or law ; to raise them altogether out of the sphere of petty detail into the life of all-embracing principles ; . . . It is essential to our understanding of Christ's meaning to observe that He designs to give a spiritual turn, if we may say so, to the old specific law. . . . So we cannot regard the extension which the law ' Thou shalt not kill ' received from Jesus as a comprehensive denial of the right of man ever to deprive a fellow-creature—in the beautiful language of the sermon on the mount, a brother—of his earthly life." Arguing in this way, the author has no difficulty in proving that Christ " countenanced and sanctioned war " (15, 18). Something will be said later in regard to this antithesis between letter and spirit and the use here made of it (p. 23).

have ye? do not even the taxgatherers do the same? (47) and if ye greet your brothers only, what extra (thing) do ye do? do not even the gentiles do the same? (48) Ye then shall be perfect, as your heavenly Father is perfect." [1] Volumes of controversy have been written as to the real import and implications of these critical words, and great care is necessary in order to discover exactly how much they mean. The obvious difficulties in the way of obeying them have led to more than one desperate exegetical attempt to escape from them. There is, for instance, the familiar plea (already alluded to) that Jesus meant his followers to adopt the spirit of his teaching, without being bound by the letter [2]—a plea which, as has been pointed out by no less an authority than Bishop Gore, commonly results in ignoring both letter and spirit

[1] The Lucan parallel (vi. 27-36) adds to 'Love your enemies' the words: 'do good to them that hate you, bless them that curse you.' Its other additions and differences are unimportant, and on the whole it has perhaps less claim to originality than the Matthaean version. It is worth remarking that the word used for enemies ($\dot{\epsilon}\chi\theta\rho o\iota$), besides being used for private and personal enemies, is also used in the Septuagint, the New Testament, and elsewhere, for *national* foes (Gen xiv. 20, xlix. 8, Exod xv. 6, Levit xxvi. 7, 8, 17, 1 Sam iv. 3, etc., etc.; Lk i. 71, 74, xix. 43: also Orig *Cels* ii. 30, viii. 69).

[2] Thus C. E. Luthardt (*History of Christian Ethics before the Reformation*, ET p. 187) criticizes Tertullianus' view that Christians ought not to wield the sword as soldiers or as magistrates as "the necessary consequence of the standpoint that makes the words of Christ which refer to the internal attitude of the disposition directly into a law for the external orders of life." Cf Magee, in *The Fortnightly Review*, January 1890, pp. 38 f. B.-Baker's view to the same effect has already been quoted (see previous p., n 1). The reader may judge for himself how far astray the latter author's method of dealing with the teaching of Jesus leads him, from the following statement, taken from the same context (*ICW* 12): "The theory upon which the Inquisition acted, that physical sufferings are of no moment in comparison with the supreme importance of the spiritual welfare, is quite consonant with the tone of Christ's commands and teaching." The error here arises from the neglect of the vital distinction between the glory of *enduring* suffering and the guilt of *inflicting* it.

alike.[1] Granting that the spirit is the more important side of the matter, we may well ask, If in our Lord's view the right spirit issues in a 'letter' of this kind, how can a 'letter' of a diametrically opposite kind be consonant with the same spirit? Another hasty subterfuge is to say that these precepts are counsels of perfection valid only in a perfect society and not seriously meant to be practised under existing conditions.[2] The utter impossibility of this explanation becomes obvious as soon as we recollect that in a perfect state of society there would be no wrongs to submit to and no enemies to love.

A less shallow misinterpretation argues that Jesus meant this teaching to govern only the personal feelings and acts of the disciple in his purely private capacity, and left untouched his duty—as a member of society and for the sake of social welfare—to participate in the authoritative and official restraint and punishment of wrongdoers.[3] Whether or no this

---

[1] See Bishop Gore's article on *The Social Doctrine of the Sermon on the Mount* in *The Economic Review* for April 1892, p. 149 : "The vast danger is that we should avail ourselves of a popular misinterpretation of St. Paul's language, and observe these precepts, as we say, "in the spirit,"—which is practically not at all in the actual details of life. . . .Therefore we must apply Christ's teaching in detail to the circumstances of our day."

[2] See for example Bigelmair 165 : "The abolition of war and therewith the necessity of forming armies was indeed certainly one of those ideals which the Divine Master foreshadowed in the Sermon on the Mount and which will be reached some day in the fulness of time. But just as such an ideal appears to be still remote from our present day, so its fulfilment was unrealizable in the earliest times," etc. (see below, p. 253): cf also this author's treatment (100) of Jesus' prohibition of oaths : "The Divine Master had in the Sermon on the Mount . . . held out the abolition of all swearing as an ideal for humanity, an ideal which will first become attainable, when the other ideals of the Kingdom of God . . ., namely that unselfishness, of which the Saviour spoke in connection with the oath, shall have succeeded in getting carried out " (zur Durchführung gelangt sein werden).

[3] See, for instance, an article by Bishop Magee in *The Fortnightly Review* for January 1890 (pp. 33-46) on *The State and the Sermon on the Mount*. Dr. Charles Mercier (*The Irrelevance of Christianity and War*,

interpretation be sound ethical teaching for the present day, the idea that it represents the meaning of Jesus cannot be allowed to pass unchallenged. For in this very passage, Jesus exhibits society's authorized court of justice, not as duly punishing the offender whom the injured disciple has lovingly pardoned and then handed over to its jurisdiction, but as itself committing the wrong that has to be borne: "if anyone wishes *to go to law* with thee, and take away thy tunic," and so on. But further than that, the Lex Talionis—that ancient Mosaic law requiring, in a case of strife between two men resulting in injury to one of them, "life for life, eye for eye, tooth for tooth, hand for hand, foot for foot, burning for burning, wound for wound, stripe for stripe" [1]—was no mere authorization of private revenge, permitting within certain limits the indulgence of personal resentment, but a public measure designed in the interests of society as a restraint upon wrong-doing, and doubtless meant to be carried out by (or under the supervision of) the public officers of the community. Yet this law Jesus quotes for the sole purpose of forbidding his disciples to apply it. We are therefore driven to the conclusion that he regarded the duty of neighbourly love as excluding the infliction of public penalties on behalf of society, as well as the indulgence of personal resentment.[2]

in *The Hibbert Journal*, July 1918, pp. 555–563) frankly recognizes that Jesus' teaching of gentleness cannot be harmonized with war ; but he cuts the Gordian knot by dividing ethics into the Moral realm and the Patriotic realm, penning up the words of Jesus within the former as applicable only to individuals within the same community, and therefore as not forbidding war, which belongs wholly to the latter !

[1] Exod xxi. 23–25 ; there is some difficulty about the literary setting (see Driver's note on this passage in the *Cambridge Bible*), but the scope and purport of the enactment are clear.

[2] Troeltsch (40) remarks, à propos of the teaching of Jesus about love :

III. In entire harmony with this conclusion is Jesus' *refusal to advance his ideals by political or coercive means.* In the one corner of the Roman world where the passion for an independent national state still survived, he had no use for that passion. As the incident of the tribute-money shows, he felt but coldly towards the fierce yearning of his fellow-countrymen for national independence and greatness, and he rejected the idea of the Messiah which was framed in conformity with these aspirations. At his Temptation, if we may so paraphrase the story, he refused to take possession of the kingdoms of the world, feeling that to do so would be equivalent to bowing the knee to Satan. It is difficult to imagine any other ground for this feeling than the conviction that there was something immoral, something contrary to the Will of God, in the use of the only means by which world-rule could then be obtained, namely, by waging a successful war. The idea that the wrong he was tempted to commit was the indulgence of pride or an eagerness for early success does not meet the point: for was he not in any case invested by God with supreme authority over men, and was it not his life's work to bring in the Kingdom as speedily as possible? Assuming that the use of military force did not appear to him to be in itself illegitimate, why should he not have used it? Had he not the most righteous of causes? Would not the enterprise have proved in his hands a complete success? Would he not have ruled the world much better than Tiberius was doing? Why then should

" Thus there exists for the children of God no law and no compulsion, no war and struggle, but only an untiring love and an overcoming of evil with good—demands, which the Sermon on the Mount interprets in extreme cases."

the acquisition of political ascendancy be ruled out as involving homage to Satan? But on the assumption that he regarded the use of violence and injury as a method that was in itself contrary to the Will of God, which contained among its prime enactments the laws of love and gentleness, his attitude to the suggestion of world-empire becomes easily intelligible.[1] Other incidents bear out this conclusion. He refuses to be taken and made a king by the Galilaeans[2] : he does not stir a finger to compel Antipas to release the Baptist or to punish him for the Baptist's death or to prevent or avenge any other of the many misdeeds of "that she-fox."[3] He was not anxious to exact from Pilatus a penalty for the death of those Galilaeans whose blood the governor had mingled with their sacrifices.[4] He made no attempt to constrain men to do good or desist from evil by the application of physical force or the infliction of physical injuries. He did not go beyond a very occasional use of his personal ascendancy in order to put a stop to proceedings that appeared to him unseemly.[5] He pronounces a blessing on peace-makers as the children of God and on the gentle as the inheritors of the earth.[6] He laments the ignorance of Jerusalem as to 'the (things that make) for peace.'[7] He demands the forgiveness of all injuries as the condition of receiving the divine pardon for oneself.[8] His own conduct on the last day of his

---

[1] This view of the third temptation (Mt iv. 8–10 = Lk iv. 5–8) is substantially that suggested by Seeley in *Ecce Homo*, ch. ii.

[2] John vi. 15.

[3] Mk i. 14 f, vi. 14–29, etc., and parallels; Lk iii. 19 f, xiii. 31

[4] Lk xiii. 1–3.

[5] The incident of Jesus' clearing the Temple-courts—often regarded as an exception to his usual policy of abstaining from violence—will be discussed later (see pp. 34 f).   [6] Mt v. 5, 9.   [7] Lk xix. 41 f ($\tau\grave{\alpha}$ $\pi\rho\grave{o}\varsigma$ $\epsilon\grave{\iota}\rho\acute{\eta}\nu\eta\nu$).

[8] Mt vi. 12, 14 f; Mk xi. 25. The context shows that this type of for-

life is the best comment on all this teaching. He does not try to escape, he offers no resistance to the cruelties and indignities inflicted upon him, and forbids his followers to strike a blow on his behalf.[1] He addresses mild remonstrances to the traitor and to his captors,[2] and at the moment of crucifixion prays to God to pardon his enemies: " Father, forgive them ; for they know not what they do." [3]

IV. The words in which Jesus expressed his *disapproval of gentile 'authority'* point in the same direction. " Ye know that those who are reckoned to rule over the gentiles lord it over them, and their great men overbear them. But it is not so among you ; but whoever wishes to become great among you shall be your servant, and whoever wishes to be first among you shall be slave of all. For the Son of Man did not come to be served, but to serve, and to give his life (as) a ransom for many." [4]   The service rendered by the Master was thus to be the pattern of that rendered by the disciples. That this service did not mean the abnegation of all authority as such is clear from the fact that Jesus himself exercised authority over his disciples and others,[5] and furthermore expected the former to exercise it as leaders of his Church.[6]   What sort of authority then was Jesus condemning in this passage ? What difference was there between the authority of the gentile ruler and that of himself and his apostles ? Surely this, that the latter rested on spiritual ascend-

---

giveness at all events is irrespective of the wrongdoer's repentance, though there may be another type which requires it (Lk xvii. 3 f; cf Mt xviii. 15-17, 21-35).   [1] Mt xxvi. 51 f ||s ; John xviii. 36.
    [2] Mt xxvi. 50 || ; John xviii. 22 f.   [3] Lk xxiii. 34.
    Mk x. 42-45 ||s.   [5] Mt xi. 27, xxiii. 10, xxviii. 18 ; John xiii. 13.
    [6] Mt v. 5, xvi. 19, xviii. 17 f, xxiv. 45-47, xxv. 21, 23 ; Lk xix. 17, 19.

ancy and was exercised only over those who willingly submitted to it, whereas the former was exercised over all men indiscriminately whether they liked it or not, and for this reason involved the use of the sanctions of physical force and penalties. There can be no doubt that it was this fact that caused Jesus to tell his disciples : " It is not so among you."

V. Further evidence to the same effect is furnished by *three incidental utterances of Jesus.* (*a*) The first of these occurs in the episode of the adulteress who was brought to Him for judgment—an admittedly historical incident.[1] The Pharisees who brought her were quite right in saying that the Law of Moses required the infliction of the death-penalty as a punishment for her offence.[2] With all his reverence for the Mosaic Law and his belief in its divine origin,[3] Jesus here refuses to have any hand in giving effect to it, and sets it on one side in favour of an altogether different method of dealing with the guilty party. "Neither do I condemn thee," he says to her, "go, and sin no more."[4] The incident reveals the determination of Jesus to take no part in the use of physical violence in the judicial punishment of wrongdoers. (*b*) The second utterance expresses a corresponding disapproval of participation in warfare on the part of his disciples. It occurs in his apocalyptic discourse, in which he

---

[1] John vii. 53–viii. 11 : cf Moffatt *INT* 555 f.
[2] Levit xx. 10 ; Deut xxii. 22–24.
[3] Mk vii. 8–13 ||.
[4] Compare Jesus' announcement—perhaps literally meant—that he had been sent " to proclaim release to captives and restoration of sight to the blind, to set the oppressed at liberty " (Lk iv. 18), and his words in the Sermon on the Mount about judging others (Mt vii. 1 f ; Lk vi. 37 f : the Lucan version has a distinctly legal ring about it). His refusal to be a ' judge and divider ' in a case of disputed inheritance (Lk xii. 13 f) may have an indirect bearing on the subject.

depicts the devastation of Judaea and the defilement of
the Temple at the hands of a foreign foe, and bids his
followers in the midst of these distresses 'flee to the
mountains.'[1] It is true that too much ought not to
be built on this saying; for it occurs in a highly pro-
blematical context, and many scholars refuse to regard
it as an actual utterance of Jesus at all,[2] and the
whole passage, even if authentic, is not very easily explained. Still, if it be a fact that Jesus anticipated a
gentile attack on Judaea and Jerusalem, and bade his
followers flee instead of resisting it, that fact is not
without significance for the question before us. (*c*) The
third utterance forbids the use of the sword in a case
which, in many respects, appeals most strongly to the
modern mind, namely, the defence of others. When
Jesus was being arrested in the garden of Gethsemane,
Peter drew a sword on his Master's behalf and attacked
one of the High Priest's servants. Jesus, however,
checked him: "Put back thy sword into its place: for
all who take the sword shall perish by the sword." [3]
It is only by an unreal isolation of the events of Jesus'
passion from the operation of all the usual moral and
spiritual laws which govern humanity, that one can deny
some sort of general application to the words here used.
The circumstances of the case were of course in a
measure special, but so is every incident in actual life:
and, inasmuch as the grim truth with which Jesus
supported his injunction was perfectly general, one

---

[1] Mk xiii. 2, 7–9, 14–20 ‖s ; cf Lk xvii. 31–37.
[2] On the theory that Mk xiii contains (7 f, 14–20, 24–27) a 'little
apocalypse,' dating from 60–70 A.D., see Moffatt *INT* 207–209.
[3] Mt xxvi. 51 ff : cf Lk xxii. 50 f; John xviii. 10 f, 36 (Jesus says to
Pilatus : " If my Kingdom were of this world, my servants would fight,
in order that I should not be handed over to the Jews : but now my
Kingdom is not from thence ").

might reasonably argue that the injunction itself was more than an order meant to meet a particular case, and had in it something of the universality of a general principle of conduct.[1]

To sum up, whatever may be thought of the weakness or the strength of any one of the various arguments that have just been adduced, it can hardly be questioned that, in conjunction with one another, they constitute a strong body of evidence for the belief that Jesus both abjured for himself and forbade to his disciples all use of physical violence as a means of checking or deterring wrongdoers, not excluding even that use of violence which is characteristic of the public acts of society at large as distinct from the individual. On this showing, participation in warfare is ruled out as inconsistent with Christian principles of conduct.[2]

STATEMENTS OF JESUS AND OTHER CONSIDERATIONS APPARENTLY LEGITIMIZING WARFARE FOR CHRISTIANS.—There are, however, a number of passages and incidents in the Gospels, which are thought by many to show that Jesus' disuse of violence and disapproval of war were not absolute, or at any rate are not binding on his followers to-day; and it re-

[1] The question has been asked, how Peter came to be carrying a sword at all, if his Master discountenanced the use of weapons (J. M. Lloyd Thomas, *The Immorality of Non-resistance*, p. ix : E. A. Sonnenschein, in *The Hibbert Journal*, July 1915, pp. 865 f). The answer is that Peter may very well have failed to understand his Master's real meaning (particularly perhaps the 'two swords' saying—which we shall discuss presently), and, apprehending danger, may have put on a sword without Jesus noticing it.

[2] Well may a present-day scholar, not himself a pacifist, say : " I think, then, it must in fairness be admitted that there is a real case for the plea of the conscientious objector that Jesus totally forbade war to his followers. . . . I cannot shut my eyes to the possibility that Jesus Himself may have been a pacifist " (Dr. A. S. Peake, *Prisoners of Hope*, pp. 28, 30).

mains to be seen whether any of them constitutes a valid objection to the conclusion we have just reached.

I. To begin with, in the very passage in which the non-resistance teaching is given, occurs the precept : "Whoever 'impresses' thee (to go) one mile, go two with him."[1] It is urged that the word translated 'impresses' is a technical term for *the requirement of service by the State*, and that Jesus' words therefore enjoin compliance even with a compulsory demand for military service. But it is clear that military service, as distinct from general state-labour, is not here in question : for (1) the technical term here used referred originally to the postal system of the Persian Empire, the ἄγγαρος not being a soldier or recruiting officer, but the king's mounted courier ; (2) instances of its later usage always seem to refer to forced labour or service in general, not to service as a soldier [2] ; and (3) the Jews were in any case exempt from service in the Roman legions, so that if, as seems probable, the Roman 'angaria' is here referred to, military service proper cannot be what is contemplated.

II. Secondly, it is pointed out that, in the little intercourse Jesus had with soldiers, we find *no mention made of any disapproval on his part of the military calling*. His record in this respect is somewhat similar to that of the Baptist,[3] whose example, however, must

---

[1] Mt v. 41 : καὶ ὅστις σε ἀγγαρεύσει μίλιον ἕν, ὕπαγε μετ' αὐτοῦ δύο.

[2] Mt xxvii. 32 || (the soldiers 'impressed'—ἠγγάρευσαν—Simon of Cyrene to carry the cross). See the article 'angaria' in Smith's *Dictionary of Greek and Roman Antiquities*: "The Roman *angaria* . . . included the maintenance and supply, not only of horses, but of ships and messengers, in forwarding both letters and burdens." The Lexicons give no hint that the word was used for impressing soldiers.

[3] See Lk iii. 14 : "And men on service" (στρατευόμενοι, who had received his baptism) "asked him, saying, 'And what are we to do?' and he said to them, 'Never extort money from anyone (μηδένα διασείσητε), or falsely accuse anyone ; and be content with your pay.'"

not be taken as indicating or determining the attitude of his greater successor. When Jesus was asked by a gentile centurion, in the service of Herodes at Capernaum, to cure his servant, he not only did so, without (as far as the record goes) uttering any disapproval of the man's profession, but even expressed appreciation of his faith in believing (on the analogy of his own military authority) that Jesus could cure the illness at a distance by a simple word of command.[1] No conclusion, however, in conflict with the position already reached can be founded on this incident. The attempt to draw such a conclusion is at best an argument from silence. Considering the number of things Jesus must have said of which no record has been left, we cannot be at all sure that he said nothing on this occasion about the illegitimacy of military service for his own followers. And even supposing he did not, is it reasonable to demand that his views on this point should be publicly stated every time he comes across a soldier? Allowance has also to be made for the fact that the centurion was a gentile stranger, who, according to Luke's fuller narrative, was not even present in person, and in any case was not a candidate for discipleship. The utmost we can say is that at this

---

[1] Mt viii. 5–13 ||. Seeley (*Ecce Homo*, pref. to 5th edn, p. xvi), says of the centurion: "He represented himself as filling a place in a graduated scale, as commanding some and obeying others, and the proposed condescension of one whom he ranked so immeasurably above himself in that scale shocked him. This spirit of order, this hearty acceptance of a place in society, this proud submission which no more desires to rise above its place than it will consent to fall below it, was approved by Christ with unusual emphasis and warmth." This misses the point: the centurion's words about being under authority and having others under him expressed, not his humility or reverence for Jesus, who was *not* above him in military rank, but his belief in Jesus' power to work the cure by word of command; and it was this belief that Jesus approved so heartily.

particular moment the mind of Jesus was not focussed
on the ethical question now before us : but even that
much is precarious, and moreover, if true, furnishes
nothing inconsistent with our previous conclusion.

III. *The expulsion of the traders from the Temple-
courts* [1] is often appealed to as the one occasion on
which Jesus had recourse to violent physical coercion,
thereby proving that his law of gentleness and non-
resistance was subject to exceptions under certain
circumstances. Exactly what there was in the situation
that Jesus regarded as justifying such an exception
has not been shown. If however the narratives given
by the four evangelists be attentively read in the
original, it will be seen (1) that the whip of cords
is mentioned in the Fourth Gospel only, which is
regarded by most critical scholars as historically less
trustworthy than the other three, and as having in this
instance disregarded historical exactitude by putting
the narrative at the beginning instead of at the close of
Jesus' ministry,[2] (2) that even the words of the Fourth
Gospel do not necessarily mean that the whip was used
on anyone besides the cattle,[3] (3) that the action
of Jesus, so far as the men were concerned, is described in all four accounts by the same word, ἐκβάλλω.
This word means literally 'to cast out,' but is also
used of Jesus being sent into the wilderness,[4] of him
expelling the mourners from Jairus' house,[5] of God
sending out workers into his vineyard,[6] of a man

---

[1] Mk xi. 15–17 ; Mt xxi. 12 f ; Lk xix. 45 f ; John ii. 13–17.

[2] I mention this argument for what it is worth, though personally I
incline to accept the historicity of the Fourth Gospel here, both as regards
chronology and details.

[3] John ii. 15 says : καὶ ποιήσας φραγέλλιον ἐκ σχοινίων πάντας ἐξέβαλεν
ἐκ τοῦ ἱεροῦ, τά τε πρόβατα καὶ τοὺς βόας, κτλ.

[4] Mk i. 12.   [5] Mk v. 40 ||.   [6] Mt ix. 38 ||.

taking out a splinter from the eye,[1] of a householder
bringing forth things out of his store,[2] of a man taking
money out of his purse,[3] and of a shepherd sending
sheep out of the fold.[4] Here therefore it need mean
no more than an authoritative dismissal. It is obviously
impossible for one man to drive out a crowd *by
physical force* or even by the threat of it. What he
can do is to .overawe them by his presence and the
power of his personality, and expel them by an
authoritative command. That apparently is what
Jesus did.[5] In any case, no act even remotely com-
parable to wounding or killing is sanctioned by his
example on this occasion.

IV. In his prophecies of the Last Things, Jesus spoke
of *the wars of the future.* He said that nation would
rise against nation and kingdom against kingdom, that
wars and rumours of wars would be heard of, that
Judaea would be devastated, Jerusalem besieged and
taken by the gentiles, and the Temple defiled and
destroyed.[6] It is difficult to separate these announcements from those other general prophecies in which
calamity is foretold as the approaching judgment
of God upon the sins of communities and individuals.[7] In this connection too we have to consider
the parabolic descriptions of the king who, angered at

[1] Mt vii. 4 ||.   [2] Mt xii. 35, xiii. 52.
[3] Lk x. 35.   [4] John x. 4.
[5] "It is the very point of the story, not that He, as by mere force, can
drive so many men, but that so many are seen retiring before the moral
power of one—a mysterious being, in whose face and form the indignant
flush of innocence reveals a tremendous feeling they can nowise compre-
hend, much less are able to resist " (Horace Bushnell, *Nature and the
Supernatural,* p. 219).
[6] Mk xiii. 2, 7 f, 14–20 ||s; Mt xxiv. 28 ; Lk xvii. 22–37, xix. 41–44,
cf xxiii. 28–31.
[7] Mt xi. 23 f ||, xiii. 37–43, 49 f, xxi. 41 ||s, xxiii. 33–36 ; Lk xii. 54–
xiii. 9, xix. 44b, xxi. 22.

the murder of his slaves, sent his armies, destroyed the murderers, and burnt their city,[1] of the other king who executed the citizens that did not wish him to rule over them,[2] and of other kings and masters who punished their offending servants with more or less violence.[3]   These passages seem to prove beyond question that, in Jesus' view, God under certain conditions punishes sinners with terrible severity, and that one notable example of such punishment would be the complete overthrow of the Jewish State as the result of a disastrous war with Rome.   That being so, may we not infer from God's use of the Roman armies as fhe rod of His anger, that Jesus would have granted that under certain circumstances his own followers might make themselves the agents of a similar visitation by waging war?   As against such an inference, we have to bear in mind (1) that wherever the infliction appears as the direct act of God, the language is always highly parabolic, and the exact interpretation proportionately difficult; nothing more than the single point of divine punishment is indicated by these parables; even the more fundamental idea of divine love—the context in which the divine severity must admittedly be read—is omitted. Can we infer from the parable of the hardworked slave,[4] illustrating the extent of the service we owe to God, that Jesus approves of a master so treating his slaves, or from the parabolic description of himself plundering Satan,[5] that he sanctions burglary?   (2) that the difference between divine and human prerogatives in the matter of punishing sin is deep and vital, God's power,

---

[1] Mt xxii. 7.   [2] Lk xix. 27.
[3] Mt xviii. 34 f, xxii. 13, xxiv. 50 f ||, xxv. 30 ; cf Lk xviii 7 f.
[4] Lk xvii. 7–10 (Moffatt's trans).   [5] Mk iii. 27 ||s.

love, knowledge, and authority making just for Him what would be unjust if done by man [1] ; (3) that, in the case of the Jewish war, the instruments of God's wrath were unenlightened gentiles who in a rebellion could see nothing better to do than to crush the rebels ; duty might well be very different for Christian disciples ; (4) that the conception of foreign foes being used to chastise God's people was one familiar to readers of the Hebrew Scriptures, and did not by any means imply the innocence of the foes in question [2] ; (5) that, while Jesus holds up the divine perfection in general as a model for our imitation, yet, when he descends to particulars, it is only the gentle side of God's method of dealing with sinners—to the express exclusion of the punitive side—which he bids us copy, [3] and which he

---

[1] For this view, cf 1 Sam xxiv. 12 : "The Lord judge between me and thee, and the Lord avenge me of thee : but mine hand shall not be upon thee."   [2] Isa x. 5–19 ; Jer l. 23, li. 20–26 ; Zech i. 15, etc.

[3] Mt v. 44–48 ||, cf vii. 11. A similar distinction appears in Paul (Rom xii. 17–xiii. 7), which we shall have to discuss later. I cannot refrain from quoting here an interesting conversation that occurs in Dickens' *Little Dorrit* (Bk ii, ch. 31) :

"I have done," said Mrs. Clennam, "what it was given me to do. I have set myself against evil ; not against good. I have been an instrument of severity against sin. Have not mere sinners like myself been commissioned to lay it low in all time ? "

"In all time ? " repeated Little Dorrit.

"Even if my own wrong had prevailed with me, and my own vengeance had moved me, could I have found no justification ? None in the old days when the innocent perished with the guilty, a thousand to one ? When the wrath of the hater of the unrighteous was not slaked even in blood, and yet found favour ? "

"Oh, Mrs. Clennam, Mrs. Clennam," said Little Dorrit, "angry feelings and unforgiving deeds are no comfort and no guide to you and me. My life has been passed in this poor prison, and my teaching has been very defective ; but let me implore you to remember later and better days. Be guided only by the healer of the sick, the raiser of the dead, the friend of all who were afflicted and forlorn, the patient Master who shed tears of compassion for our infirmities. We cannot but be right if we put all the rest away, and do everything in remembrance of Him. There is no vengeance and no infliction of suffering in His life, I am sure. There can be no confusion in following Him, and seeking for no other footsteps, I am certain."

himself copied in that supreme act in which he revealed God's heart and moved sinners to repentance, namely, his submission to the cross.

V. Difficulty has sometimes been raised over *Jesus' illustrative allusions to war*. There cannot be any question as to the purely metaphorical character of his picture of the two kings at war with unequal forces—given to enforce the duty of counting in advance the cost of discipleship,[1] or of his allusion to violent men snatching the Kingdom or forcing their way into it [2]—a demand for eagerness and enterprise in spiritual things.[3] The parabolic description of the king sending his armies to avenge his murdered slaves [4] has already been dealt with. More easily misunderstood is the passage in which Jesus states that he was sent not to bring peace to the earth, but a sword.[5] But there is no real difficulty here : Jesus is simply saying that, as a result of his coming, fierce antipathies will arise against his adherents on the part of their fellow-men. The context clearly reveals the meaning ; the word 'sword' is used metaphorically for dissension, and a result is announced as if it were a purpose, quite in accordance with the deterministic leanings of the Semitic mind. No sanction for the Christian engaging in war can be extracted from the passage, any more than a sanction of theft can

---

[1] Lk xiv. 31–33.   [2] Mt xi. 12 ; Lk xvi. 16.

[3] Seeley, in the passage quoted above (p. 33 n 1), says : " As Christ habitually compared his Church to a state or kingdom, so there are traces that its analogy to an army was also present to his mind." Seeley has, as I have pointed out, misunderstood the words of Jesus and the centurion about each other ; but Jesus' approval of the centurion's ascription to him of quasi-military power on the analogy of his (the centurion's) own power lends a little colour to the view which Seeley here expresses.

[4] Mt xxii. 6f.   [5] Mt x. 34 : cf Lk xii. 51.

be drawn from Jesus' comparison of his coming to that of a thief in the night.[1] More serious difficulty is occasioned by an incident narrated by Luke in his story of the Last Supper. After reminding his disciples that they had lacked nothing on their mission-journeys, though unprovided with purse, wallet, and shoes, Jesus counsels them now to take these necessaries with them, and adds : "And let him who has no sword sell his cloak and buy one. For I tell you that this which has been written must be accomplished in me, 'And he was reckoned with the lawless.' For that which concerneth me has (its own) accomplishment" ($\tau\epsilon\lambda o\varsigma$). They tell him there are two swords there, and he replies abruptly: "It is enough."[2] No entirely satisfactory explanation of this difficult passage has yet been given.[3] The obvious fact that two swords were *not* enough to defend twelve men seems to rule out a literal interpretation ; and the closing words of Jesus strongly suggest that the disciples, in referring to actual swords, had misunderstood him. The explanation suggested by Harnack,[4] that the sword was meant metaphorically to represent the stedfast defence of the Gospel under the persecution now approaching, is perhaps the best within our reach at present : at all events, until one obviously

[1] Mt xxiv. 43 ||.   [2] Lk xxii. 35–38.

[3] One recent attempt may be referred to. B. W. Bacon distinguishes two sections in Jesus' Messianic programme ; first, the gathering of the flock, when premature Zealotism was guarded against by non-resistance ; secondly, when the flock would have to defend itself. Thus, Peter's sword is " returned to its sheath to await the predicted day of need " (*Christus Militans*, in *The Hibbert Journal*, July 1918, pp. 542, 548, 550 f). But Peter had to sheathe his sword, because " all they that take the sword will perish by the sword," not simply because his act was badly timed : and beyond this precarious reading of the 'two-swords' passage, there is nothing in the Gospels to support the idea of a coming period of violent self-defence, and much that is highly inconsistent with it.

[4] Harnack *MC* 4 f.

better has been produced, we cannot infer from the passage that Jesus was really encouraging his disciples to go about armed. Peter took a sword with him that very night, but on the first occasion on which he used it, he was told by Jesus not to do so.[1]

VI. It is clear that *Jesus accorded a certain recognition to the civil governments of his day*. It is doubtful whether the Temptation-story compels us to believe that he regarded the Roman Empire as objectively Satanic : an explanation of the story has been offered which involves no such supposition.[2] He called the Roman coins 'the things that belong to Caesar,'[3] and bade the Jews pay them to their owner : in the Fourth Gospel he is made to tell Pilatus that the latter's magisterial power over him had been given to him 'from above'[4] : he revered King David and the Queen of Sheba[5] : he spoke of the old Mosaic Law, with its pains and penalties, as 'the word of God'[6] : he reckoned 'judgment' (? = the administration of justice) among the weightier matters of the Law, and rebuked the scribes and Pharisees for neglecting it[7] : courtiers, judges, rulers, and councillors were numbered among his friends and admirers[8] : he was scrupulously obedient to the Jewish Law,[9] and paid the Temple-tax, even though he thought it unfair[10] : he enjoined compliance with the State's demand for forced labour[11] : he would undertake no sort of active opposition to the

---

[1] See above, p. 30.
[2] See above, pp. 26 f.
[3] Mk xii. 17 ‖s : τὰ Καίσαρος.
[4] John xix. 11.
[5] Mk ii. 25 f ‖s, xii. 35–37 ‖s ; Mt xii. 42 ‖.
[6] Mk vii. 8–13 ‖.
[7] Mt xxiii. 23 ‖.
[8] Mk xv. 43 ; Lk vii. 2–6, viii. 3, xiv. 1, xxiii. 50 f ; John iii. 1, 10, iv. 46 ff, vii. 50–52, xii. 42, xix. 38 f.
[9] Mt v. 17–19 ‖, viii. 4 ‖s, xxiii. 2,23 fin ; Lk xvii. 14.
[10] Mt xvii. 24–27.
[11] Mt v. 41 ; cf xxvii. 32.

governments of his day : he submitted meekly to the
official measures that led to his own death ; and his
refusal to be made a king by the Galilaeans [1] marks
a certain submissiveness even towards Herodes, for
whom he seems to have had much less respect than
for other rulers.   Does not all this—it may be asked—
does not, in particular, the command to ' Give back to
Caesar the things that are Caesar's,' carry with it the duty
of rendering military service if and when the government demands it ?   Important as the words about
Caesar doubtless are, they must not be made to bear
more than their fair weight of meaning.   Caesar, it was
well understood, had formally exempted the Jews from
service in his legions ; and the question was, not whether
they should fight for him, but whether they should bow
to his rule and pay his taxes.   To part with one's property at the demand of another person does not make
one responsible for all that person's doings, nor does it
imply a readiness to obey any and every command that
that person may feel he has a right to issue.   Jesus
sanctioned disobedience to Caesar in forbidding his
followers to deny him before kings and governors [2] ;
and refusal to disobey his ethical teaching at Caesar's
bidding would be but a natural extension of this precept.
If it be urged that the phrase $\tau\grave{\alpha}$ $K\alpha\acute{\iota}\sigma\alpha\rho\sigma\varsigma$ and the other
evidence quoted point to some sort of real justification
on Jesus' part of the imperial and other governments,
it may be replied that that justification was relative
only—relative, that is, to the imperfect and unenlightened state of the agents concerned.   The fact
that they were not as yet ready to be his own followers was an essential condition of his approval of

[1] John vi. 15.   [2] Mt x. 17 f, 28–33 ||s.

their public acts. That approval, therefore, did not affect the ethical standard he demanded from his own disciples.[1]

VII. It is commonly assumed that obedience to the non-resistance teaching of Jesus is so *obviously inconsistent with the peace and well-being of society* that he could not have meant this teaching to be taken literally. Thus Professor Bethune-Baker says: " If the right of using force to maintain order be denied, utter social disorganization must result. Who can imagine that this was the aim of one who . . .? It was not Christ's aim ; and He never gave any such command."[2] " The self-forgetting altruism, the ideal humanity and charity," says Schell, " would, by a literal fulfilment of certain precepts of the Sermon on the Mount, offer welcome encouragement to evil propensities, and by its indulgence would even provoke the bad to riot in undisciplined excess."[3] " A country," says Loisy, " where all the good people conformed to these maxims would, instead of resembling the kingdom of heaven, be the paradise of thieves and criminals."[4] This plausible argument is however erroneous, for it ignores in one way or another three important facts: (1) The ability to practise this teaching of Jesus is strictly relative to the status of discipleship: the Teacher issues it for

---

[1] John indeed tells us (xii. 42) that ' many of the rulers believed on him ' and (xix. 38) calls Joseph of Arimathaea, who we know was a councillor (Mk xv. 43), a disciple ; but how much does this prove ? These people were afraid to let their discipleship be publicly known, and the rulers ' loved the glory of men more than the glory of God ' (xii. 43). We certainly cannot argue from silence that Jesus approved of any regular disciple of his pronouncing or executing judicial penalties or acting as a soldier.

[2] B.-Baker *ICW* 13.

[3] Quoted by Holtzmann, *Neutestamentliche Theologie* (1911), i. 229 f.

[4] Ibid.

immediate acceptance, not by the whole of unredeemed humanity, still less by any arbitrarily chosen local group of people (one nation, for instance, as distinct from others), but by the small though growing company of his own personal disciples. It is essentially a law for the Christian community. (2) The negative attitude which this teaching involves is more than compensated for by its positive counterpart. Jesus and his disciples use no force, but they are on that account by no means ciphers in the struggle against sin. The changes wrought by Jesus in the Gerasene maniac, the prostitute, the adulteress, the extortionate tax-gatherer, and the thief on the cross, show what a far more efficient reformer of morals he was than the police. As we shall see later, his first followers worked on the same lines, and met with the same splendid success. Nor is it very difficult to see how enfeebled would have been this policy of Jesus and the early Christians, if it had been combined by them with a use of coercion or of the punitive power of the state. True, as long as man's will is free, moral suasion is not bound to succeed in any particular case; but the same is true also of the use of force. The point is that the principles of Jesus, as a general policy, so far from leaving human sin unchecked, check it more effectively than any coercion or penalization can do. (3) The growth of the Christian community is a gradual growth, proceeding by the accession of one life at a time. Two gradual processes have thus to go on pari passu, firstly, a gradual diminution in the number of those who use violence to restrain wrong, and secondly, a gradual diminution in the number of those who seem to them to need forcible restraint.[1]   The concomitance of these processes obviously means no such "utter social disorganisation" as is often imagined, but a gradual and steady transition to greater social security.

VIII. Lastly, we have to consider the view which frankly admits that the teaching of Jesus is inconsistent with the use of arms, but regards that teaching as an '*interim ethic*,' framed wholly with an eye to the approaching break-up of the existing world-order (when by God's intervention the Kingdom would be set up), and therefore as having no claim to the strict obedience of modern Christians who perforce have to take an entirely different view of the world.   Dr. Wilhelm Herrmann of Marburg presents this view in a paper which appears in an English form in *Essays on the Social Gospel* (London, 1907).[2]   On the ground of the supposed historical discovery that Jesus looked upon human society as near its end, he cheerfully emancipates the modern Christian from the duty of "absolutely obeying in our rule of life to-day, the traditional words of Jesus."[3] "Endeavours to imitate Jesus in points inseparable from His especial mission in the world, and His position—which is not ours,—towards that world— efforts like these lacking the sincerity of really necessary tasks, have so long injured the cause of Jesus, that our joy will be unalloyed when scientific study at last reveals to every one the impossibility of all such attempts."[4]   "As a result of that frame of mind whereby we are united with Him, we desire the existence of a national State, with a character and

[1] The power of Christianity to extirpate crime was insisted on by Tolstoi in his novel *Work while ye have the Light* (ET published by Heinemann, 1890).
[2] pp. 176–185, 202–225.   [3] p. 182.   [4] p. 181.

with duties with which Jesus was not yet acquainted; we will not let ourselves be led astray, even if in this form of human nature various features are as sharply opposed to the mode of life and standpoint of Jesus as is the dauntless use of arms."[1] This view, though quoted from a German author, represents the standpoint of a good deal of critical opinion in this country, and is in fact the last stronghold of those who realize the impossibility of finding any sanction for war in the Gospels, but who yet cling to the belief that war is in these days a Christian duty. In regard to it we may say (1) that 'scientific study' has not yet proved that the mind of Jesus was always dominated by an expectation of a world-cataclysm destined to occur within that generation. The Gospels contain non-apocalyptic as well as apocalyptic sayings, and there are no grounds for ruling out the former as ungenuine. Early Christian thought tended to over-emphasize the apocalyptic element, a fact which argues strongly for the originality of the other phase of Jesus' teaching. His ethics cannot be explained by reference to his expectation of the approaching end. On the contrary, "where He gives the ground of His command, as in the case of loving enemies, forgiveness, and seeking the lost, it is the nature of God that He dwells upon, and not anything expected in the near or distant future."[2] (2) Herrmann maintains that "the command to love our enemies" and the words of Jesus "dealing with the love of peace" are not to be included among the

---

[1] pp. 217 f.
[2] I borrow these words from a private pamphlet by my friend Mr. J. A. Halliday, of Newcastle, and others.

sayings which have to be explained by the idea of the approaching end.[1]   But he does not point to anything in these sayings which entitles him to treat them as exceptional ; nor does he explain how obedience to them—seeing that after all they are to be obeyed —can be harmonized with " the dauntless use of arms."   (3) The appeal to the interim-ethic theory, however sincere, has a pragmatic motive behind it, as Herrmann's words about the *desire* for a national state clearly reveal.   " Thus Jesus brings us into conflict," he confesses, "with social duties to which *we all wish* to cling."[2]   He takes no account at all of the three facts which have just been referred to[3] as governing compliance with Jesus' teaching.   These facts, when properly attended to and allowed for, show how utterly baseless is the prevalent belief that to adopt the view of Jesus' teaching advocated in these pages is to ensure the immediate collapse of one state or another and to hand society over to the control of any rascals who are strong enough to tyrannize over their fellows.   When that pragmatic motive is shown to be based on a misapprehension, no ground will remain for withholding, from our Lord's prohibition of the infliction of injury upon our neighbour, that obedience which all Christian people willingly admit must be accorded to his more general precepts of truthfulness, service, and love.

The interim-ethic theory is, as we have said, the last fortress of militarism on Christian soil.   Driven from that stronghold, it has no choice but to take refuge over the border.   Its apologists eventually find

[1] pp. 178 f., 202 f.   [2] p. 163 (italics mine).   [3] See above, pp. 42 ff.

that they have no option but to argue on grounds inconsistent with the supremacy of Christianity as a universal religion or as a final revelation of God. Most of the arguments we hear about 'the lesser of two evils,' 'living in an imperfect world,' 'untimely virtues,' and so on, reduce themselves in the last analysis to a renunciation of Christianity, at least for the time being, as the real guide of life. In the fierce agony of the times, the inconsistency is unperceived by those who commit it; or, if it is perceived, the sacrifice of intellectual clearness becomes part of the great sacrifice for which the crisis calls. But he, to whose words men have so often fled when the organized Christianity of the hour appeared to have broken down or at any rate could not solve the riddle or point the way, will, when the smoke has cleared from their eyes, be found to possess after all the secret for which the human race is longing; and the only safe 'Weltpolitik' will be seen to lie in simple and childlike obedience to him who said: "Happy are the gentle, for they will inherit the earth."

In chalking out the main divisions of our subject from this point onwards, it is not proposed to give the first place to any set of chronological landmarks between the death of Jesus about 29 A.D. and the triumph of Constantinus about 313 A.D. This does not mean that the Christian attitude to war underwent no change in the course of that long period; but such changes as there were it will be convenient to study within subdivisions founded on the subject-matter rather than on the lapse of time. The material —excluding the final summary and comments—falls naturally into two main divisions, firstly, the various forms in which the Christian disapproval of war expressed itself, such as the condemnation of it in the abstract, the emphasis laid on the essential peacefulness of Christianity, the place of gentleness and non-resistance in Christian ethics, the Christians' experience of the evils of military life and character, and their refusal to act as soldiers themselves; and secondly, the various forms of what we may call the Christian acceptance or quasi-acceptance of war, ranging from such ideal realms as Scriptural history, spiritual warfare, and so on, right up to the actual service of Christians in the Roman armies.[1] When we have examined these two complementary phases of the subject, we shall be in a position to sum up the situation —particularly the settlement involved in the Church's alliance with Constantinus, and to offer a few general observations on the question as a whole.

[1] The reader is reminded that the dates of the early Christian authors and books quoted and events referred to are given in the chronological table at the beginning of the book, in order to avoid unnecessary explanations and repetitions in the text, and that with the same object full particulars of works quoted are given in another list, the references in the footnotes being mostly in an abbreviated form.

PART II

FORMS OF THE EARLY CHRISTIAN DISAPPROVAL OF WAR

THE CONDEMNATION OF WAR IN THE ABSTRACT.[1]— The conditions under which the books of the New Testament were written were not such as to give occasion for Christian utterances on the wrongfulness of war. The few New Testament passages expressing disapprobation of 'wars' and 'battles'[2] probably refer in every case, not to military conflicts, but to strife and dissension in the more general sense. Reflection is, however, cast on the incessant wars of men in 'The Vision of Isaiah': the prophet ascends to the firmament, "and there I saw Sammael and his hosts, and there was great fighting therein, and the angels of Satan were envying one another. And as above, so on the earth also; for the likeness of that which is in the firmament is here on the earth. And I said unto the angel who was with me: 'What is this war, and what is this envying?' And he said unto me: 'So has it been since this world

[1] No purpose would be served by retailing to the reader passages in which war is cited simply as a calamity or as a mere historical incident, without any direct hint of moral blame or of divine visitation.

[2] 2 Cor vii. 5 ("wrangling all round me"—Moffatt); Jas iv. 1 f (even if the proposed substitution of φθονεῖτε (ye envy) for φονεύετε (ye kill) in verse 2 be rejected, and the latter given its literal meaning (so Mayor), the reference can hardly be to warfare as usually understood); 2 Tim ii. 23 f; Tit iii. 9.

was made until now, and this war will continue till He whom thou shalt see will come and destroy him.'"[1] Aristeides attributed the prevalence of war—chiefly among the Greeks—to the erroneous views of men as to the nature of their gods, whom they pictured as waging war: "for if their gods did such things, why should they themselves not do them? thus from this pursuit of error it has fallen to men's lot to have continual wars and massacres and bitter captivity."[2] He specially mentions Ares and Herakles as discredited by their warlike character.[3] Justinus said that it was the evil angels and their offspring the demons who "sowed murders, wars, adulteries, excesses, and every wickedness, among men."[4] Tatianus equated war and murder, and said that the demons excited war by means of oracles. "Thou wishest to make war," he says to the gentile, "and thou takest Apollon (as thy) counsellor in murder" (σύμβουλον τῶν φόνων). He refers to Apollon as the one "who raises up seditions and battles" and "makes announcements about victory in war."[5] Athenagoras instances the usages of unjust war—the slaughter of myriads of men, the razing of cities, the burning of houses with their inhabitants, the devastation of land, and the destruction of entire populations—as samples of the worst sins, such as could not be adequately punished by any amount of suffering in this life.[6] He also says that Christians cannot endure to see a man put to death, even justly.[7] In the apocryphal Acts of

---

[1] Charles, *The Ascension of Isaiah* (vii. 9–12) p. 48, cf 74 (x. 29–31).
[2] Arist 8 (104).   [3] Arist 10 (106 and—Syriac—43).
[4] Just 2 *Ap* v. 4. When the martyr Karpos at Pergamum accused the devil of preparing wars (*Karp* 17), he was referring to the persecutions carried on against the Christians.   [5] Tat 19 (849).   [6] Athenag *Res* 19 (1013).
[7] Athenag *Legat* 35 (969). We shall discuss later the qualification 'even justly.'

John, the apostle tells the Ephesians that military conquerors, along with kings, princes, tyrants, and boasters, will depart hence naked, and suffer eternal pains.[1]

Clemens of Alexandria casts aspersions on the multifarious preparation necessary for war, as contrasted with peace and love, and on the type of music patronized by " those who are practised in war and who have despised the divine fear."[2]   He likens the Christian poor to " an army without weapons, without war, without bloodshed, without anger, without defilement."[3]   In the Pseudo-Justinian ' Address to the Greeks,' the readers are exhorted : " Be instructed by the Divine Word, and learn (about) the incorruptible King, and know His heroes, who never inflict slaughter on (the) peoples."[4] Tertullianus says that when Peter cut off Malchus' ear, Jesus " cursed the works of the sword for ever after."[5]   He criticizes the gentiles' greed of gold in hiring themselves out for military service.[6]   He objects to the literal interpretation of Psalm xlv. 3 f as applied to Christ : ' Gird the sword upon (thy) thigh . . . extend and prosper and reign, on account of truth and gentleness and justice ': " Who shall produce these (results) with the sword," he asks, " and not rather those that are contrary to gentleness and justice, (namely), deceit and harshness and injustice, (which are) of course the proper business of battles ? "[7]   " Is the laurel of triumph," he asks elsewhere, " made up of leaves. or of corpses ? is it decorated with ribbons, or tombs ? is it besmeared with

---

[1] *Acts of John* 36 fin (ii. 169 ; Pick 148).
[2] Clem *Paed* I xii. 99, II iv. 42.
[3] Clem *Quis Dives* 34.   [4] Ps-Just *Orat* 5 init.
[5] Tert *Pat* 3 (i. 1254) : itaque et gladii opera maledixit in posterum.
[6] Tert *Pat* 7 (i. 1262).   [7] Tert. *Marc* iii. 14 (ii. 340), *Jud* 9 (ii. 621).

ointments, or with the tears of wives and mothers, perhaps those of some men even (who are) Christians— for Christ (is) among the barbarians as well?"[1]   Hippolutos, in his commentary on Daniel, explains the wild beasts that lived under the tree in Nebuchadnezzar's dream as "the warriors and armies, which adhered to the king, carrying out what was commanded (them), being ready like wild beasts for making war and destroying, and for rending men like wild beasts."[2]   One of the features of the Roman Empire, when viewed by this writer as the Fourth Beast and as a Satanic imitation of the Christian Church, was its preparation for war, and its collection of the noblest men from all countries as its warriors.[3]   The Bardesanic 'Book of the Laws of the Countries' mentions the law of the Seres (a mysterious Eastern people) forbidding to kill, and the frequency with which kings seize countries which do not belong to them, and abolish their laws.[4]   Origenes spoke depreciatively of the military and juridical professions as being prized by ignorant and blind seekers for wealth and glory.[5]

Cyprianus declaims about the "wars scattered everywhere with the bloody horror of camps.   The world," he says, "is wet with mutual blood(shed): and homicide is a crime when individuals commit it, (but) it is called a virtue, when it is carried on publicly.   Not the reason of innocence, but the magnitude of savagery, demands impunity for crimes."   He censures also the vanity and

---

[1] Tert *Cor* 12 (ii. 94 f). In *Pudic* 10 (ii. 999), he groups soldiers with tax-gatherers as those to whom, besides the sons of Abraham, the Baptist preached repentance.   [2] Hipp *Dan* III viii. 9.
[3] Hipp *Dan* IV viii. 7, ix. 2.   [4] *ANCL* xxiib. 101, 108.
[5] Greg Thaum *Paneg* vi. 76 f.   On the low idea entertained of the soldier's calling in the third century, and particularly by philosophers and Christians, see Harnack *MC* 69 f.

deceitful pomp of the military office.[1] "What use is it," asks Commodianus, "to know about the vices of kings and their wars?"[2] Gregorios censures certain Christians for seizing the property of others in compensation for what they had lost in a raid made by the barbarians : just as the latter, he says, had "inflicted the (havoc) of war" on these Christians, they were acting similarly towards others.[3] The Didaskalia forbids the receipt of monetary help for the church from "any of the magistrates of the Roman Empire, who are polluted by war."[4] The Pseudo-Justinian Cohortatio censures the god Zeus as being in Homer's words "disposer of the wars of men."[5] In the Clementine Homilies, Peter asks, if God loves war, who wishes for peace?,[6] speaks obscurely of a female prophecy, who, "when she conceives and brings forth temporary kings, stirs up wars, which shed much blood,"[7] and points his hearers to the continual wars going on even in their day owing to the existence of many kings[8] ; Zacchaeus depicts the heretic Simon as 'standing like a general, guarded by the crowd'[9]; and Clemens tells the Greeks that the lusts of the flesh must be sins, because they beget wars, murders, and confusion.[10] Similarly in the Recognitions, Peter pleads that a decision by truth and worth is better than a decision by force of arms,[11] and says : " Wars and con-

---

[1] Cypr *Donat* 6, 10 f. In *Ep* 73 (72) 4 he calls heretics pestes et gladii.
[2] Commod *Carm* 585 f; cf *Instr* i. 34 (l. 12), ii. 3 (ll. 12 f), 22.
[3] Greg Thaum *Ep Can* 5 (τὰ πολέμου εἰργάσαντο).
[4] *Didask* IV vi. 4 (omni magistratu imperii Romani, qui in bellis maculati sunt). We are left uncertain as to whether all—or only some—magistrates are spurned as bloodstained : but probably the latter is meant.
[5] Ps-Just *Cohort* 2 (Hom *Il* xix. 224) : ἀνθρώπων ταμίης πολέμοιο. Cf 17 (wars etc. represented by Homer as the result of a multiplicity of rulers).   [6] *Clem Hom* ii. 44.   [7] op cit iii. 24, cf 25 fin, 26.
[8] *op cit* iii. 62 ; cf ix. 2 f.   [9] op cit iii. 29.
[10] *op cit* iv. 20.   [11] *Clem Recog* ii. 24.

tests are born from sins ; but where sin is not committed, there is peace to the soul,"[1] "hence" (i.e. from idol-worship) "the madness of wars blazed out"[2]; and Niceta remarks that implacable wars arise from lust.[3] Methodios says that the nations, intoxicated by the devil, sharpen their passions for murderous battles,[4] and speaks of the bloody wars of the past.[5]

The treatise of Arnobius abounds in allusions to the moral iniquity of war. Contrasting Christ with the rulers of the Roman Empire, he asks : " Did he, claiming royal power for himself, occupy the whole world with fierce legions, and, (of) nations at peace from the be-ginning, destroy and remove some, and compel others to put their necks beneath his yoke and obey him?"[6] "What use is it to the world that there should be . . . generals of the greatest experience in warfare, skilled in the capture of cities, (and) soldiers immoveable and invincible in cavalry battles or in a fight on foot?"[7] Arnobius roundly denies that it was any part of the divine purpose that men's souls, "forgetting that they are from one source, one parent and head, should tear up and break down the rights of kinship, overturn their cities, devastate lands in enmity, make slaves of free-men, violate maidens and other men's wives, hate one another, envy the joys and good fortune of others, in a word all curse, carp at, and rend one another with the biting of savage teeth."[8] He rejects with indignation the pagan idea that divine beings could patronize, or take pleasure or interest in, human wars. Speaking of Mars, for instance, he says : " If he is the one who allays

[1] *op cit* ii. 36.　　　　[2] *op cit* iv. 31.　　　　[3] *op cit* x. 41.
[4] Method *Symp* v. 5.　　[5] *op cit* x. 1, 4.　　　[6] Arnob ii. 1.
[7] id ii. 38.　　　　　　[8] id ii. 45.

the madness of war, why do wars never cease for a day? But if he is the author of them, we shall therefore say that a god, for the indulgence of his own pleasure, brings the whole world into collision, sows causes of dissension and strife among nations separated by distance of lands, brings together from different (quarters) so many thousands of mortals and speedily heaps the fields with corpses, makes blood flow in torrents, destroys the stablest empires, levels cities with the ground, takes away liberty from the freeborn and imposes (on them) the state of slavery, rejoices in civil broils, in the fratricidal death of brothers who die together and in the parricidal horror of mortal conflict between sons and fathers." [1]

Lactantius also, in his 'Divine Institutes,' again and again alludes to the prevalence of war as one of the great blots on the history and morals of humanity. I quote three only of the numerous passages. Speaking of the Romans, he says: "They despise indeed the excellence of the athlete, because there is no harm in it; but royal excellence, because it is wont to do harm extensively, they so admire that they think that brave and warlike generals are placed in the assembly of the gods, and that there is no other way to immortality than by leading armies, devastating foreign (countries), destroying cities, overthrowing towns, (and) either slaughtering or enslaving free peoples. Truly, the more men they have afflicted, despoiled, (and) slain, the more noble and renowned do they think themselves; and, captured by the appearance of empty glory, they give the name of excellence to their

---

[1] Arnob iii. 26. Rhetorical allusions to this and other aspects of the wrongfulness of war occur in ii. 39, 76, iii. 28, v. 45, vi. 2, vii. 9, 36, 51.

crimes. Now I would rather that they should make gods for themselves from the slaughter of wild beasts than that they should approve of an immortality so bloody. If any one has slain a single man, he is regarded as contaminated and wicked, nor do they think it right that he should be admitted to this earthly dwelling of the gods. But he who has slaughtered endless thousands of men, deluged the fields with blood, (and) infected rivers (with it), is admitted not only to a temple, but even to heaven." [1] "They believe that the gods love whatever they themselves desire, whatever it is for the sake of which acts of theft and homicide and brigandage rage every day, for the sake of which wars throughout the whole world overturn peoples and cities." [2] In criticizing the definition of virtue as that which puts first the advantages of one's country, he points out that this means the extension of the national boundaries by means of aggressive wars on neighbouring states, and so on: "all which things are certainly not virtues, but the overthrowing of virtues. For, in the first place, the connection of human society is taken away; innocence is taken away; abstention from (what is) another's is taken away; in fact, justice itself is taken away; for justice cannot bear the cutting asunder of the human race, and, wherever arms glitter, she must be put to flight and banished. . . . For how can he be just, who injures, hates, despoils, kills? And those who strive to be of advantage to their country do all these things." [3] Eusebios ascribed the incessant occurrence of

---

[1] Lact *Inst* I xviii. 8–10 ; cf 11–17.   [2] Lact *Inst* II vi. 3.
[3] Lact *Inst* VI vi. 18–24.   The words quoted are taken from 19 f, 22. For other passages dealing with the subject, see *Inst* I xix. 6, V v. 4, 12–14, vi. 6 f, VI v. 15, xix. 2 f, 10, VII xv. 9 ff.

furious wars in pre-Christian times, not only to the multiplicity of rulers before the establishment of the Roman Empire, but also to the instigation of the demons who tyrannized over the nations that worshipped them.[1] He refers to Ares as "the demon who is the bane of mortals and the lover of war"[2] and remarks that "the din of strife, and battles, and wars, are the concern of Athena, but not peace or the things of peace."[3]

This collection of passages will suffice to show how strong and deep was the early Christian revulsion from and disapproval of war, both on account of the dissension it represented and of the infliction of bloodshed and suffering which it involved. The quotations show further how closely warfare and murder were connected in Christian thought by their possession of a common element—homicide ; and the connection gives a fresh significance for the subject before us to the extreme Christian sensitiveness in regard to the sin of murder—a sensitiveness attested by the frequency with which warnings, prohibitions, and condemnations in regard to this particular sin were uttered and the severity with which the Church dealt with the commission of it by any of her own members. The strong disapprobation felt by Christians for war was due to its close relationship with the deadly sin that sufficed to keep the man guilty of it permanently outside the Christian community.[4]

---

[1] Eus *PE* 10b–11a, 179ab.   [2] Eus *PE* 163b.   [3] Eus *PE* 192c.

[4] I have not attempted to quote or give references to the numerous allusions to murder in Christian literature. The attitude of condemnation is, as one might expect, uniform and unanimous.

Archdeacon Cunningham's summary statements on the early Christian attitude to war are completely at variance with the facts we have just been surveying : thus, "there was not in primitive times any definite protest against this particular symptom in society of the evil disease in human

THE ESSENTIAL PEACEFULNESS OF CHRISTIANITY. ——The natural counterpart of the Christian disapproval of war was the conception of peace as being of the very stuff and substance of the Christian life. Peace, of course, meant a number of different things to the early Christian. It meant reconciliation between himself and God ; it meant the stilling of turbulent passions and evil desires in his own heart ; it meant the harmony and concord that normally reigned within the Christian community ; it meant (to Paul, for instance, in writing 'Ephesians') the reconciliation of Jew and gentile ; it meant immunity from annoyance and persecution at the hands of pagans ; it meant also freedom from the distractions, toils, and dangers of actual war. Little purpose would be served by attempting an analysis of all occurrences of the word 'peace' in early Christian literature according to the particular shade of meaning in each case, with the object of dissolving out the exact amount said about peace as the antithesis and correlative of war. The result would be little more than a general impression of the Christian inclination towards, and approval of, peace. That fact in itself is not without significance : for, while there are many places in which peace is mentioned without any apparent reference to the military calling—for instance, where Peter, shortly before baptizing the centurion Cornelius, gave him the pith of the Christian gospel as "the word which God sent to the sons of Israel, giving the good news of peace

hearts" (*Christianity and Politics*, 249) ; the first four centuries are taken as a single period under the heading "The acceptance of War as inevitable in an evil world" (249 f) ; "so far as we can rely on the argument from silence, *Christians do not appear to have been repelled by bloodshed in war*. Pliny does not complain of them, and there seem to be no special warnings in regard to un-Christian conduct in connection with military service" (251) (italics mine : the argument from Plinius will be touched on later).

through Jesus Christ"[1]—yet the close and repeated identification of Christianity with peace even in a vague sense (e.g., in the opening and closing salutations of letters, and in phrases like 'the God of Peace') has an important bearing on the Christian attitude to war, particularly in view of the many direct and explicit allusions we find to peace in the military sense. It will be sufficient for our present purpose to quote only a few of the more explicit passages. Paul, for instance, tells the Romans: "If possible, as far as lies in your power, be at peace with all men"[2]: similarly, the author of Hebrews: "Pursue peace with all (men)."[3] The evangelist 'Matthew' quotes the words of Jesus: "Happy are the peace-makers"[4]; and Luke tells us that at the birth of Jesus the host of angels sang: "Glory in the highest to God and on earth peace among men whom He favours,"[5] and represents Zacharias as praying God "to guide our feet into (the) way of peace."[6] In the liturgical prayer at the end of the epistle of Clemens of Rome occurs a petition for world-wide peace among men generally: "Give concord and peace to us and to all who inhabit the earth, as Thou gavest to our fathers."[7] Then he prays specially for the rulers: "Give them, Lord, health, peace, concord, stability, that they may administer without offence the government given to them by Thee. . . . Do Thou, Lord, direct their counsel . . . in order that they, administering piously with peace and gentleness the authority given them by Thee, may find favour with

---

[1] Ac x. 36, 48.
[2] Rom xii. 18.
[3] Heb xii. 14.
[4] Mt v. 9.
[5] Lk ii. 14: are the ἄνθρωποι εὐδοκίας men generally, or Christians only, or Jews?
[6] Lk i. 79; cf the reference to national enemies in vv. 71, 74.
[7] 1 Clem lx. 4.

Thee." [1]   Ignatius exclaims : " Nothing is better than
peace, by which all war of those in heaven and those
on earth is abolished." [2]   A Christian Elder quoted by
Eirenaios said that King Solomon "announced to the
nations that peace would come and prefigured the-reign
of Christ." [3]   Justinus told the Emperors that the
Christians were the best allies and helpers they had in
promoting peace, [4] on the ground that their belief in
future punishment and in the omniscience of God
provided a stronger deterrent from wrongdoing than
any laws could do.

The Christian Church appropriated to itself that old
prophecy, found both in Isaiah and Micah, of the
abolition of war in the Messianic age. " And many
peoples shall go and say, Come ye, and let us go up
to the mountain of the Lord, to the house of the God of
Jacob ; and He will teach us of His ways, and we
will walk in His paths : for out of Zion shall go forth
the law, and the word of the Lord from Jerusalem.
And He shall judge among the nations, and convict
many peoples ; and they shall beat their swords into
ploughshares, and their spears into pruning-knives ;
nation shall not lift sword against nation, neither shall
they learn war any more." [5]   This prophecy is quoted,
in whole or in part, by a succession of Christian writers,
who all urge that it is being fulfilled in the extension
of Christianity, the adherents of which are peace-loving
people, who do not make war. Thus Justinus quotes
it in his Apology, and goes on : " And that this has
happened, ye can be persuaded. For from Jerusalem

[1] I Clem lxi. I f.   [2] Ig *E* xiii. 2.
[3] Eiren IV xxvii. i (ii. 240) : the reference is apparently to Ps. lxxii. 7.
[4] Just I *Ap* xii. I : Ἀρωγοὶ δ'ὑμῖν καὶ σύμμαχοι πρὸς εἰρήνην ἐσμὲν
πάντων μᾶλλον ἀνθρώπων.   [5] Isa ii. 3 f ; cf Mic iv. 2 f,

twelve men went out into the world, and these (were) unlearned, unable to speak ; but by (the) power of God they told every race of men that they had been sent by Christ to teach all (men) the word of God. And we, who were formerly slayers of one another, not only do not make war upon our enemies, but, for the sake of neither lying nor deceiving those who examine us, gladly die confessing Christ." [1] He quotes it again in his Dialogue with Truphon the Jew, and insists in opposition to the Jewish interpretation that it is already being fulfilled : "and we," he goes on, "who had been filled with war and mutual slaughter and every wickedness, have each one—all the world over— changed the instruments of war, the swords into ploughs and the spears into farming instruments, and we cultivate piety, righteousness, love for men, faith, (and) the hope which is from the Father Himself through the Crucified One." [2] Eirenaios quotes it, and comments upon it as follows : "If therefore another law and word, issuing from Jerusalem, has thus made peace among those nations which received it, and through them convinced many a people of folly, it seems clear that the prophets were speaking of someone else (besides Jesus). But if the law of liberty, that is, the Word of God, being proclaimed to the whole earth by the Apostles who went out from Jerusalem, effected a change to such an extent that (the nations) themselves wrought their swords and lances of war into ploughs and changed them into sickles, which He gave for reaping corn, (that is), into instruments of peace, and if they now know not how to fight, but, (when they are) struck, offer the other cheek also, (then) the prophets

[1] Just I *Ap* xxxix. 1-3.   [2] Just *Dial* 109 f (728 f).

did not say this of anyone else, but of him who did it. Now this is our Lord," etc.[1] Tertullianus quotes it, and asks : " Who else therefore are understood than ourselves, who, taught by the new law, observe those things, the old law—the abolition of which the very action (of changing swords into ploughs, etc.) proves was to come—being obliterated ? For the old law vindicated itself by the vengeance of the sword, and plucked out eye for eye, and requited injury with punishment ; but the new law pointed to clemency, and changed the former savagery of swords and lances into tranquillity, and refashioned the former infliction of war upon rivals and foes of the law into the peaceful acts of ploughing and cultivating the earth. And so . . . the observance of the new law and of spiritual circumcision has shone forth in acts of peaceful obedience."[2] He quotes it again clause by clause in his treatise against Markion, inserting comments as he goes along : " ' And they shall beat their swords into ploughs, and their spears into sickles,' that is, they shall change the dispositions of injurious minds and hostile tongues and every (sort of) wickedness and blasphemy into the pursuits of modesty and peace. ' And nation shall not take sword against nation,' namely, (the sword) of dissension. ' And they shall not learn to make war any more,' that is, to give effect to hostile feelings : so that here too thou mayest learn that Christ is promised not (as one who is) powerful in war, but (as) a bringer of peace ; " and he goes on to insist that it is Christ who must be referred

---

[1] Eiren IV xxxiv. 4 (ii. 271 f). Cf the use made by Eirenaios of Isa xi. 6–9 in *Demonstr* 61 (35).

[2] Tert *Jud* 3 (ii. 604) : the last words are in pacis obsequia eluxit.

to.[1] He adverts to the prophecy again a little later:
"And then 'they beat their swords into ploughs . . .,'
that is, minds (that were) once wild and savage they
change into feelings (that are) upright and productive
of good fruit."[2] Origenes quotes it: "To those who
ask us whence we have come or whom we have (for)
a leader, we say that we have come in accordance with
the counsels of Jesus to cut down our warlike and
arrogant swords of argument into ploughshares, and
we convert into sickles the spears we formerly used
in fighting. For we no longer take 'sword against
a nation,' nor do we learn 'any more to make war,'
having become sons of peace for the sake of Jesus,
who is our leader, instead of (following) the ancestral
(customs) in which we were strangers to the covenants."[3]
It is quoted in the Pseudo-Cyprianic treatise 'Against
the Jews' and in the 'Dialogus de Recta Fidei' as a
reference to the state of affairs inaugurated by Christ.[4]
Lastly, Eusebios quotes it—after referring to the
multiplicity of rulers in pre-Christian times and the
consequent frequency of wars and universality of
military training—as prophesying the change that
was actually introduced at the advent of Christ. True,
he conceives the fulfilment to lie—in part at least—
in the unification of all governments in that of
Augustus and the resultant cessation of conflicts;
but he goes on to point out that, while the demons
goaded men into furious wars with one another, "at
the same time, by our Saviour's most pious and most
peaceful teaching, the destruction of polytheistic error

---

[1] Tert *Marc* iii. 21 (ii. 351).   [2] Tert *Marc* iv. 1 (ii. 361).
[3] Orig *Cels* v. 33.   What exactly Origenes means by τὰς πολεμικὰς ἡμῶν λογικὰς μαχαίρας καὶ ὑβριστικάς I do not know: anyhow, the reference to actual warfare is clear.   [4] Ps-Cypr *Jud* 9; Adamant i. 10.

began to be accomplished, and the dissensions of the nations immediately began to find rest from former evils. Which (fact)," he concludes, " I regard as a very great proof of our Saviour's divine and irresistible power." [1]

Resuming our account of the various laudatory allusions of Christian authors to peace, we find Athenagoras saying to the Emperors : " By your sagacity the whole inhabited world enjoys profound peace." [2] Clemens of Alexandria says of the Christians : " We are being educated, not in war, but in peace " ; " We, the peaceful race " are more temperate than " the warlike races " ; among musical instruments, " man is in reality a pacific instrument," the others exciting military and amorous passions ; " but we have made use of one instrument, the peaceful word only, wherewith we honour God." [3] Tertullianus, defending the Christian meetings, asks : " To whose danger did we ever meet together ? What we are when we are separated, that we are when we are gathered together : what we are as individuals, that we are as a body, hurting no one, troubling no one " [4] : he calls the Christian " the son of peace." [5] The devil, says Hippolutos, " knows that the prayer of the saints produces peace for the world." [6] The Pseudo-Melitonian Apologist prescribed the knowledge and fear of the one God as the only means by which a kingdom could be peaceably governed.[7] The Bardesanic ' Book of the Laws of the Countries ' foretold the coming

---

[1] Eus *PE* 10b–11a, cf 179ab.
[2] Athenag *Legat* 1 (892), cf 37 fin (972).
[3] Clem *Paed* I xii. 98 fin, II ii. 32, iv. 42.
[4] Tert *Apol* 39 (i. 478).   [5] Tert *Cor* 11 (ii. 92).
[6] Hipp *Dan* III xxiv. 7.   [7] Ps-Mel 10 (*ANCL* xxiib. 121.)

of universal peace as a result of the dissemination of new teaching and by a gift from God.[1]   In the Pseudo-Justinian 'Address to the Greeks,' the Word of God is invoked as : " O trumpet of peace to the soul that is at war ! " [2]   Commodianus says to the Christian : " Make thyself a peace-maker to all men." [3] Cyprianus commends patience as that which " guards the peace." [4] Arnobius tells the pagans : " It would not be difficult to prove that, after Christ was heard of in the world, those wars, which ye say were brought about on account of (the gods') hatred for our religion, not only did not increase, but were even greatly diminished by the repression of furious passions. For since we— so large a force of men—have received (it) from his teachings and laws, that evil ought not to be repaid with evil, that it is better to endure a wrong than to inflict (it), to shed one's own (blood) rather than stain one's hands and conscience with the blood of another, the ungrateful world has long been receiving a benefit from Christ, through whom the madness of savagery has been softened, and has begun to withhold its hostile hands from the blood of a kindred creature. But if absolutely all who understand that they are men by virtue, not of the form of their bodies, but of the power of their reason, were willing to lend an ear for a little while to his healthful and peaceful decrees, and would not, swollen with pride and arrogance, trust to their own senses rather than to his admonitions, the whole world would long ago have turned the uses of iron to milder works and be living in the softest tranquillity, and would have come together in healthy concord

---

[1] *ANCL* xxiib. 111.   [2] Ps-Just *Orat* 5.   [3] Commod *Instr* ii. 22.
[4] Cypr *Bon Pat* 20 : cf *Clem Hom* iii. 19, *Recog* ii. 27–31.

without breaking the sanctions of treaties."[1]   The martyr Lucianus told the judge at Nicomedia that one of the laws given by Christ to Christians was that they should "be keen on peace."[2]

It might of course be urged that these expressions or at least the bulk of them voiced the sentiments of a community that bore no political responsibility and had been disciplined by no political experience.   "The opinions of the Christians of the first three centuries," says Lecky, "were usually formed without any regard to the necessities of civil or political life ; but when the Church obtained an ascendancy, it was found necessary speedily to modify them."[3]   It must of course be frankly admitted that the passages we have quoted do not explicitly handle the ultimate problems with which the philosophy of war and penal justice has to deal : but it is quite another question whether the policy of conduct dictated by what many might consider this blind attachment to peace and this blind horror of war did not involve a better solution of those problems than had yet been given to the world.   The modifications of which Lecky speaks were due to other causes than the enlargement of the Church's vision and experience. The grave relaxation of her early moral purity had a good deal to do with it : and, as we shall see later, the early Church was not without at least one competent thinker who was fully equal to giving a good account of the peace-loving views of himself and his brethren in face of the objections raised by the practical pagan critic.

---

[1] Arnob i. 6 : the general prevalence of peace since the time of Christ is alluded to by Methodios (*Symp* x. 1 fin).

[2] Routh iv. 6 (studere paci).

[3] Lecky ii. 39.

THE CHRISTIAN TREATMENT OF ENEMIES AND WRONGDOERS.—A very interesting sidelight is cast on the attitude of the early Christians to war by the serious view they took of those precepts of the Master enjoining love for all, including enemies, and forbidding retaliation upon the wrongdoer, and the close and literal way in which they endeavoured to obey them. This view and this obedience of those first followers of Jesus are the best commentary we can have upon the problematic teaching in question, and the best answer we can give to those who argue that it was not meant to be practised save in a perfect society, or that it refers only to the inner disposition of the heart and not to the outward actions, or that it concerns only the personal and private and not the social and political relationships of life. The Christian emphasis on the duty of love may be thought by some to have little bearing on the question of war, inasmuch as it is possible to argue that one can fight without bitterness and kill in battle without hatred. Whatever may be thought on that particular point, the important fact for us to notice just now is, not only that the early Christians considered themselves bound by these precepts of love and non-resistance in an extremely close and literal way, but that they did actually interpret them as ruling out the indictment of wrongdoers in the law-courts and participation in the acts of war. And when we consider that these same simple-minded Christians of the first generations did more for the moral purification of the world in which they lived than perhaps has ever been done before or since, their principles will appear to be not quite so foolish as they are often thought to be.

We proceed to quote the main utterances of the early

Christian writers on this subject. The Apostle Paul writes to the Thessalonians: "May the Lord make you to increase and abound in love towards one another and towards all.[1] . . . See (to it) that no one renders to any evil in return for evil, but always pursue what is good towards one another and towards all."[2] To the Galatians: "As then we have opportunity, let us work that which is good towards all."[3] To the Corinthians: "What (business) is it of mine to judge outsiders? . . . outsiders God will judge."[4] To the Romans: "Render to no one evil for evil. . . . If possible, as far as lies in your power, be at peace with all men. Do not avenge yourselves, beloved, but leave room for the wrath (of God); for it is written: 'Vengeance is mine, I will repay, saith the Lord.' But if thine enemy hunger, feed him; if he thirst, give him drink; for by doing this thou wilt heap coals of fire on his head. Be not conquered by evil, but conquer evil with (what is) good. . . . Owe no man anything, except mutual love: for he who loves his neighbour has fulfilled the Law. For the (commandment): 'Thou shalt not commit adultery,' 'Thou shalt not kill,' 'Thou shalt not steal,' 'Thou shalt not covet,' and whatever other commandment there is, is summed up in this saying: 'Thou shalt love thy neighbour as thyself.' Love does not work evil on a neighbour: love therefore is the fulfilment of the Law."[5] To the Philippians: "Let your forbearance be known to all men."[6] A practical

---

[1] 1 Th iii. 12.   [2] 1 Th v. 15.   [3] Gal vi. 10.
[4] 1 Cor v. 12 f. The allusions in 2 Cor vi. 6 to 'longsuffering' and 'love unfeigned' refer to Paul's attitude to outsiders in his missionary work.
[5] Rom xii. 17-21, xiii. 8-10. I postpone for the present all commen on the intervening passage on the State (Rom xiii. 1-7).
[6] Phil iv. 5 (τὸ ἐπιεικὲς ὑμῶν).

instance of the way in which Paul 'conquered evil with what is good' appears in his treatment of Onesimos, the slave who had robbed his Christian master and then run away from him : Paul, who came across him at Rome, called him ' My child, whom I have begotten in my bonds,' and gained by love so great and good an influence over him as to be able to send him back with a letter of apology and commendation to his offended master.[1] In the Pastorals we read : " The servant of God ought not to fight, but to be mild to all, a (skilled) teacher, patient of evil (ἀνεξίκακον), gently admonishing his opponents—God may possibly give them repentance (leading) to a knowledge of truth, and they may return to soberness out of the snare of the devil "[2] ; " Remind them . . . to be ready for every good work, to rail at no one, to be uncontentious, forbearing, displaying all gentleness towards all men."[3] In the Epistle of James : " With it (the tongue) we bless the Lord and Father, and with it we curse men who are made in the likeness of God. Out of the same mouth issues blessing and cursing. My brothers, this ought not to be so."[4] In the Epistle of Peter : " Honour all men.[5] . . . For unto this were ye called, because Christ suffered for you, leaving you an example in order that ye might follow in his footsteps : . . . who, when he was reviled, did not revile in return, when he suffered, did not threaten, but entrusted himself to Him who judges righteously.[6] . . . Finally, (let) all (be) . . . humble, not rendering evil in return for evil or reviling

---

[1] Philemon, passim.   [2] 2 Tim ii. 24 ff (but see above, p. 49).
[3] Tit iii. 1 f.   [4] Jas iii. 9 f.   [5] 1 Pet ii. 17.
[6] 1 Pet ii. 21, 23 : the words are actually addressed to slaves, who (vv. 18–20) are exhorted to submit patiently to unjust treatment from their masters, but, as the next quotation shows, the words apply to all Christians.

in return for reviling, but on the contrary blessing (those who revile you): for unto this were ye called, in order that ye might inherit a blessing.[1] . . . For it is better, if the Will of God wills (it so), to suffer for doing right rather than for doing wrong: because Christ also suffered once for sins, the righteous for the unrighteous, in order that he might bring us to God." [2]   We do not need to quote over again the passages in the Gospels bearing upon this aspect of Christian conduct, as they have already been fully considered in our examination of the teaching of Jesus; but it is important to bear in mind the immense significance which those passages would have for the evangelists who embodied them in their Gospels and for the contemporary generation of Christians.   Echoes of them are heard in other Christian writings of the time.   Thus the Didache says: " This is the way of life: first, thou shalt love the God who made thee, secondly, thy neighbour as thyself: and all things whatsoever thou wouldest not should happen to thee, do not thou to another.   The teaching of these words is this: Bless those who curse you, and pray for your enemies, and fast on behalf of those who persecute you: for what thanks (will be due to you), if ye love (only) those who love you? do not the gentiles also do the same?   But love ye those who hate you, and ye shall not have an enemy. . . . If anyone give thee a blow upon the right cheek, turn the other also to him, and thou shalt be perfect: if anyone impress thee (to go) one mile, go two with him: if anyone take away thy cloak, give him thy tunic also: if anyone take from thee what is thine, do not demand it back.[3] . . . Thou shalt not plan any evil against thy neighbour.   Thou

---

[1] I Pet iii. 8 f.   [2] I Pet iii. 17 f.   [3] *Did* i. 2–4.

shalt not hate any man; but some thou shalt reprove, on some thou shalt have mercy, for some thou shalt pray, and some thou shalt love above thine own soul.[1] . . . Thou shalt not become liable to anger—for anger leads to murder—nor jealous nor contentious nor passionate, for from all these things murders are born." [2] "Every word," says the Epistle of Barnabas, "which issues from you through your mouth in faith and love, shall be a means of conversion and hope to many." [3]

An eloquent practical example of the true and typical Christian policy towards sinful and wayward paganism, is that beautiful story told by Clemens of Alexandria about the aged apostle John. The story has every appearance of being historically true, at least in substance; but, even if fictitious, it must still be 'in character,' and therefore have value as evidence for the approved Christian method of grappling with heathen immorality. The story is briefly as follows. John, while visiting the Christians in some city—perhaps Smyrna—saw in the church a handsome heathen youth, and feeling attracted to him, entrusted him, in the presence of Christian witnesses, to the bishop's care. The bishop took the youth home, taught, and baptized him; and then, thinking him secure, neglected him. When thus prematurely freed from restraint, bad companions got hold of him, and by degrees corrupted and enticed him into evil ways and finally into the commission of some great crime. He then took to the mountains with them as a brigand-chief, and committed acts of bloodshed and cruelty. Some time after, John visited

---

[1] *Did* ii. 6 f : cf Barn xix. 3 ff.   [2] *Did* iii. 2.
[3] Barn xi. 8. Cf. also the allusions to meekness, forbearance, long-suffering, etc., in I Clem xiii. I, xix. 3, xxx. I, 3.

the same city again, and, learning on enquiry what had happened, called for a horse and guide, and at length found his way unarmed into the young captain's presence. The latter fled away in shame ; but the apostle pursued him with entreaties : " Why, my child, dost thou flee from me, thine own father, unarmed (and) aged (as I am) ? Have mercy on me, my child ; fear not. Thou still hast hope of life. I will give account to Christ for thee. If need be, I will willingly endure thy death (for thee), as the Lord endured it for us. I will give my life for thine. Stand ; believe ; Christ has sent me." The youth halted, looked downwards, cast away his weapons, trembled, and wept. When the apostle approached, the youth embraced him, and poured forth confessions and lamentations. John assured him of the Saviour's pardon, and, falling on his knees, and kissing the right hand which the youth had concealed in shame, prevailed upon him to suffer himself to be led back to the church. There the apostle spent time with him in intercessory prayer, prolonged fasting, and multiplied counsels, and did not depart until he had restored him to the church, ' a trophy of visible resurrection.' [1]

Ignatius writes to the Ephesians : " And on behalf of the rest of men, pray unceasingly. For there is in them a hope of repentance, that they may attain to God. Allow them therefore to become disciples even through your works. Towards their anger (be) ye gentle ; towards their boasting (be) ye meek ; against their railing (oppose) ye your prayers ; against their error (be) ye steadfast in the faith : against their savagery (be) ye mild, not being eager to imitate them. Let us

[1] Clem *Quis Dives* xlii. 1–15 ; Eus *HE* III xxiii. 6–19.

be found their brothers in forbearance : and let us be eager to be imitators of the Lord, (to see) who can be most wronged, who (most) deprived, who (most) despised, in order that no plant of the devil be found in you, but in all chastity and temperance ye may remain in Jesus Christ as regards both flesh and spirit." [1] He says to the Trallians of their bishop : " His gentleness is a power : I believe even the godless respect him." [2] " I need gentleness," he tells them, " by which the Ruler of this age is brought to nought." [3] He exhorts his friend Polukarpos, the bishop of Smyrna : " Forbear all men in love, as indeed thou dost." [4] Polukarpos himself tells the Philippians that God will raise us from the dead if we " do His will and walk in His commandments . . . not rendering evil in return for evil, or reviling in return for reviling, or fisticuff in return for fisticuff, or curse in return for curse." [5] " Pray also," he says, " for kings and authorities and rulers and for those who persecute and hate you and for the enemies of the cross, that your fruit may be manifest among all, that ye may be perfect in Him." [6] Aristeides says of the Christians : " They appeal to those who wrong them and make them friendly to themselves ; they are eager to do good to their enemies ; they are mild and conciliatory." [7] Diognetos is told that the Christians " love all (men), and are persecuted by all ; . . . they are reviled, and they bless ; they are insulted, and are respectful." [8] Hermas includes in his enumeration of Christian duties those of " withstanding no one, . . . bearing insult, being longsuffering, having no remembrance of

---

[1] Ig *E* x. 1–3. [2] Ig *T* iii. 2. [3] Ig *T* iv. 2. [4] Ig *P* i. 2.
[5] Pol ii. 2 : on the duty of love, cf iii. 3, iv. 2, (xii. 1).
[6] Pol xii. 3. [7] Arist 15 (111), cf 17 (Syriac, 51). [8] *Diog* v. 11, 15.

wrongs." [1] The author of the so-called second Epistle of Clemens reproves his readers for not being true to these principles : " For the gentiles, hearing from our mouth the words of God, are impressed by their beauty and greatness : then, learning that our works are not worthy of the things we say, they turn to railing, saying that it is some deceitful tale. For when they hear from us that God says : ' No thanks (will be due) to you, if ye love (only) those who love you; but thanks (will be due) to you, if ye love your enemies and those that hate you'— when they hear this, they are impressed by the overplus of goodness : but when they see that we do not love, not only those who hate (us), but even those who love (us), they laugh at us, and the Name is blasphemed." [2]

" We," says Justinus, " who hated and slew one another, and because of (differences in) customs would not share a common hearth with those who were not of our tribe, now, after the appearance of Christ, have become sociable, and pray for our enemies, and try to persuade those who hate (us) unjustly, in order that they, living according to the good suggestions of Christ, may share our hope of obtaining the same (reward) from the God who is Master of all. [3] . . . And as to loving all (men), he has taught as follows : ' If ye love (only) those who love you, what new thing do ye do ? for even fornicators do this. But I say to you : Pray for your enemies and love those who hate you and bless those who curse you and pray for those who act spitefully towards you.' [4] . . . And as to putting up with evil and being serviceable to all and without

[1] Herm *M* VIII 10.   Hermas has many inculcations of gentleness, longsuffering, etc., etc.
[2] 2 Clem xiii. 3 f.   [3] Just 1 *Ap* xiv. 3.   [4] Just 1 *Ap* xv. 9.

anger, this is what he says : 'To him that smiteth thy cheek, offer the other (cheek) as well, and do not stop (the man) that takes away thy tunic or thy cloak. But whoever is angry is liable to the fire. Every one who impresses thee (to go) a mile, follow (for) two (miles). Let your good works shine before men, that seeing (them) they may worship ($\theta \alpha \upsilon \mu \acute{\alpha} \zeta \omega \sigma \iota$) your Father in heaven.' For (we) must not resist : nor has (God) wished us to be imitators of the wicked, but has bidden (us) by patience and gentleness lead all (men) from (the) shame and lust of the evil (things). And this we are able to show in the case of many who were (formerly) on your side. They changed from (being) violent and tyrannical, conquered either (through) having followed the constancy of (their Christian) neighbours' life, or (through) having noticed the strange patience of fellow-travellers when they were overreached, or (through) having experienced (it in the case) of those with whom they had dealings." [1]

"We have learnt," says Athenagoras, "not only not to strike back and not to go to law with those who plunder and rob us, but with some, if they buffet us on the side of the head, to offer the other side of the head to them for a blow, and with others, if they take away our tunic, to give them also our cloak.[2] . . . What then are those teachings in which we are brought up ? " He then quotes the familiar words of Mt v. 44 f, and asks what logician ever loved and blessed and prayed for his enemies, instead of plotting some evil against them : but among the Christians, he says, there are those who

---

[1] Just I *Ap* xvi. 1–4. Similar professions are made by Justinus in *Dial* 96 (704), 133 fin (785), *Res* 8 fin (1588).
[2] Athenag *Legat* I (893).

" do not rehearse speeches, but display good deeds, (viz.) not hitting back when they are struck, and not going to law when they are robbed, giving to those that ask, and loving their neighbours as themselves." [1]   He speaks of the Christians later as those " to whom it is not lawful, when they are struck, not to offer themselves (for more blows), nor, when defamed, not to bless : for it is not enough to be just—and justice is to return like for like —but it is incumbent (upon us) to be good and patient of evil." [2]   Speratus, the martyr of Scilli, told the proconsul : " We have never spoken evil (of others), but when ill-treated we have given thanks—because we pay heed to our Emperor " (i.e. Christ).[3]   Theophilos wrote : " In regard to our being well-disposed, not only to those of our own tribe, as some think (but also to our enemies), Isaiah the prophet said : ' Say to those that hate and loathe you, Ye are our brothers, in order that the name of the Lord may be glorified and it may be seen in their gladness.'   And the Gospel says : ' Love your enemies, and pray for those who treat you spitefully. For if ye love (only) those that love you, what reward have ye ? even the robbers and the taxgatherers do this.' " [4]

Eirenaios refers on several occasions to this teaching. One of the passages we have already had before us.[5] Elsewhere he quotes Jesus' prayer, ' Father, forgive them . . .' as an instance of obedience to his own com-

---

[1] Athenag *Legat* 11 (912 f), cf 12 (913, 916).
[2] Athenag *Legat* 34 fin (968).
[3] *P Scill* 112.   A little later, when persuaded by the proconsul to give up his Christianity, Speratus replies : Mala est persuasio homicidium facere, falsum testimonium dicere (114).   I am not clear to what exactly the first clause alludes.   [4] Theoph iii. 14.
[5] Eiren IV xxxiv. 4 (ii. 271 f), quoted on pp. 61 f, and illustrating the direct bearing, according to the Christian view, of this teaching on the subject of war.

mand to love and pray for enemies. He argues from
the prayer that the sufferings of Jesus could not have
been in appearance only, as the Docetic errorists maintained : if they were, then his precepts in the Sermon on
the Mount would be misleading, and "we shall be even
above the Master, while we suffer and endure things
which the Master did not suffer and endure."[1] The
Lord bade us, he says later, "love not neighbours only,
but even enemies, and be not only good givers and
sharers, but even givers of free gifts to those who take
away what is ours. 'For to him that takes away (thy)
tunic from thee,' he says, 'give to him thy cloak also ;
and from him who takes away what is thine, demand (it)
not back ; and as ye wish that men should do to you, do
ye to them' : so that we may not grieve as if we did not
want to be defrauded, but rejoice as if we gave willingly,
rather conferring a favour on neighbours, than bowing
to necessity. 'And if any one,' he says, 'impress thee
(to go) a mile, go two more with him,' so that thou
mayest not follow as a slave, but mayest go in front like
a free man, showing thyself ready in all things and useful
to (thy) neighbour, not regarding their badness, but
practising thy goodness, conforming thyself to the
Father, 'who makes His sun rise on bad and good, and
rains on just and unjust.'"[2] Eirenaios in another work
remarks that the Law will no longer say "'Eye for eye,
and tooth for tooth' to him who regards no one as his
enemy, but all as his neighbours : for this reason he can
never stretch out his hand for vengeance."[3] Apollonius
told the Roman Senate that Christ "taught (us) to

---

[1] Eiren III xviii. 5 f (ii. 99 f).
[2] Eiren IV xiii. 3 (ii. 182). Another paraphrase of the teaching of the
Sermon on the Mount in regard to returning good for evil occurs in
Eiren II xxxii. 1 (i. 372). [3] Eiren *Demonstr* 96 (50).

allay (our) anger, . . . to increase (our) love (for others)
(φιλίαν), . . . not to turn to (the) punishment (ἄμυναν)
of those who wrong (us). . . ." [1]

Clemens of Alexandria alludes several times to the
teaching of Mt v. 44 f, Lk vi. 27 f,[2] and says further that
the Gnostic, by which he means the thorough-going
Christian, "never bears a grudge (μνησικακεῖ), nor is
vexed (χαλεπαίνει) with anyone, even though he be
worthy of hatred for what he does : for he reveres the
Maker, and loves the one who shares in life, pitying and
praying for him because of his ignorance." [3]   Those who
pray that the wrongs they suffer should be visited upon
the wrongdoers, Clemens considers as better than those
who wish to retaliate personally by process of law ; but
he says that they " are not yet passionless, if they do not
become entirely forgetful of wrong and pray even for
their enemies according to the Lord's teaching."   After
some further words about forgiveness, he goes on to say
that the Gnostic " not only thinks it right that the good
(man) should leave to others the judgment of those who
have done him wrong, but he wishes the righteous man
to ask from those judges forgiveness of sins for those
who have trespassed against him ; and rightly so." [4]
" Above all," he says elsewhere, " Christians are not
allowed to correct by violence sinful wrongdoings.   For
(it is) not those who abstain from evil by compulsion,
but those (who abstain) by choice, (that) God crowns.
For it is not possible for a man to be good steadily
except by his own choice." [5]

Tertullianus adverts to the command to love enemies

---

[1] *Acts of Apollonius* 37 (Gebhardt 56 ; Conybeare 46).
[2] Clem *Strom* II i. 2, xviii. 88, IV xiv. 95.
[3] Clem *Strom* VII xi. 62.   [4] Clem *Strom* VII xiv. 84 f.
[5] Clem *frag* in Maximus Confessor, *Serm* 55 (Migne *PG* xci. 965).

and not to retaliate, and reassures the pagans that, although the numbers of the Christians would make it easy for them to avenge the wrongs they suffer, this principle puts an actual revolt out of the question : "For what war," he asks, "should we not be fit (and) eager, even though unequal in numbers, (we) who are so willing to be slaughtered—if according to that discipline (of ours) it was not more lawful to be slain than to slay?"[1]   "The Christian does not hurt even his enemy."[2]   In his treatise on patience, he quotes the words about turning the other cheek, rejoicing when cursed, leaving vengeance to God, not judging, etc., and insists on the duty of obeying them in all cases.   "It is absolutely forbidden to repay evil with evil."[3]   It is true that Tertullianus smirches somewhat the beauty of the Christian principle of the endurance of wrongs, by inviting the injured one to take pleasure in the disappointment which his patience causes to the wrong-doer.   The spirit of retaliation is kept, and   coals of fire' selected as the most poignant means of giving effect to it.   But his failure to catch the real spirit of Christian love renders his testimony to what was the normal Christian policy all the more unimpeachable. He calls the Christian the son of peace, for whom it will be unfitting even to go to law, and who does not avenge his wrongs.[4]   The Bardesanic 'Book of the Laws of the Countries' compares those who take it upon themselves to inflict vengeance, to lions and leopards.[5]

Origenes has several important allusions to this aspect

---

[1] Tert *Apol* 37 (i. 463).   [2] Tert *Apol* 46 (i. 512).
[3] Tert *Pat* 8 (i. 1262 f), 10 (i. 1264) (absolute itaque praecipitur malum malo non rependendum).
[4] Tert *Cor* 11 (ii. 92) : . . . filius pacis, cui nec litigare conveniet . . . nec suarum ultor iniuriarum.   [5] *ANCL* xxiib. 94.

of Christian teaching. I select three only for quotation. He points out that God united the warring nations of the earth under the rule of Augustus, in order that by the suppression of war the spread of the gospel might be facilitated : for "how," he asks, "would it have been possible for this peaceful teaching, which does not allow (its adherents) even to defend themselves against [1] (their) enemies, to prevail, unless at the coming of Jesus the (affairs) of the world had everywhere changed into a milder (state)?"[2] Later he says : "If a revolt had been the cause of the Christians combining, and if they had derived the(ir) origin from the Jews, to whom it was allowed (ἐξῆν) to take arms on behalf of the(ir) families and to destroy (their) enemies, the Lawgiver of (the) Christians would not have altogether forbidden (the) destruction of man, teaching that the deed of daring (on the part) of his own disciples against a man, however unrighteous he be, is never right—for he did not deem it becoming to his own divine legislation to allow the destruction of any man whatever" (ὁποιανδήποτε ἀνθρώπου ἀναίρεσιν).[3] Later still, in dealing with the difference between the Mosaic and Christian dispensations, he says : "It would not be possible for the ancient Jews to keep their civil economy unchanged, if, let us suppose, they obeyed the constitution (laid down) according to the gospel. For it would not be possible for Christians to make use, according to the Law of Moses, of (the) destruction of (their) enemies or of those who had acted contrary to the Law and were judged worthy of destruction by fire or stoning. . . . Again, if thou wert to take away from the Jews of that time, who

---

[1] Or possibly, 'take vengeance on'—ἀμύνεσθαι.
[2] Orig *Cels* ii. 30.   [3] Orig *Cels* iii. 7.

had a civil economy and a land of their own, the (right)
to go out against the(ir) enemies and serve as soldiers
on behalf of their ancestral (institutions) and to destroy
or otherwise punish the adulterers or murderers or (men)
who had done something of that kind, nothing would be
left but for them to be wholly and utterly destroyed,
the(ir) enemies setting upon the nation, when they
were weakened and prevented by their own law
from defending themselves against the(ir) enemies." [1]
These statements of Origenes are important for several
reasons—for the clear indication they give that in the
middle of the third century the 'hard sayings' of the
Sermon on the Mount were still adhered to as the proper
policy for Christians, for the direct bearing which those
sayings were felt to have on the question of war, and for
the frank recognition which Origenes accords to the
place of sub-Christian ethical standards in the world's
development.

Cyprianus lays it down that "when an injury has
been received, one has to remit and forgive it," "requital
for wrongs is not to be given," "enemies are to be loved,"
"when an injury has been received, patience is to be kept
and vengeance left to God." [2] He was horror-struck at
the torture that went on in the law-courts : "there at
hand is the spear and the sword and the executioner,
the hook that tears, the rack that stretches, the fire that
burns, more punishments for the one body of man than

---

[1] Orig *Cels* vii. 26. Origenes refers in *Cels* ii. 10 to the incident of
Peter's sword ; in v. 63 he quotes the beatitudes about the meek and the
peace-makers, etc., in order to demonstrate the gentleness of the Christian
attitude to opponents and persecutors ; in vii. 25 he proves from Lamentations that the command to turn the other cheek was not unknown to the
O.T. ; in viii. 35 he quotes Mt v. 44 f and gives a couple of illustrations
from pagan history of kindness to enemies.
[2] Cypr *Test* iii. 22 f, 49, 106.

(it has) limbs!"[1]   "None of us," he says, "offers resistance when he is seized, or avenges himself for your unjust violence, although our people are numerous and plentiful . . . it is not lawful for us to hate, and so we please God more when we render no requital for injury . . . we repay your hatred with kindness," and so on.[2] In his treatise on patience, he takes occasion to quote Mt v. 43–48 in full.[3]   When a plague broke out and the pagans fled, he urged the Christians not to attend to their co-religionists only, saying "that he might be made perfect, who did something more than the taxgatherer and the gentile, who, conquering evil with good and practising something like the divine clemency, loved his enemies also, who prayed for the safety of his persecutors, as the Lord advises and exhorts."   Cyprianus drove this lesson home, we are told, with arguments drawn from Mt v. 44–48.[4]   Commodianus utters the brief precept: "Do no hurt."[5]   The Didaskalia lays it down: "Those who injure you, injure not in return, but endure (it), since Scripture says: 'Say not: I will injure my enemy since he has injured me; but bear it, that the Lord may help thee, and exact vengeance from him who has injured thee.'   For again it says in the Gospel: 'Love those who hate you and pray for those who curse you, and ye shall have no enemy.'"[6]   "Be prepared therefore to incur a loss, and try hard to keep the peace; for if thou incurrest any loss in secular affairs for the sake of peace, there shall accrue a gain with God to thee as to one who fears God and lives according to His com-

---

[1] Cypr *Donat* 10.   [2] Cypr *Demetr* 17, 25.   [3] Cypr *Bon Pat* 5.
[4] Pont *Vit Cypr* 9.   [5] Commod *Instr* ii. 22 (noli nocere).
[6] *Didask* I ii. 2 f: cf I ii. 1 (on blessing those who curse) and V xiv. 22 (on praying for enemies).

mandment."[1]   In the Clementine Homilies Peter disclaims all wish to destroy the heretic Simon, saying that he was not sent to destroy men, but that he wished to befriend and convert him ; and he touches on the Christian custom of praying for enemies in obedience to Jesus' example : and Clemens rehearses to his father the teaching of Mt v. 39–41.[2]

Lactantius refers to the Christians as "those who are ignorant of wars, who preserve concord with all, who are friends even to their enemies, who love all men as brothers, who know how to curb anger and soften with quiet moderation every madness of the mind.[3] . . . This we believe to be to our advantage, that we should love you and confer all things upon you who hate (us)."[4] Since the just man, he says, " inflicts injury on none, nor desires the property of others, nor defends his own if it is violently carried off, since he knows also (how) to bear with moderation an injury inflicted on him, because he is endowed with virtue, it is necessary that the just man should be subject to the unjust, and the wise man treated with insults by the fool," etc.[5]   "God has commanded that enmities are never to be contracted by us, (but) are always to be removed, so that we may soothe those who are our enemies by reminding them of (their) relationship (to us)."[6]   The just man, once again, must return only blessings for curses : " let him also take careful heed lest at any time he makes an enemy by his own fault ; and if there should be anyone so impudent as to inflict an injury on a good and

---

[1] *Didask* II xlvi. 2 ; cf II vi. 1 (bishop not to be angry or contentious).
[2] *Clem Hom* vii. 10 f, xi. 20 fin, xv. 5.   Arnobius (iv. 36) also mentions the Christian custom of praying regularly for enemies.
[3] Lact *Inst* V x. 10.
[4] Lact *Inst* V xii. 4.
[5] Lact *Inst* V xxii. 10.
[6] Lact *Inst* VI x. 5.

just man, let him (i.e. the just man) bear it kindly and temperately, and not take upon himself his own vindication, but reserve (it) for the judgment of God." After more to the same effect, Lactantius proceeds: " Thus it comes about that the just man is an object of contempt to all: and because it will be thought that he cannot defend himself, he will be considered slothful and inactive. But he who avenges himself on (his) enemy— he is judged to be brave (and) energetic : all reverence him, (all) respect him." [1] A little later comes the famous passage, in which he deals with the divine command about homicide, and interprets it as prohibiting both capital charges and military service : " And so in (regard to) this commandment of God no exception at all ought to be made (to the rule) that it is always wrong to kill a man, whom God has wished to be a sacrosanct creature." Of this application of the teaching we must speak later.[2]

Probably one of the first things that will strike a modern reader on surveying this remarkable body of evidence is the apparent absence of any treatment of the question of *the defence of others* as a special phase of the general question concerning the treatment of wrongdoers. The silence of Christian authors on this particular point is certainly remarkable. Tertullianus even takes it for granted that, if a man will not avenge his own wrongs, à fortiori he will not avenge those of others [3]—a sentiment pointedly at variance with the

---

[1] Lact *Inst* VI xviii. 10–13 : cf also xi. 1 f (against injuring others generally), and xviii. 6 (about speaking the truth to one's enemy).

[2] Lact *Inst* VI xx. 15–17. The martyr Pollio told his judge that the divine laws demanded pardon for enemies (*Passio Pollionis* 2, in Ruinart 435) ; the martyr Lucianus that they required Christians "to cultivate mildness, to be keen on peace, to embrace purity of heart, to guard patience " (Routh iv. 6).

[3] Tert *Cor* 11 (ii. 92) : Et vincula et carcerem et tormenta et supplicia administrabit, nec suorum ultor injuriarum ?

spirit of modern Christianity, which is at times disposed to accept (as an ideal at all events, if not always as a practicable policy) absolute non-resistance in regard to one's own wrongs, but which indignantly repudiates such a line of action when the wrongs of others—particularly those weaker than oneself—are in question. It is on the validity of this distinction that the whole case of the possibility of a Christian war is felt by many to rest. The point is so important that we may be pardoned for devoting a few lines to it, even though it carries us a little beyond the strictly historical treatment of the subject. In the first place, it needs to be borne in mind that the question is not the general one, whether or no the Christian should try to prevent others being wronged. That question admits of only one answer. The life of a Christian is a constant and effective check upon sin ; and he is therefore at all times, in a general though in a very real way, defending others. The question is, Which is the right method for him to use— the gentle moral appeal or violent physical coercion ? Whatever method he may choose, that method is not of course bound to succeed in any particular case, for circumstances may at any time be too strong for him : possibility of failure, therefore, is not to be reckoned a fatal objection to a policy of defence, for it tells in some measure against all policies. And be it remembered that the restraining power of gentleness is largely diminished, if not entirely destroyed, if the user of it attempts to combine it with the use of coercion and penalty.[1] We are therefore driven to make our choice

[1] Consider how little influence for good would have remained to Jesus and the Apostles over the Gerasene maniac, the prostitute, the adulteress, the extortionate tax-gatherer, the thief on the cross, Onesimos, and the young robber of Smyrna (see above, pp. 43, 69, 71 f), if they had tried to

between two policies of conduct, which to all intents and purposes are mutually exclusive.[1] Now in the use of violence and injury for the defence of others, the Christian sees a policy which he is forbidden, ex hypothesi, to use in his own defence—and that for a reason as valid in the case of others' sufferings as in that of his own, viz. the absolute prohibition of injury [2] —and which is furthermore a less effective policy than that of bringing the force of his own Christian spirit to bear on the wrongdoer, as the Salvationist, for instance, often does with the violent drunkard. If the objection be raised that few people possess this powerful Christian spirit capable of restraining others, I reply that we are discussing the conduct of those alone who, because or in so far as they are faithful Christians, do possess it. Again, when the wrongs of innocent sufferers are brought in in order to undermine obedience to the Sermon on the Mount, a fictitious distinction always has to be made between wrongs inflicted on others in one's very presence and the possibly far more horrible wrongs that go on out of one's sight. " Pity for a horse o'er-driven " easily evaporates when once the poor animal has turned the corner. Many a man would feel it a duty to use his fists to defend a woman from being knocked about under his own eyes, but would not by any means feel called upon to use either his fists or his powers of persuasion on behalf of the poor wife being

combine with the spiritual means of regeneration any form of physical coercion or penalty.

[1] It may be mentioned in passing that we are here dealing solely with the behaviour of Christians towards adult and responsible human beings. God's treatment of man, and man's treatment of his children, are, in some important respects, different problems.

[2] What else can the Golden Rule mean here but that the Christian must defend his neighbour, not as his neighbour wishes, but as he himself —the Christian—wishes to be protected, viz. without violence ?

beaten in her home a few streets off or on the other side of the town. Still less would he admit it as a general principle that he must not rest as long as there is any injustice going on in the world, which he might feel disposed to rectify by the use of violence if it were happening close at hand : and though he may allow himself to be swayed by this particular plea in a political crisis, it is obvious that it could never be taken and is never taken as a general guide for conduct. Unfortunately, we have to recognize the fact that countless acts of cruelty and injustice are going on every day, all around us, near and far ; and the practical demands of Christian usefulness forbid the sensitive man to allow his spirit to be crushed by the awful thought that he cannot yet put a stop to these things. The sentiment which bids a man stick at nothing in order to check outrageous wrongdoing is entitled to genuine respect, for it is closely akin to Christian love ; but it is misleading when it comes into conflict with a considered Christian policy for combating sin, for, as we have seen, it operates only within the compass of a man's vision and in certain occasionally and arbitrarily selected areas beyond, and, when erected into a general principle of conduct, immediately breaks down. The rejection of this sentiment does not mean the rejection of the Christian duty " to ride abroad redressing human wrong " : it means the adoption, not only of gentler, but of more effective, tactics, calling—as the Christian persecutions show—for their full measure of danger and self-sacrifice ; it means too a refusal to stultify those tactics under the impulse of a rush of feeling which so soon fails to justify itself as a guide to conduct.

The early Christians therefore were not guilty, either

of selfish cowardice or of an error of judgment, in interpreting the Master's words as ruling out the forcible defence of one another against the manifold wrongs which pagan hatred and cruelty and lust brought upon them. It was clear indeed that the Master had so interpreted his words himself. He did nothing to avenge John the Baptist or the slaughtered Galilaeans; and when he forbade the use of the sword in Gethsemane, the occasion was one on which it had been drawn in a righteous cause and for the defence of an unarmed and innocent man. The way in which the Christians endured the injuries inflicted upon them in persecution had the effect—so Christian authors continually tell us—of evoking pagan admiration and sympathy, and even adding considerably to the number of converts. By the time the victory over the persecutors was won, Christian ethics had largely lost their early purity; but we see enough to be able to say that that victory was in no small measure due to the power of the Christian spirit operating against tremendous odds without the use of any sort of violent resistance. It took time of course to win the victory, and during that time countless acts of unthinkable cruelty and horror were endured: but would anyone seriously argue that that suffering would have been diminished, or better results achieved for the world at large or for the sufferers themselves, if from the first Christian men had acted on the principle that, while ready themselves to submit meekly, it was their duty to defend others if need be by force and bloodshed? When Plinius tortured the two Bithynian deaconesses, and when Sabina was threatened at Smyrna with being sentenced to the brothel, no Christian knight came forward to prevent the wrong by force of arms or perish in the attempt. Sabina said simply, in answer to the threat: " The holy God will see about that." There must have been innumerable instances of Christians deliberately abstaining from the defence of one another. Such conduct, amazing as it may seem to us, does not argue callousness, still less cowardice, for cowards could never have endured torture with the constancy normally shown by the Christian martyrs. It simply means a strenuous adherence to the Master's teaching—an adherence based indeed on a simple sense of obedience to him, but issuing, as posterity can see, in the exertion of an immense positive moral power, and involving, in a situation from which conflict and suffering in some measure were inseparable, probably a less severe conflict and a smaller amount of suffering than any other course of conduct consistent with faithfulness to the Christian religion would have involved.

THE CHRISTIANS' EXPERIENCE OF EVIL IN THE CHARACTER OF SOLDIERS.—Before we enter upon an examination of the course actually pursued by Christians in regard to service in the Roman legions, there is one more introductory study we shall have to undertake, viz. that of the unfavourable criticisms passed by Christians on the seamy side of the military character as they knew it in practical life, and the harsh treatment they received at the hands of soldiers with whom they came into conflict. The reader will of course understand that what we are here concerned with constitutes only one side of the picture ; the other side, showing us instances of kind treatment and so on on the part of soldiers, will come to light at a later stage of our enquiry. At the same time, the aspect now before us was a very real and a very painful one, and is not without a fairly direct bearing on the early Christian attitude to war.

The main fact in the situation was that the soldier, being charged with ordinary police duties as well as with military functions in the narrower sense, was the normal agent of governments in giving effect to their measures of persecution. While the illegality of Christianity did not become a part of the imperial policy until 64 A.D., numerous acts of persecution were committed before that date. John the Baptist had been beheaded in prison by one of Antipas' guards.[1] Jesus himself had been mocked, spat upon, scourged, and crucified by soldiers.[2] James, the son of Zebedee, was executed by one of Agrippa's soldiers.[3] Peter was guarded in chains by others, and escaped a like fate only by a miraculous deliverance.[4] Paul endured long confinement in the hands of the military; and, when the ship in which he and other prisoners were being taken to Rome was wrecked, the soldiers advised that they should all be killed to prevent any of them escaping.[5] Both Paul and Peter were eventually martyred at Rome, doubtless by the hands of soldiers. In 64 A.D. Nero's act in persecuting the Christians in order to divert from himself the suspicion of having set Rome on fire, inaugurated what proved to be the official policy of the Empire until the

---

[1] Mk vi. 27 f.

[2] Mk xv. 16–20, 24 ; Mt xxvii. 27 ff ; Lk xxiii. 11, 36 f ; John xix. 2, 32 ff. The soldiers of Antipas, as well as the Roman soldiers, were implicated.

[3] Ac xii. 2 : this is surely implied when it is said that Herodes slew him *with a sword*.

[4] Ac xii. 6, 18 f.   [5] Ac xxvii. 42, xxviii. 16, etc. Cf xvi. 23 f.

time of Constantinus. That policy was that the profession of Christianity was regarded as in itself a crime against society—like piracy, brigandage, theft, and arson—and as such was punishable with death by virtue of the ordinary administrative powers of the Roman Governor. Refusal to participate in the widely practised worship of the Emperor or to recognize any other of the pagan gods, strong disapproval of idolatry and all other manifestations of pagan religion, dissent and aloofness from many of the social customs of paganism, secret meetings, nocturnal celebration of 'love-feasts,' disturbance caused to family life by conversions—all these had resulted in making the Christians profoundly unpopular, and brought upon them the suspicion of being guilty of detested crimes, such as cannibalism and incest, and the stigma of being regarded as thoroughly disloyal and dangerous members of society. Such was the basis upon which the imperial policy rested. As individual Emperors varied in their attitude to Christianity (some even going so far as to grant it a de facto toleration), as the popular hatred would flame out and die down at different times and in different places, and lastly as the provincial governors had large discretionary powers and would differ widely in their personal views, the imperial policy of stern repression was not carried out consistently or uniformly. There would be extensive regions and lengthy intervals in which it would lie dormant. Here and there, now and then, it would break forth in varying degrees of severity: and whenever it did so, the task of carrying out the state's decrees devolved upon the soldiers, as the policemen of the Empire. More than that, it is easy to see that, inasmuch as the conduct of official proceedings against the Christians rested in the hands of the military, they must often have borne the main responsibility for the occurrence of persecution.[1] We come across many traces of their activities in this direction. Thus Ignatius of Antioch wrote to his friends at Rome : "From Syria as far as Rome I am fighting with beasts, by land and sea, night and day, having been bound to ten leopards, that is (to say), a squad of soldiers, who become worse even when they are treated well. By the wrongs they do me, I am becoming more of a disciple."[2]   The arrest and burning of Polukarpos at Smyrna were evidently carried out by the military.[3] When Karpos was burnt at Pergamum, it was a soldier's hand that lit the faggots.[4]   In the dreadful persecution at Lugdunum (Lyons) in 177–8 A.D., we are told that "all the wrath of populace and governor and soldiers fell in exceeding measure" upon certain of the martyrs, whose appalling sufferings cast a sinister light upon the character of their tormentors.[5]   Clemens and Origenes group soldiers with kings, rulers, etc., as

---

[1] There is no need here to discuss in greater detail the legal aspect of persecution or to give a sketch of the different outbreaks.   The reader will find the former excellently dealt with in E. G. Hardy's *Christianity and the Roman Government* (London, 1894), and the latter in any good Church History.

[2] Ig *R* v. 1.   Gibbon, writing in 1776, said of the imperial Roman armies : "The common soldiers, like the mercenary troops of modern Europe, were drawn from the meanest, and very frequently from the most profligate, of mankind" (Gibbon, *Decline and Fall*, i. 9 f, ed. Bury). Harnack says : "The conduct of the soldiers during peace (their extortion, their license, their police duties) was as opposed to Christian ethics as their wild debauchery and sports (*e.g.* "the Mimus") at the Pagan festivals" (*ME* ii. 52).   Marcus Aurelius (*Medit* x. 10) called successful soldiers robbers ; but he was a soldier himself, and was obliged to fill his ranks with gladiators, slaves, and Dalmatian brigands (Capitolinus, *Hist. Aug. Life of M. Antoninus Philosophus* xxi. 6 f).

[3] *M. Pol* vii. 1 mentions διωγμῖται καὶ ἱππεῖς μετὰ τῶν συνήθων αὐτοῖς ὅπλων, ὡς ἐπὶ λῃστὴν τρέχοντες ; xviii. 1 ὁ κεντυρίων burns the body.

[4] *Karp* 40.   [5] *M Lugd* in Eus *HE* V i. 17 ff.

one of the parties regularly implicated in the futile persecution of Christianity.[1] Tertullianus numbers them as strangers and therefore enemies of the truth, their motive being the desire for gain.[2] Christians seem to have been exposed to as much danger from the interference of the military as from the hatred of the mob.[3] It seems to have been not unusual for imperilled or imprisoned Christians or their friends to secure better treatment or even release or immunity by secretly bribing an influential soldier, justifying their action by saying that they were rendering to Caesar the things that were Caesar's : Tertullianus disapproved of the practice.[4] The apocryphal Acts of Thomas (225–250 A.D.) tell how the Apostle, being sentenced to death, was struck by four soldiers and slain.[5] When Pionios was burnt at Smyrna in the persecution of Decius (250 A.D.), a soldier nailed him to the stake.[6] The sufferings of Dionusios of Alexandria in the same persecution were due to his treatment by the military.[7] In the persecution of Valerianus (258–9 A.D.) the same story is told : the arrest, custody, and execution of Cyprianus at Carthago were carried out by the proconsul's soldiers[8] : the martyracts of Marianus and Jacobus, who suffered in Numidia, tell us that in the region of the martyrdom " the attacks

---

[1] Clem *Strom* VI xviii. 167 ; Orig *Cels* i. 3.

[2] Tert *Apol* 7 (i. 308) : Tot hostes ejus quot extranei, et quidem proprii ex aemulatione Judaei, ex concussione milites, ex natura ipsi etiam domestici nostri.

[3] Thus Tertullianus warns those who wished to buy themselves off : neque enim statim et a populo eris tutus, si officia militaria redemeris (Tert *Fug* 14 (ii. 119)).   [4] Tert *Fug* 12–14 (ii. 110–120).

[5] *Acts of Thomas* 168 (iii. 282 ; Pick 360).

[6] *M Pionii* xxi. 2.   [7] Dion Alex in Eus *HE* VII xi. 22, VI xl. 2, 4.

[8] Pont *Vit Cypr* 15, 18. Similarly in the *Passio Montani et Lucii* iii. 1, iv. 2, vi. 3, xi. 2, xxi. 9 (Gebhardt 146 ff).

of persecution swelled up, like waves of the world, with
the blind madness and military offices of the gentiles,"
that " the madness of the bloody and blinded governor
sought for all the beloved of God by means of bands of
soldiers with hostile and aggressive minds," that the
martyrs were guarded by "a violent band of centurions," and that they were "assailed with numerous
and hard tortures by a soldier on guard, the executioner
of the just and pious, a centurion and the magistrates
of Cirta being present also to help his cruelty." [1]   Fructuosus, who suffered death in Spain, was hurried to
prison by the soldiers.[2]   In the interval of comparative
peace between 259 and 303 A.D., the bigotry of certain
pagan soldiers was more than once the cause of death
to Christians in the army.[3]   The great persecution
begun by Diocletianus and his colleagues in 303 A.D.
and continued in some parts of the Empire until
313 A.D. opened with the sack of the great church
at Nicomedia by military and other officials, and the
complete destruction of the building by the Praetorian
Guards, who " came in battle array with axes and other
instruments of iron." [4]   In the account given by Eusebios of the sufferings of the Christians, particularly in
the East, soldiers appear at every turn of the story, as
the perpetrators either of the diabolical and indescribable
torments inflicted on both sexes [5] or of the numerous
other afflictions and annoyances incidental to the per-

---

[1] *Passio Mariani et Jacobi* ii. 2, 4, iv. 3, vi. 1 (Gebhardt 135 ff).

[2] *Passio Fructuosi* 1 (Ruinart 264).

[3] See the facts reported by Eusebios in *HE* VII xv. and VIII iv., and
cf below, pp. 151 ff.   [4] Lact *Mort Pers* xii.

[5] Eus *HE* VIII x. 3 ff, *Mart* iv. 8–13, vii. 2, ix. 7 : cf *Passio Tarachi*,
etc. 2 (Ruinart 454).   It is fairly safe to assume that the infliction of torture
referred to in other passages (Eus *HE* VIII iii. 1, v. 2, vi. 2–4, 6, viii,
ix., etc., etc.) was carried out by soldiers, even though they are not
explicitly mentioned.

secution.[1] In Phrygia, for instance, they committed to the flames the whole population of a small town which happened to be entirely Christian.[2]

Besides these allusions to the iniquities of persecution and besides the expressions of horror at the barbarities of war in general, we come across other references to the evil characters and evil deeds of soldiers. The Didaskalia forbids the acceptance of money for the church " from soldiers who behave unrighteously or from those who kill men or from executioners[3] or from any (of the) magistrate(s) of the Roman Empire who are stained in wars and have shed innocent blood without judgment, who pervert judgments," etc.[4] Lactantius alludes to the calamities caused by the multiplication of armies under Diocletianus and his colleagues,[5] to the misdeeds of the Praetorians at Rome in slaying certain judges and making Maxentius Emperor,[6] to the terrible ravages committed by the troops of Galerius in his retreat from Rome,[7] and to the rapacity of the soldiers of Maximinus Daza in the East.[8] Eusebios gives us similar information in regard to the last-named ruler,[9] and tells us of the massacre committed in Rome by the guards of Maxentius.[10]

Let us repeat that the grim indictment of the military character constituted by this long story of cruelty and outrage forms only one side of the picture, and obviously does not of itself imply any view as to the abstract rightfulness or otherwise of bearing arms :

---

[1] Eus *HE* VIII iii. 3 f, *Mart* ix. 2, xi. 6, *HE* IX ix. 20.
[2] Eus *HE* VIII xi. 1 : cf Lact *Inst* V xi. 10.
[3] I suppose this is the meaning of speculatoribus condemnationis.
[4] *Didask* IV vi. 4 (see above, p. 53 n 4).
[5] Lact *Mort Pers* vii. 2 ff.
[6] *op cit* xxvi. 3.
[7] *op cit* xxvii. 5 ff.
[8] *op cit* xxxvii. 5 f.
[9] Eus *HE* VIII xiv. 11.
[10] Eus *HE* VIII xiv. 3.

on the contrary, its sharpest charges belong to a time when there were certainly many Christian soldiers. Nevertheless, our study of the Christian view of war would be incomplete without the inclusion of this aspect of the case on the debit side of the account, an aspect which is more or less closely connected with the central question to which we have just alluded. It is to an examination of the view taken by the early Christians of that question that we have now to turn.

THE CHRISTIAN REFUSAL TO PARTICIPATE IN WAR.—The evidence as to the actual refusal of the early Christians to bear arms cannot be properly appreciated, or even fully stated, without a consideration of the parallel evidence touching the extent to which they were willing to serve as soldiers. The material of the present section will therefore be found to a certain extent to interlace with that of the corresponding section in our next part. For the sake, however, of simplicity of arrangement, it will be best to marshal the facts as we have them, first on one side, and then on the other, and to postpone our final generalizations until we have given full consideration to both.

It will probably be agreed by all that the substance of the last four sections creates at least a strong prima facie presumption that the persons who expressed themselves in the way explained in those sections would decline on principle to render military service. This presumption becomes very much stronger when we are reminded that there was practically nothing in the conditions of the time which would put such pressure on any early Christian as to compel him either to be a soldier against his will or to suffer the consequences of refusing to do so. We should expect therefore to find these Christians, at all events during the first few generations, refusing to serve as soldiers. With that expectation the little information that we possess is in almost entire harmony.[1] Apart from Cornelius and the one or two soldiers who may have been baptized with him by Peter at Caesarea (? 40 A.D.) and the gaoler baptized by Paul at Philippi (circ A.D. 49),[2] we have no direct or reliable evidence for the existence of a single Christian soldier until after 170 A.D.

Partly in justification, partly in amplification, of this negative statement, a few words must be said in regard to one or two incidents and epochs within the period indicated. Thus it is stated that Sergius Paulus, the proconsul of Cyprus, 'believed' as a result of the teaching of Paul on his first mission journey[3] (47 A.D.). If this meant that Sergius Paulus became a Christian in the ordinary sense, he would have to be reckoned as another Christian soldier, for the proconsul of Cyprus was a military, as well as a civil, official : but the adherence of a man of proconsular rank to the Christian faith at this early date would be a very extraordinary occurrence ; no other event of the same significance occurs till nearly the end of the century ; no

---

[1] Such is the conclusion of Harnack, who is not likely to be suspected of exaggerating the evidence in its favour. See his *ME* ii. 52 ("The position of a soldier would seem to be still more incompatible with Christianity than the higher offices of state, for Christianity prohibited on principle both war and bloodshed "), *MC* 11 ("We shall see that the Christian ethic forbade war absolutely (überhaupt) to the Christians "), 47 f ("Had not Jesus forbidden all revenge, even all retaliation for wrong, and taught complete gentleness and patience ? and was not the military calling moreover contemptible on account of its extortions, acts of violence, and police-service ? Certainly : and from that it followed without question, that a Christian might not of his free will become a soldier. It was not however difficult to keep to this rule, and certainly the oldest Christians observed it ").

[2] Ac x. 1 ff, 7 ff, 47 f, xvi. 27–34.   [3] Ac xiii. 12.

mention is made of the baptism of Sergius Paulus ; and when it is said that he 'believed,' what is probably meant is that he listened sympathetically to what the apostles said and expressed agreement with some of their most earnest utterances.[1] In writing from Rome to his friends at Philippi (60 A.D.), Paul says : " My bonds became manifest in Christ in the whole praetorium and to (or among) all the rest."[2] Various opinions have been held as to the exact meaning of 'praetorium' here[3] ; but, even if it means the camp of the Praetorian Guards, the passage would not imply that some of the guards became Christians, but only that it became known to all of them that Paul was in custody because he was a Christian, and not for any political offence.

A more positive piece of information consists in the fact that, shortly before the siege of Jerusalem by the Romans (70 A.D.), the Christians of that city, in obedience to " a certain oracular response given by revelation to approved men there,"[4] left Jerusalem, and settled at Pella in Peraea beyond the Jordan, thus taking no part in the national struggle against Rome. We are too much in the dark as to the details to be able to ascertain the motive that really prompted this step. How far was it due to a disapproval of the national policy of the Jews ? how far to a sense of a final break with Mosaism ? how far to a simple desire for personal safety ? how far to a recollection of the Master's words, " Flee to the mountains " ? or how far, possibly, to a feeling that the use of the sword was

---

[1] Cf. Knowling's note on Ac xiii. 12 in *The Expositor's Greek Testament*; McGiffert, *Apostolic Age*, 175 ; Bartlet, *Apostolic Age*, 68 n 2. Bigelmair (125) believes in his full conversion.

[2] Phil i. 13 : ἐν ὅλῳ τῷ πραιτωρίῳ καὶ τοῖς λοιποῖς πᾶσιν.

[3] See Purves in *HDB* iv. 33.   [4] Eus *HE* III v. 3.

forbidden them? None of these reasons can be either definitely affirmed or definitely denied. The one last suggested is by no means impossible or unnatural. It is in keeping with what we know of the facts of the case. At all events the flame of Jewish patriotism was extinct in the hearts of these Jerusalemite Christians. Their policy on this occasion formed a contrast to that of a certain section of the Essenes, who, despite the fact that they were not usually over-patriotic and that they abjured the use of arms on principle, yet joined with their fellow-countrymen in the revolt against Rome.[1]

The letter written about 112 A.D. by Plinius, proconsul of Bithynia, to the Emperor Trajanus concerning the Christians, does not refer either to their willingness or unwillingness to serve in the legions, and there would therefore be no occasion to mention it in this connection, were it not for the attempt which has been made to represent its silence as implying that the Christians of that time had no objection to bearing arms. Thus, Professor Bethune-Baker says: " Pliny's letter shows that there was no complaint against the Christians then with regard to their view of war "; and in this judgment he is followed by the Venerable Archdeacon of Ely.[2] But inasmuch as there was nothing in the circumstances of the time to bring about a collision between the imperial government and the Christians on the subject of military service, and very probably nothing even to bring the views of the latter to the governor's notice at all, the silence of the letter is perfectly compatible with the supposition that the Christians would not serve; and the attempt to deduce

---

[1] Holtzmann, *Neutestamentliche Theologie* (1911) i. 147.
[2] B.-Baker *ICW* 21 ; Cunningham 251 (quoted above, p. 58 n).

the opposite conclusion from it can only be described as entirely unwarranted.   While we are speaking of the reign of Trajanus, it may be mentioned that in the Acts of Phokas, who is said to have been put to death in Pontus under this Emperor, the martyr-bishop baptizes a number of soldiers at their own request.[1]   But the acts as a whole are of very questionable authority as history[2]; and least of all could an ornamental detail like this be accepted on such slender grounds.

The idea has also been entertained that there is evidence for the existence of Christian soldiers in the time of the Emperor Hadrianus (117–138 A.D.).   The late Dr. J. Bass Mullinger of Cambridge says : " Aringhi (*Antiq. Christianae*, i. 430) gives an epitaph of a soldier of the time of Hadrian, and (ii. 170) that of a soldier in the praetorian guard ; Boldetti (*Osservazioni sopra i cimiteri*, &c., p. 432), one of a VETERANUS EX PRO-TERIORIBUS (? "protectorioribus "), and also (p. 415) one " Pyrrho militi," and (p. 416) that of one who is described as "felicissimus miles."   Marangoni (*Act. S. Vict.* p. 102) gives us that of a centurion, and Ruinart (*Act. Mart.* i. 50) that of two brothers, Getulius and Amantius, who were military tribunes under Hadrian."[3] The first of these inscriptions, (which occurs, by the bye, on p. 525, not on p. 430, of Aringhi's first volume), reads as follows : " Tempore Hadriani Imperatoris : Marius adolescens dux militum, qui satis vixit dum vitam pro Ch(rist)o cum sanguine consunsit, in pace tandem quievit.   Benemerentes cum lacrimis et metu

---

[1] Conybeare 118.
[2] Harnack (*C* i. 317 n 3) says that Conybeare has not convinced him that the Armenian text of these acts contains a genuine ancient document. The acts were rejected even by the Bollandists.
[3] *DCA* ii. 2028b (Art. *War*).

posuerunt." It is, I am informed on competent authority, unquestionably a forgery. As regards the second inscription from Aringhi, there is not only no evidence of its pre-Constantinian date, but none even of its Christian origin. As regards the three inscriptions given by Boldetti, there is no evidence that any one of them is as early as the second century. That given by Marangoni is probably post-Constantinian, as it contains the nomen Flavius in the contracted form FL.[1] As for Getulius and Amantius, their existence rests on the witness of the highly-coloured Acts of Symphorosa.[2] The names of Symphorosa and her seven sons are those of real martyrs : but that apparently is all that can be affirmed in support of the historicity of the story. Lightfoot, after a full discussion, decides that "the story condemns itself both in its framework and in its details," and that "there is no sufficient ground for assigning their martyrdom to the reign of Hadrian."[3]

It has already been remarked that the sentiments expressed by Christian authors in regard to the iniquity of war, the essentially peaceful character of Christianity, the fulfilment of the great ploughshare prophecy in the birth and growth of the Church, the duty of loving enemies, and so on, all point to the refusal to bear arms as their logical implicate in practice. What has already been said, therefore, on these various points has a certain

---

[1] On the evidence of the inscriptions for Christians in military service, cf *DCA* ii. 2028 f, Brace, *Gesta Christi*, 91, Harnack *MC* 121 n, Bigelmair 182 f.

[2] Ruinart 71 (ET in *ANCL* ixb. 192–194) : Symphorosa says to Hadrianus, Vir meus Getulius, cum fratre suo Amantio, tribuni tui cum essent, pro Christi nomine passi sunt diversa supplicia, ne idolis consentirent ad immolandum. . . . Elegerunt enim magis decollari quam vinci, etc.

[3] Lightfoot *AF* II i. 503–505.

place in the consideration of the concrete topic now before us. While this is so, it would be merely tedious to reiterate all the evidence previously adduced: but there are certain pieces of that evidence which are more direct and explicit than others, and which therefore deserve to be either repeated or referred to here.

First in order among these are one or two passages in Justinus. What view, we may ask, in regard to military service must have been taken by the man who said: "We who hated and slew one another, and because of (differences in) customs would not share a common hearth with those who were not of our tribe, now, after the appearance of Christ, have become sociable, and pray for our enemies, and try to persuade those who hate (us) unjustly, in order that they, living according to the good suggestions of Christ, may share our hope of obtaining the same (reward) from the God who is Master of all"?[1] "We, who had been filled with war and mutual slaughter and every wickedness, have each one—all the world over—changed the instruments of war, the swords into ploughs and the spears into farming implements, and we cultivate piety, righteousness, love for men, faith, (and) the hope which is from the Father Himself through the Crucified One."[2] Hefele[3] maintains that the language of Justinus in his (first) Apology, ch. xiv, does not necessarily imply a general disapproval of the profession of the warrior; and Professor Bethune-Baker, referring to ch. xi (where Justinus denies that the Christians are looking for a human kingdom) and xiv ff, remarks that he "expresses

---

[1] Just I *Ap* xiv. 3: cf xxxix. 3: "We who were formerly slayers of one another, not only do not make war upon our enemies, but," etc. (see above, p. 61).

[2] Just *Dial* 110 (729).   [3] Quoted in *DCA* ii. 2028a.

no definite view on the subject of war. . . . What he says . . . really only amounts to a general repudiation of warlike aims or methods on behalf of Christians. Had he regarded war as actually incompatible with Christian sentiment he would probably have taken this opportunity of disposing absolutely of the suspicion to which the Christians were exposed by their Master's use of earthly metaphors to shadow forth eternal spiritual relations."[1] This reasoning is, in my opinion, faulty. Justinus said all that was necessary in order to controvert the suspicion in question, and also, I would add, quite enough to show where he stood on the subject of military service: he would needlessly have prejudiced the Emperor against his main plea, viz. for toleration, had he gone out of his way to say that, if ever the attempt were made to compel Christians to serve in the legions, they would refuse to obey the Emperor's order. It is worth while to notice, though Justinus does not mention the point in connection with war, that he regarded the Christians as making a positive contribution to the maintenance of peace by their very Christianity, and he commends them to the Emperor's favour on this ground.[2]

Tatianus, as we have seen, condemned war as murderous,[3] and, as Harnack says, " was undoubtedly opposed to the military calling." He wrote: " I do not want to be a king: I do not wish to be rich: I decline military command: I hate fornication."[4]

---

[1] B.-Baker *ICW* 21. [2] Just I *Ap* xii. 1 (see above, p. 60 n 4).
[3] See above, p. 50.
[4] Tat 11 (829). Harnack (*ME* ii. 55 n 5) understands the word translated ' military command ' ($\tau\grave{\eta}\nu \ \sigma\tau\rho\alpha\tau\eta\gamma\acute{\iota}\alpha\nu$) to indicate the praetorship, i.e. a magisterial office. But Tatianus has already dealt with magistracy in his first clause ($\beta\alpha\sigma\iota\lambda\epsilon\acute{\upsilon}\epsilon\iota\nu \ o\grave{\upsilon} \ \theta\acute{\epsilon}\lambda\omega$); and in a list of this sort some reference to military life is almost desiderated.

What again must have been thė attitude of Athenagoras, who declared that the Christians could not endure to see a man put to death, even justly, considering that to do so was practically equivalent to killing him, and that for this reason they could not attend the gladiatorial games? [1]

The heathen philosopher Celsus in the 'True Discourse' which he wrote against the Christians about 178 A.D. (the approximate date of Athenagoras' 'Legatio' also), not only exhorts the Christians to take part in civil government, but "urges us" (so Origenes said later, quoting Celsus' words) "to help the Emperor with all (our) strength, and to labour with him (in maintaining) justice, and to fight for him and serve as soldiers with him, if he require (it), and to share military command (with him)." Celsus argued that, if all did as the Christian, nothing would prevent the Emperor being left alone and deserted and earthly affairs getting into the hands of the most lawless and savage barbarians, so that the glory neither of Chris-. tianity nor of true wisdom would be left among men. [2] "It is quite obvious from this," Harnack says, "that Christians were charged with a disinclination to serve in the army, and the charge was undoubtedly well founded." [3]

[1] Athenag *Legat* 35 (969). Hefele (quoted above) does not regard this as disapproving of the warrior's profession : but Bigelmair (166) recognizes that it is at least possible that Athenagoras had war in mind.

[2] Orig *Cels* viii. 73, 68 : cf 74, 75 (see below, pp. 131 ff).

[3] Harnack *ME* ii. 57 n 1. Guignebert (190 f) imagines that Celsus is attacking the doctrines of the Christians rather than the "applications pratiques qu'ils en peuvent déjà faire." Professor B.-Baker (*ICW* 21 ff) ignores the evidence of Celsus for the latter part of the second century : he does not mention his date, but treats him along with Origenes, as if they were contemporaries (*ib*. 27 : cf 29 : "By this time, therefore," (i.e. the time of Origenes' reply, 248 A.D.) "many Christians shrank from military service ").

The first reliable evidence for the presence of Christians in any number in the Roman army belongs, as we shall see later, to the reign of Marcus Aurelius (161–180 A.D.), more precisely to about the year 174 A.D. This epoch is therefore an important landmark in the history of the subject, and we may pause here for a moment to summarize one or two aspects of the situation. It is only in this period that the question of service or abstention becomes one of real and practical significance to Christian people. Up to that time the conditions had constituted no challenge for anyone. "It is not therefore surprising," says Harnack, "that until about the time of the Antonines, in particular Marcus Aurelius, a question of military service (Soldatenfrage) did not exist in the churches: the baptized Christian did not become a soldier; and those who were caught by the Christian faith in the camp had to see how they could come to terms with their military profession." [1] The same scholar gives a useful enumeration of the various features of military life, which could not have failed to thrust themselves on the Christian's notice as presenting, to say the least, great ethical difficulty. The shedding of blood on the battlefield, the use of torture in the law-courts, the passing of death-sentences by officers and the execution of them by common soldiers, the unconditional military oath, the all-pervading worship of the Emperor, the sacrifices in which all were expected in some way to participate, the average behaviour of soldiers in peace-time, and other idolatrous and offensive customs—all these would constitute in combination an exceedingly powerful deterrent against any Christian joining the army on his own initiative.[2]

[1] Harnack *MC* 51. [2] Cf Harnack *MC* 46 f.

As a transition from this point to the full material furnished by Tertullianus, we may recall in passing the phrase in the Pseudo-Justinian ' Address to the Greeks,' exhorting them thus : " Learn (about) the incorruptible King, and know his heroes who never inflict slaughter on (the) peoples," [1] the passage in Eirenaios, in which he applies the ploughshare prophecy to the Christians and says that they " now know not how to fight, but, (when they are) struck, offer the other cheek also," [2] and the remark of Clemens of Alexandria : " We do not train women like Amazons to be manly in war, since we wish even the men to be peaceable." [3]

The writings of Tertullianus make it abundantly clear that in his time there were considerable numbers of Christians serving in the Roman army. This fact, the nature and significance of which will be considered later, is one of great importance, but it is very far from exhausting the contribution of this great writer to our subject. He testifies not only to the willingness of many to serve, but also to the unwillingness of many others ; and the views he expresses on the question are more than mere statements of a personal opinion —they represent the convictions of a very large proportion of his fellow-Christians. Our best plan will be, first, to quote the pertinent passages from his works in chronological order, and then to add a few necessary comments. It may, however, be stated here that, bound up with the problem of military service was the problem of undertaking public office as a magistrate. The police-work of society was done largely by soldiers, and the magistrate was not so sharply

[1] Ps-Just *Orat* 5.
[2] Eiren IV xxxiv. 4 (ii. 271 f), quoted above, pp. 61 f.
[3] Clem *Strom* IV viii. 61.

distinguished from the army officer as he is now. In any case, the Christian difficulty was pretty much the same with the one as with the other : common to both were the two great stumbling-blocks of idolatrous contamination and the shedding of blood (either judicially or in battle). It will therefore help us to understand the Christian position if we include a few passages bearing upon the question of the Christian's abstention from public office.

We recall first the passage in Tertullianus' 'Apologeticus,' in which he tells the pagans that, though the Christians are numerous and reckless enough to avenge their wrongs, there is no fear of their doing so. "For what war," he asks them, "should we not be fit (and) eager, even though unequal in numbers, (we) who are so willing to be slaughtered—if, according to that discipline (of ours), it was not more lawful to be slain than to slay?"[1] It is doubtless in the light of this sentiment that we are to read the assumption earlier in his apology that Caesars could not be Christians.[2] In his 'De Idololatria,' written

---

[1] Tert *Apol* 37 (i. 463). The Latin runs : Cui bello non idonei, non prompti fuissemus, etiam impares copiis, qui tam libenter trucidamur, si non apud istam disciplinam magis occidi liceret quam occidere ? The meaning is sufficiently clear, viz. that the Christians, though few, were so careless of death that they would fight their pagan enemies, were it not for their rule that it is better to be killed than to kill. Professor B.-Baker, however, translates (*ICW* 23) : "Tell me a war for which we *have not been* useful and ready, even when inferior in numbers ; ready to be cut down, as none would be whose tenets were not that it is more lawful to be killed than to kill," and quotes it as showing that "the chief thing by which they " (*i.e.* Christians in the Army) " were distinguished from their Pagan comrades—so far as concerned their action in the field—was their greater readiness to encounter death, *in proportion as they had received a more excellent hope for the future*" (italics mine). This surprising misinterpretation of Tertullianus has been followed by Cunningham (251 f).

[2] Tert *Apol* 21 (i. 403) : Sed et Caesares credidissent super Christo, si aut Caesares non essent saeculo necessarii, aut si et Christiani potuissent esse Caesares. Further reference will have to be made later to this important passage.

while he was still a loyal Catholic, he states the conditions under which he believes it to be possible for
a Christian to be a magistrate. " And so let us grant,"
he says, " that it is possible for anyone to succeed,
in whatever office (he may happen to hold), in going
on under the mere name of the office, without sacrificing, or lending his authority to sacrifices, or contracting
for sacrificial victims, or assigning (to others) the care
of the temples, or seeing after their revenues, or giving
shows at his own (expense) or at that of the public,
or presiding at them when they have to be given, or
making a proclamation or an edict for any solemnity,
or even swearing (oaths), or—as regards (his magisterial) power—judging anyone on a capital or criminal
charge[1]—for thou mightest allow (him to judge) about
(questions of) money—or condemning (anyone),[2] binding anyone, imprisoning anyone, or torturing (anyone): if it can be believed that these things are
possible."[3]   In the next chapter he brands all magisterial garb and pomp as idolatrous and diabolic, but
does not touch on the objection of violence and
bloodshed.   In the following chapter he deals specifically with the question of military service.   " (The
question) also concerning military service, which is
concerned both with rank and power,[4] might seem (to
have been) definitely settled in that (last) chapter.   But
now the question is asked on that (very point), whether
a believer may turn to military service, and whether
the military—at least the rank and file or (say) all the
inferior (grades), who are under no necessity of (offer-

---

[1] Latin : neque judicet de capite alicujus vel pudore.
[2] neque damnet neque praedamnet.   [3] Tert *Idol* 17 (i. 687).
    de militia, quae inter dignitatem et potestatem est.

ing) sacrifices or (passing) capital sentences—may be admitted to the faith. There is no congruity between the divine and human 'sacramentum,' the sign of Christ and the sign of the devil, the camp of light and the camp of darkness: one soul cannot be owed to two, God and Caesar. And (yet, some Christians say), Moses carried a rod, and Aaron (wore) a buckle, and John was girt with a leather belt,[1] and Joshua (the son of) Nun led a line of march, and the people waged war—if it is your pleasure to sport (with the subject). But how will (a Christian) make war—nay, how will he serve as a soldier in peace(-time)—without the sword, which the Lord has taken away? For, although soldiers had come to John and received the form of a rule, although also a centurion had believed, (yet) the Lord afterwards, in disarming Peter, ungirded every soldier. No dress is lawful among us which is assigned to an unlawful action."[2] In 'Adversus Judaeos,' which belongs roughly to the same period as 'De Idololatria,' Tertullianus says: "The old law vindicated itself by the vengeance of the sword, and plucked out eye for eye, and requited injury with punishment ; but the new law pointed to clemency, and changed the former savagery of swords and lances into tranquillity, and refashioned the former infliction of war upon rivals and foes of the law into the peaceful acts of plough-ing and cultivating the earth. And so . . . the ob-servance of the new law and of spiritual circumcision has shone forth in acts of peaceful obedience."[3] In the treatise 'Adversus Marcionem,' which came a few years later, about the time when Tertullianus broke with the

---

[1] The allusions are to various items in the Roman soldier's equipment.
[2] Tert *Idol* 19 (i. 690 f).   [3] Tert *Jud* 3 (ii 604) : see above, p. 62.

Church and became a Montanist, he asks : " Who shall produce these (results, viz. truth, gentleness, and justice) with the sword, and not rather that which is contrary to gentleness and justice, (namely), deceit and harshness and injustice, (which are) of course the proper business of battles ? "[1]   A little later in the same work, he says : " ' And they shall not learn to make war any more,' that is, to give effect to hostile feelings ; so that here too thou mayest learn that Christ is promised not (as one who is) powerful in war, but (as) a bringer of peace."[2]   In ' De Pallio,' written about 210 A.D., he confesses, in the person of his philosophic mantle, that he is " no barking pleader, no judge, no soldier."[3]

We next come to his important treatise ' De Corona Militis,' written—in 211 A.D., some years after his attachment to Montanism—in defence of a Christian soldier who had refused to wear a garland on the Emperor's birthday.   Tertullianus takes occasion to touch on the prior question whether a Christian ought to be a soldier at all.   " And in fact, in order that I may approach the real issue of the military garland, I think it has first to be investigated whether military service is suitable for Christians at all.   Besides, what sort (of proceeding) is it, to deal with incidentals, when the (real) fault lies with what has preceded them ?   Do we believe that the human ' sacramentum ' may lawfully be added to the divine, and that (a Christian) may (give a promise in) answer to another master after Christ, and abjure father and mother and every kins-

[1] Tert *Marc* iii. 14 (ii. 340), cf *Jud* 9 (ii. 621).
[2] Tert *Marc* iii. 21 (ii. 351).
[3] Tert *Pall* 5 (ii. 1047) : caussas non elatro, non judico, non milito, secessi de populo, etc.

man, whom even the Law commanded to be honoured and loved next to God, (and) whom the Gospel also thus honoured, putting them above all save Christ only? Will it be lawful (for him) to occupy himself with the sword, when the Lord declares that he who uses the sword will perish by the sword? And shall the son of peace, for whom it will be unfitting even to go to law, be engaged in a battle? And shall he, who is not the avenger even of his own wrongs, administer chains and (im)prison(ment) and tortures and executions? Shall he now go on guard for another more than for Christ, or (shall he do it) on the Lord's Day, when (he does) not (do it even) for Christ? And shall he keep watch before temples, which he has renounced? and take a meal there where the Apostle has forbidden it?[1] And those whom he has put to flight by exorcisms in the daytime, shall he defend (them) at night, leaning and resting upon the pilum with which Christ's side was pierced? And shall he carry a flag, too, that is a rival to Christ? And shall he ask for a watchword from his chief, when he has already received one from God? And (when he is) dead, shall he be disturbed by the bugler's trumpet—he who expects to be roused by the trumpet of the angel? And shall the Christian, who is not allowed to burn (incense), to whom Christ has remitted the punishment of fire, be burned according to the discipline of the camp? (And) how many other sins can be seen (to belong) to the functions of camp(-life)—(sins) which must be explained as a transgression (of God's law). The very transference of (one's) name from the camp of light to the camp of darkness, is a transgression. Of

[1] An allusion to 1 Cor. viii. 10.

course, the case is different, if the faith comes subsequent(ly) to any (who are) already occupied in military service, as (was, for instance, the case) with those whom John admitted to baptism, and with the most believing centurions whom Christ approves and whom Peter instructs : all the same, when faith has been accepted and signed, either the service must be left at once, as has been done by many, or else recourse must be had to all sorts of cavilling, lest anything be committed against God—(any, that is, of the things) which are not allowed (to Christians) outside the army, or lastly that which the faith of (Christian) civilians has fairly determined upon must be endured for God.[1]   For military service will not promise impunity for sins or immunity from martyrdom.   The Christian is nowhere anything else (than a Christian). . . . With him (i.e. Christ) the civilian believer is as much a soldier as the believing soldier is a civilian.   The state of faith does not admit necessities.   No necessity of sinning have they, whose one necessity is that of not sinning. . . . For (otherwise) even inclination can be pleaded (as a) necessity, having of course an element of compulsion in it.   I have stopped up that very (appeal to necessity) in regard to other cases of (wearing) garlands of office, for which (the plea of) necessity is a most familiar defence ; since either (we) must flee from (public) offices for this reason, lest we fall into sins, or else we must

---

[1] dum tamen, suscepta fide atque signata, aut deserendum statim sit, ut a multis actum, aut omnibus modis cavillandum, ne quid adversus Deum committatur, quae nec extra militiam permittuntur, aut novissime perpetiendum pro Deo, quod aeque fides pagana condixit.   The phrase 'quae nec extra militiam permittuntur' is difficult to construe ; but by retaining this reading instead of the suggested 'ex militia' (so Rigaltius and Migne), one does not get rid of the proposal to desert, as the Translator in *ANCL* xi. 348 n seems to imagine.

endure martyrdoms, that we may break (off our tenure of public) offices. On (this) first aspect of the question, (namely) the illegitimacy of the military life itself, I will not add more, in order that the second (part of the question) may be restored to its place—lest, if I banish military service with all my force, I shall have issued a challenge to no purpose in regard to the military garland."[1] In the following chapter, he asks : "Is the laurel of triumph made up of leaves, or of corpses ? is it decorated with ribbons, or tombs? is it besmeared with ointments, or with the tears of wives and mothers, perhaps those of some men even (who are) Christians—for Christ (is) among the barbarians as well?"[2]

The clear, thorough-going, and outspoken opinions of Tertullianus have naturally attracted a good deal of attention and criticism ; and there are one or two points in connection with them which it will be well briefly to consider and emphasize.

1. The 'De Idololatria' (198–202 A.D.) is the earliest evidence we have for the enlistment in the army of Christians who were already baptized.[3] Any Christian soldiers mentioned in documents of an earlier date may well have consisted, for aught we know to the contrary, of men converted when already engaged in military life.

2. He recognizes only two practicable alternatives for the converted soldier : he must either leave the

---

[1] Tert *Cor* 11 (ii. 91–93).   [2] Tert *Cor* 12 (ii. 94 f).

[3] It will be seen (p. 108) that he asks the question " whether a believer may turn to military service," which almost certainly implies that some believers had already done so. Similarly in *De Corona* (211 A.D.) (see p. 111) he speaks of ' transferring one's name from the camp of light to the camp of darkness,' and mentions those converted when they were already soldiers as a special class, thus making it evident that there were others who had enlisted after conversion.

service, or suffer martyrdom. Harnack indeed says that Tertullianus displays some uncertainty in regard to converts who were already soldiers, and that he does not present them this dilemma of either leaving the army or dying as martyrs, "but opens to them yet a third possibility, namely that of avoiding pollution by heathenism as much as they can." [1] But it has to be remembered that the pollution was, in Tertullianus' view, practically inseparable from military life ; he runs over a large number of the commonest duties of the soldier, and raises objections to them one after another ; and his third alternative must therefore be regarded as an ironical concession of a bare abstract possibility, which would be obviously impossible in practice, like his concession that a Christian may hold office, provided he has nothing to do with sacrifices, temples, public shows, oaths, judgment of capital or criminal cases, pronunciation and infliction of penalties, and so on.

3. The emphasis which he lays on the danger of contamination by idolatry has led some authors to represent this as his one real objection to military service and to use it for the purpose of dissociating him from those who in later times have objected to war on humanitarian grounds. Thus Professor Bethune-Baker says : "It is important to notice what Tertullian means by those offences against God which are inseparable from the soldier's life. *It is not the modern idea at all.* The special objections which he feels, *the only offences against Christian sentiment that seem to really weigh with him*, are the military oath—over which the heathen gods presided—and the pagan

[1] Harnack *MC* 67.

ceremonial with which so many military acts and operations were invested." [1] This remarkable statement is approvingly quoted by Archdeacon Cunningham.[2] The passages just quoted from Tertullianus are sufficient proof of its amazing inaccuracy. Great as was his horror of idolatry, his conviction of the illegitimacy of all bloodshed and violence was equally great. Nor can I understand how Gass can say: "Tertullian was prepared to put up with Christian soldiers, only without the ostentatious crown of victory." [3] Even Troeltsch falls a victim to this error: he says that Tertullianus and Origenes, "despite the(ir) contention that the soldiers' handiwork of blood was absolutely unchristian, would have acquiesced, if service in the army had not brought the Christians into contact with the worship of the Emperor and (the religious customs) of the camp." [4] This statement is unwarranted even in regard to Tertullianus, and still more so in regard to Origenes, who never raises the difficulty of idolatrous contamination in the army at all.[5]

4. Tertullianus has been accused of lack of candour in boasting to pagans in one treatise [6] of the large number of Christians in the army, and after that arguing

---

[1] B.-Baker *ICW* 25. Italics mine.

[2] *Christianity and Politics*, 253. What is, I think, the one solitary allusion to the early Christian attitude to war in Dr. Forsyth's *Christian Ethic of War* contains a serious over-statement, if not a positive inaccuracy. He says (68 f): "The demand from Christian soldiers of the military oath . . . was objected to less on the grounds of the Sermon on the Mount than because it involved a confession of the Emperor's deity inconsistent with the place of Christ in His Gospel."

[3] Gass, *Geschichte der christlichen Ethik*, i. 93.

[4] Troeltsch 111 n 56.

[5] The remarks of Ramsay (*The Church in the Roman Empire*, pp. 435 f) on the subject imply that fear of participating in heathen rites was the one ground for the early Christian refusal of military service. Cf also Milman, *History of Christianity*, ii. 142.

[6] Tert *Apol* 1, 37, *Nat* i. 1, (see below, p. 234).

with his fellow-Christians that there ought not to be any Christians in the army at all.[1] But unless candour requires a writer to explain his whole mind on a subject every time he mentions it in a purely incidental way, the charge of disingenuousness is unwarranted. Each time that Tertullianus spoke to pagans of Christian soldiers without reproaching them, he was simply adverting to an obvious and admitted fact, in order to prove the numbers and ubiquity of the Christians and their readiness to take part in the activities of society. It would have been not only futile, but out of place, to introduce a topic upon which Christian opinion was divided, unless the course of the argument distinctly called for its treatment.

5. Again, Tertullianus' attempt to find an application of Christianity to every department of life has been criticized as in itself a mistake. His earnestness, it is admitted, was commendable; but he was on wrong lines: "he failed, as every. man is bound to fail, who conceives of Christianity in the light of a Rule, as a law of commandments contained in ordinances, rather than as a law of the spirit of life in Christ Jesus." [2] We may concede that the province of Christian casuistry is a strictly limited one, and that the limits are at times overpassed both by Tertullianus and others. But even the Pauline Epistles, not to mention the Synoptic Gospels, teach us that there is such a thing as the Law of Christ, which, while springing from 'the spirit of life in Christ Jesus,' issues in certain very definite and concrete principles of conduct. This being so, it becomes the duty of every Christian,

[1] So Harnack *MC* 59 f: cf B.-Baker *ICW* 23; Guignebert 192; Bigelmair 180; De Jong 9 ff.　　　[2] Scullard 212.

not only to work out the application of these principles to his own life, but also—and this is particularly the duty of the Christian teacher and writer—to assist others to do the same.

6. It is interesting to notice in Tertullianus the idea already suggested by Justinus [1] of the 'alternative service' rendered by the Christian to society and the State, despite the fact that he does not engage officially in public affairs. The idea forms, as we shall see later, a very important item in the apologia of Origenes. Tertullianus does not work it into any organic system of thought ; but his expressions of it, such as they are, are interesting. "I might deservedly say," he argues, "Caesar is more ours (than yours), inasmuch as he is appointed by our God. So that I do more for his (health and) safety (than ye do), not only because I demand it of Him who is able to give (it), nor because I who demand it am such as to deserve to obtain it, but also because, in reducing the majesty of Caesar below God, I the more commend him to God, to whom alone I subject him." [2] He makes his philosophic cloak say in reply to the charge of idleness and neglect of public affairs : "Yet to me also it will be to some extent allowed that I am of advantage to the public. I am wont, from every boundary-stone or altar, to prescribe for morals medicines that will confer good health more happily on public affairs and states and empires than your works (will). . . . I flatter no vices ; I spare no lethargy, no scabbiness ; I apply the cautery to ambition," and so on. [3]

7. Lastly, it is a mistake to regard Tertullianus as

[1] See above, pp. 60, 103.　　　　[2] Tert *Apol* 33 (i. 448).
[3] Tert *Pall* 5 (ii. 1047 f).

an individual dissenter from the Church as a whole on this question of whether Christians ought to serve in the army or not. Harnack, for instance, urges (in my opinion, without sufficient ground) that the Christian soldiers in the army had up till then never agitated as malcontents (frondiert) on account of their Christian profession, and that his "attack on the service of Christians in the army was something new, hitherto unheard of : easy as it was for him to prove the essential incompatibility of the service of Christ and service in the army, even in peace(-time), it was just as impossible for him to appeal to a rigorous custom and practice already in force hitherto." [1] It is true that no general or authoritative ruling on the point had yet been given—circumstances not having called for it, that Christian conviction in regard to it was never absolutely unanimous, that many of Tertullianus' Christian contemporaries (how many we do not know) differed from him, and that the Church on the whole ultimately agreed with them rather than with him. It must however be borne in mind that this last fact would have its own effect in submerging to some extent earlier utterances of a contrary tendency ; and this effect must be allowed for in explaining whatever paucity there is in records of this kind. Tertullianus clearly tells us that 'many' soldiers, when converted to Christianity, immediately left the service.[2] His own views are not to be set aside as those of a Montanist, for his objection to military service is as clear and emphatic in 'De Idololatria,' written before he had

---

[1] Harnack *MC* 67.

[2] See p. 112 n. 1. Harnack (*MC* 66) waters down Tertullianus' 'multis,' into 'vielleicht viele.'

adopted Montanism, as it is in ' De Corona,' written after he had adopted it.[1] And when we consider that these views, as will be shown presently, agree with the testimony of Origenes and the oldest Church-Orders as to the normal Christian practice in the earlier part of the third century, and were apparently endorsed by so representative a churchman as his own fellow-countryman and admirer Cyprianus, we shall hardly be inclined to believe that at this time he was voicing the opinion of a minority of Christians, still less that he represented the views of a mere handful of fanatical extremists.[2]

We have now to consider the evidence of the Canons of Hippolutos; but in order to do so, it is necessary to say something, by way of introduction, on a tiresome and as yet unsolved literary problem. Hippolutos was a learned Roman Christian, who flourished during the first thirty years of the third century. He was the critic and rival of Pope Kallistos (218–223 A.D.), and for a time headed a separate congregation, as opposition-bishop; in 235 A.D. he was exiled to Sardinia, where probably he died. He is known to have interested him-

---

[1] Professor B.-Baker's treatment of this point (*ICW* 22–26) is peculiarly conflicting and difficult to follow. He knows the date of ' De Idololatria,' and quotes what is said in it about Christ disarming every soldier, and so on: yet he makes much of the distinction between " Tertullian (*a*) Catholic " and " (*b*) Montanist," quotes the former as testifying to the presence of Christians in the army, adding that "in the opinion of Tertullian this redounded to their credit," speaks of " Tertullian's change of mind," points out how his Montanism is revealed in his later writings, and concludes that "the opinions recorded in them must be proportionately discounted." Some remarks have already been offered (pp. 115 f) on the real bearing to Tertullianus' boasts in *Apol* 37 and *Nat* i. 1. They cannot be taken as showing that in his Catholic period he approved of Christians acting as soldiers.

[2] Ramsay (*The Church in the Roman Empire*, pp. 435 f) speaks as if it was only a few individuals here and there who objected to Christians serving as soldiers.

self in ecclesiastical regulations and to have written περὶ χαρισμάτων ἀποστολικὴ παράδοσις. Whether this is the title of one work or of two ('Concerning Ministerial Gifts' and 'Apostolic Tradition') we do not know ; neither do we know the *exact* meaning he attached to χαρίσματα. These uncertainties have added to the difficulty of identifying Hippolutos' composition among the various extant works possessing some sort of claim to embody it. The works concerned are members of a large family of documents and fragments in different languages and of different dates, but all closely related to one another and all dealing with rules and regulations to be observed in the government of the Church. Without attempting to enter into the tangled details of the problem, we may briefly outline the chief points. Three documents are in question : (1) the so-called 'Hippolytean Canons,' which cannot have come from Hippolutos as they stand, but must in any case have been heavily interpolated :[1] (2) the so-called 'Egyptian Church-Order,' the contents of which closely resemble those of the Hippolytean Canons, and which is usually assigned to the first half of the fourth century, though it has recently been claimed (by Dom Conolly) as virtually the composition of Hippolutos himself[2]: (3) 'The Testament of our Lord,' a Syrian or Cilician version of the same general collection of rules, dating about

[1] Achelis, in *Texte und Untersuchungen* VI 4 (38–137) gives a Latin version of the Canones Hippolyti, and argues for the authorship, in the main, of Hippolitus. Riedel, in *Die Kirchenrechtsquellen des Patriarchats Alexandrien* (Leipzig, 1900) (193–230), gives a German version based on better MSS than those used by Achelis.

[2] See Krüger 360 ; Maclean 160 f : Dom R. H. Conolly in *Texts and Studies* VIII 4 (1916). The text is given in the last-named work, pp. 175–194, and also by Funk in *Didascalia et Constitutiones Apostolorum* (Paderborn, 1905) ii. 97–119.

the middle of the fourth century,[1] but in some respects preserving older material than either of the two last-named works. Even if we cannot take Conolly's theory as proven, we may yet well believe that Hippolutos did actually compose detailed regulations for Church-management, particularly if ἀποστολικὴ παράδοσις is to be regarded as the title of a separate work, distinct from περὶ χαρισμάτων, and that these regulations found their way to the East and are contained in a more or less modified form in the ' Egyptian Church-Order,' and the ' Hippolytean Canons ' and also lie at the basis of ' The Testament of our Lord ' and the still later Apostolic Constitutions (circ. 375 A.D.). It would be difficult to account for the connection of Hippolutos' name with this body of documents, unless we could regard him as the author of some of the material contained in them.[2] The reader will easily see that no investigation of the ruling given by Hippolutos on any point is adequate without a full quotation of what is said on it in each of the three documents mentioned. We must therefore proceed next to quote their respective regulations on the subject of Christians acting as magistrates and soldiers. These regulations occur in that part of each document which deals with the acceptance of new members into the Church and with the question of the trades and professions which it is legitimate or otherwise for Church-members to follow. As several versions are in question, I have set forth their contents in tabular form (pp. 122, 123) to facilitate the comparison of one with another.

[1] Cooper and Maclean 41 ; Maclean 166.
[2] The subject is more fully dealt with by the authors already quoted : cf also Krüger 341 f; Harnack *C* ii. 501–517 ; Funk *op cit* ii. xix–xxviii ; Bardenhewer, *Patrologie*, 219, 353–357 ; Maclean 156 ff.

THE EGYPTIAN CHURCH-ORDER.		THE 'HIPPOLYTEAN CANONS'.		THE TESTAMENT OF OUR LORD.7
According to Funk (Latin, based on Coptic).3	According to Ethiopic Version as given by Horner.3	According to Achelis (Latin, based on Arabic).4	According to Riedel (German, based on other Arabic MSS).5	
xi. 9. The soldier, who is under authority, thou mayest not allow him to kill men; if he is ordered (to do so), thou mayest not allow him to thrust himself forward,2 nor to swear; if however he is unwilling (to comply), let him be rejected.	A soldier of the prince they shall not receive, and if indeed they received him, if he was commanded to kill, he shall not do (it); and if he does not leave off, he shall be rejected. . . .	xiii. 71. A man who has accepted the power of killing, or a soldier, may never be received at all. xiii. 72. But those who, when they were soldiers, were ordered to fight, but otherwise have abstained from all evil speech, and have not placed garlands on their heads, but have acquired every mark of distinction (omne signum adepti sunt) [? may be received].	13. Persons who possess authority to kill, or soldiers, should not kill at all even when it is commanded them, and (should) not utter any evil word. They should not carry on their heads garlands, which they receive as marks of distinction.	If anyone be a soldier or in authority, let him be taught not to oppress or to kill or to rob, or to be angry or to rage and afflict anyone. But let those rations suffice him which are given to him. But if they wish to be baptized in the Lord, let them cease from military service or from the [post of] authority, and if not let them not be received.
xi. 10. He who has the power of the sword or is ruler of a city, clad in purple, let him either leave off or be rejected.	He who is a soldier among the believers and among the instructed, or a star-gazer or magician and the like, and a magistrate with the sword or chief of praefects, and he who is clad in red, let him leave off or be rejected.	xiii. 73. But every man, who, having been raised to the rank of prefecture or precedence or power, is not clothed with the adornment of justice which is according to the gospel, let him be separated from the flock, and let him not the	Every one who receives a distinctive (and) leading position, or a magisterial power, and does not clothe himself with the unarmedness (Waffen-losigkeit), which is becoming to the gospel, should be separated from the flock,	

xi. 11. If a catechumen or a believer wishes to become a soldier, let them be rejected, for they have despised God.

And a catechumen or believer, if they wish to be a soldier, shall be rejected, because it is far from God.

bishop pray in his presence. xiv. 74. Let not the Christian become a soldier of his own will, unless he is compelled by a commander. Let him have the sword; but let him beware lest he become guilty of the charge of shedding blood. xiv. 75. If it be found out that blood has been shed by him, let him abstain from participation in the mysteries, unless perchance he shall be corrected by a singular change in his manners, accompanied by tears and lamentation. Nevertheless, let his gift be, not a mere sham, but (given) with the fear of God.

and the bishop should not pray with him. 14. No Christian should go and become a soldier, unless he is compelled to.[6] Let not a commander, who has a sword, draw any (guilt of) bloodshed upon himself. If he has shed blood, he should not take part in the mysteries, until he is cleansed by chastisement and tears and sighs. Let him not clothe his office as commander with deceit, but with the fear of God.

Let a catechumen or a believer of the people, if he desire to be a soldier, either cease from his intention, or if not let him be rejected. For he hath despised God by his thought, and leaving the things of the Spirit, he hath perfected himself in the flesh, and hath treated the faith with contempt.

[1] Funk op cit 107: cf Horner 312 f.

[2] se obtrudere.

[3] Horner 149. The Ethiopic version is often nearer the original than the Coptic, on which the Latin of Funk is here based. It is adopted here by Conolly in his tentative version of the Egyptian Church-Order (Texts and Studies VIII 4. 181). The preceding clause in the Ethiopic excludes him who teaches hunting, or fighting, or war.

[4] Achelis op cit 81-83.

[5] Riedel op cit 206 f.

[6] Harnack (MC 73) brackets this clause [wenn es nicht notwendig für ihn ist] as 'certainly a later addition.' Riedel gives as an alternative rendering: "unless a commander, who has a sword, compels him: let him not draw," and so on.

[7] Cooper and Maclean 118, cf 208 f.

It will be observed that only 'The Testament of our Lord' is consistently rigorous in refusing baptism to soldiers and magistrates except on condition of their quitting their offices, and forbidding a Christian to become a soldier on pain of rejection. All the other documents introduce some sort of modification. The Ethiopic version of the Egyptian Church-Order seems to allow a soldier already received to remain as such in the Church, on condition that he kills no one; but immediately afterwards it goes back on this concession by requiring a soldier among the believers to leave off or be rejected. The Coptic version of the Egyptian Church-Order first forbids the Christian soldier to kill men, and then says that, if he is commanded to kill men, he is not to thrust himself forward; but, like 'The Testament,' it refuses to admit a magistrate, and forbids the Christian to become a soldier on pain of rejection. The 'Hippolytean Canons' in one form forbid soldiers and magistrates to kill, even when commanded to do so, and prescribe 'unarmedness' for the latter; in the other form they first forbid the admission of magistrates and soldiers, and then apparently accept soldiers who have fought but who have neither used bad language nor worn garlands, and magistrates who are clothed with the adornment of justice.

While we are unfortunately not able to extract with any confidence from this bewildering maze of contradictions and modifications the exact words of Hippolutos himself, or of the original regulation, by whomsoever it was framed, it is not very difficult to see what the provisions of that original regulation must have been. All that we know from other sources—and from the inherent probabilities of the case—goes to

show that the constant trend of Christian thought on
this and similar questions was from strictness towards
relaxation, from an almost complete abstention to an
almost equally complete freedom to participate.[1] An
incidental confirmation of this view comes from the
Apostolic Constitutions, which are certainly later than
the Egyptian Church-Order and almost certainly later
than the other two documents we have been dealing
with. In those Constitutions we can see that the
movement towards leniency has got still further, and
all that is required of a soldier applying for Church-
membership is that he shall " inflict injury on no one,
make no false accusation, and be content with the pay
given to him." [2] This is of course simply a repetition
of the precepts of John the Baptist, and clearly does
not imply that soldier-candidates would have to leave
the army. We shall therefore not go far wrong in
seeking for the original terms of Hippolutos' Church-
Order in the most stringent of the requirements still
embedded in the documents as we have them. As the
demand for a relaxation of this stringency made itself
felt, the terms of the original would be little by little
abbreviated, added to, or otherwise modified, so as
to provide loopholes in favour of a laxer policy.
Hence would arise that weird mixture of inconsistent

[1] Professor B.-Baker is undoubtedly mistaken in treating the Christian
objection to war on the ground of bloodshed as a comparatively new
development belonging to " the last forty years of the third century, when
the practical life and example of Christ and the Apostles was receding far
into the background," etc. (*ICW* 31 ; cf 29 : "By this time, therefore,"
(i.e. 249 A.D.), " many Christians shrank from military service "). Archdeacon Cunningham (253) follows Professor B.-Baker in this error : " there
seems to have been an increasing aversion to military service on the part of
Christians in the third century." The evidence of Celsus (see p. 104)
shows that the Christians as a general rule refused service at least as early
as 180 A.D.   [2] *Apostolic Constitutions* VIII xxxii. 10.

permissions and prohibitions which gives such a curious appearance of vacillation to most of the existing codes. The only one of them which has kept the full strictness —whether or no in the actual words—of the original is ' The Testament of our Lord,' which dates in its present form from the middle of the fourth century or a little later, and arose among the conservative Christians of Syria or south-eastern Asia Minor.[1] The substance of that original regulation must have been that a soldier or a magistrate who wielded the power of the sword could not be admitted by baptism to membership in the Christian Church, unless he had first resigned his military or quasi-military calling, that if a catechumen or a baptized Christian became a soldier, he must give it up or else suffer exclusion from the Church, and that similarly a mere desire on his part to become a soldier, showing, as it was thought, contempt for God, must be relinquished on pain of rejection or excommunication.

That some such regulations as these should have emanated—as they probably did—from so influential and representative a Churchman as Hippolutus of Rome, that the document embodying them should have been made the basis of virtually all subsequent Church-Orders, including some that were apparently highly esteemed and closely followed throughout whole regions of eastern Christendom, and that these particular rules should have survived unmodified in at least one such Church-Order until late in the fourth century and should still be so clearly visible as they are, under the moss-growths of successive editions, in other Church-Orders of approximately the same date—are facts of the first importance in the history of our subject, and

[1] Cooper and Maclean 41–45.

facts, too, which as yet have not received anything like the attention they deserve. The comparative recency of the investigation of the Church-Orders accounts, in part at least, for the total omission of all reference to them in many of the writings that deal with this topic.[1] But even in the most recent and scholarly works the place assigned to them is scarcely adequate. Bigelmair quotes the passages from the Egyptian Church-Order, the ' Hippolytean Canons,' and ' The Testament of our Lord,' and admits that "they mark clearly and distinctly the views which prevailed in wide circles": but he describes them as emanating from circles where "tertullianic views" were prevalent (aus tertullianischen Anschauungskreisen), and says that they possessed no generally binding power.[2] Even Harnack, whose work is that of an impartial, thorough, and accurate scholar, confines himself to a quotation of the ' Hippolytean Canons,' Nos. 13 and 14, as given by Riedel, combining it in a single paragraph with quotations from Origenes and Lactantius, and then remarks: "But these injunctions of the moralists were by no means followed in the third century," adding as his grounds for this statement sundry pieces of evidence showing that many Christians of the

---

[1] Grotius goes so far as to argue from the *absence* of regulations. He contends that "nothing more can be gathered from those sayings (of the Fathers) than the private opinion of certain people, not the public (opinion) of the Churches," and says : "But setting aside private authorities, let us come to the public (authority) of the Church, which ought to be of the greatest weight (with us). I say therefore that those who served as soldiers were never rejected from baptism or excommunicated by the Church, which nevertheless ought to have been done and would have been done, if military service conflicted with the conditions of the new faith " (Grotius, *De Jure Belli ac Pacis*, I ii. ix, 2 and x, 2). Cf Ramsay, *Cities and Bishoprics of Phrygia*, ii. 718 ("The Church as a whole never sanctioned this prohibition, or called on its converts to abandon the ranks or on its adherents to refuse to enter them ").

[2] Bigelmair 133, 171–173.

third century and later were either in the army themselves or knew of no objection to Christians being
there. [1]   But this latter fact, the nature and extent of
which we shall have to examine later, in no wise
invalidates the conclusion to be drawn from the
Church-Orders, viz. that in the third century the conviction that Christianity was incompatible with the
shedding of blood, either in war or in the administration of justice, was not only maintained and vigorously
defended by eminent individuals like Tertullianus of
Carthago, Hippolutos of Rome, and Origenes of Palestine and Egypt, but was widely held and acted on in
the Churches up and down Christendom. [2]   For reasons
to be stated later, the conviction was not unanimous ;
but the various indications of its absence can quite
easily be explained without adopting Harnack's view
that it was simply the personal opinion of a few uninflu-
ential 'moralists.'   That view seems to me, in face of
the evidence we have just had before us, and even in
face of the facts on the other side of the case, not only
unnecessary, but also erroneous.

Minucius Felix says : " It is not right for us either to
see or hear of a man being slain ; and so careful are we
(to abstain) from human blood, that we do not even
touch the blood of eatable animals in (our) food. . . .
Even though we refuse your official honours and
purple, yet we do not consist of the lowest dregs of
the population." [3]

[1] Harnack *MC* 72 f.
[2] Cooper and Maclean 209 : " The Church-Orders lean to the stricter
view.   But we cannot therefore ascribe them to sectarian bodies, who kept
themselves aloof from ordinary Christian life " ; etc.
[3] Minuc xxx. 6, xxxi. 6.

We turn next to Origenes, the prince of early Christian thinkers. Apart from his general eminence as scholar, theologian, apologist, and practical Christian, he is far and away the most important writer who handles the question before us. Though he yields to Tertullianus in rhetorical brilliance and to Augustinus in his influence over posterity, his defence of the early Christian refusal to participate in war is the only one that faces at all thoroughly or completely the ultimate problems involved. He has however been strangely misunderstood and misinterpreted, and certainly never answered. Our procedure will be, as before, to let our author first speak for himself, and then add a few elucidations and comments of our own. We begin, therefore, with a series of passages from Origenes' reply to Celsus (248 A.D.), some of which we have already had occasion to quote in another connection.

" How would it have been possible for this peaceful teaching (of Christianity), which does not allow (its adherents) even to defend themselves against [1] (their) enemies, to prevail, unless at the coming of Jesus the (affairs) of the world had everywhere changed into a milder (state) ? "[2] " If a revolt had been the cause of the Christians combining, and if they had derived the(ir) origin from the Jews, to whom it was allowed (ἐξῆν) to take arms on behalf of the(ir) families, and to destroy (their) enemies, the Lawgiver of (the) Christians would not have altogether forbidden (the) destruction of man, teaching that the deed of daring (on the part) of his own disciples against a man, however unrighteous he be, is never right—for he did not deem it becoming to his

---

[1] Or possibly ' take vengeance on '—ἀμύνεσθαι.
[2] Orig *Cels* ii. 30.

own divine legislation to allow the destruction of any man whatever." [1] "To those who ask us whence we have come or whom we have (for) a leader, we say that we have come in accordance with the counsels of Jesus to cut down our warlike and arrogant swords of argument into ploughshares, and we convert into sickles the spears we formerly used in fighting. For we no longer take 'sword against a nation,' nor do we learn 'any more to make war,' having become sons of peace for the sake of Jesus, who is our leader, instead of (following) the ancestral (customs) in which we were strangers to the covenants." [2] "It would not be possible for the ancient Jews to keep their civil economy unchanged, if, let us suppose, they obeyed the constitution (laid down) according to the gospel. For it would not be possible for Christians to make use, according to the Law of Moses, of (the) destruction of (their) enemies or of those who had acted contrary to the Law and were judged worthy of destruction by fire or stoning. . . . Again, if thou wert to take away from the Jews of that time, who had a civil economy and a land of their own, the (right) to go out against the(ir) enemies and serve as soldiers on behalf of their ancestral (institutions) and to destroy or otherwise punish the adulterers or murderers or (men) who had done something of that kind, nothing would be left but for them to be wholly and utterly destroyed, the(ir) enemies setting upon the nation, when they were weakened and prevented by their own law from defending themselves against the(ir) enemies." [3] "We ought, however, to despise currying favour with men and kings, not only if we curry favour with them

---

[1] Orig *Cels* iii. 7.   [2] Orig *Cels* v. 33 (see above, p. 63 n 3).
[3] Orig *Cels* vii. 26.

by means of acts of blood-guiltiness and licentiousness and savage cruelty, but also if (we do it) by means of impiety towards the God of all or any speech (uttered) with servility and obsequiousness, (which is) foreign to brave and high-principled men and to those who wish to join to the(ir) other (virtues) bravery as (the) highest virtue." [1]

Origenes, however, does not set himself seriously to grapple with the difficulties of the problem until near the end of his eighth and last book, Celsus having placed his criticism on this particular point at the end of his work and being followed in the matter of arrangement by his Christian opponent. Practically the whole of the eight chapters that come last but one in Origenes' reply are taken up in justifying the Christian attitude of aloofness from all forms of violence in the service of the state. We shall confine our quotations to the most pertinent passages. First, in replying to the objection that, if all did the same as the Christians, the Emperor would be deserted, and the Empire would fall a prey to the barbarians, Origenes says : " On this supposition " (viz. that all did the same as himself and took no part in war or magistracy), " the Emperor will not ' be left alone ' or ' deserted,' nor will ' the world's (affairs) fall into the hands of the most lawless and savage barbarians.' For if, as Celsus says, ' all were to do the same as' I (do), clearly the barbarians also, coming to the Word of God, will be most law-abiding and mild ; and every religious worship will be abolished, and that alone of the Christians will hold sway ; and indeed, one

[1] Orig *Cels* viii. 65. This is the only passage I have noticed in which Origenes alludes to idolatry as a bar to state-service. Bigelmair (136) recognizes that the risk of idolatrous contamination was not brought prominently forward by Origenes.

day it shall alone hold sway, the Word ever taking possession of more (and more) souls." [1] Then in the next chapter : " Since he puts the question : ' What would happen if the Romans, persuaded by the argument of the Christians, should neglect the (services owed) to the recognized gods and the laws formerly in force among men, and should worship the Most High ?,' hear our answer on this. We say that if two of us agree upon earth concerning anything that they shall ask, they shall receive it from the heavenly Father of the righteous : for God rejoices over the agreement of rational beings, and turns away from discord. What must (we) believe if, not only—as now—very few agree, but the whole Empire (governed) by the Romans ? For they will pray to the Word, who said of old to the Hebrews when they were pursued by the Egyptians : ' The Lord shall fight for you, and ye shall be silent ' ; and, praying with all concord, they will be able to overthrow far more enemies who pursue them than those whom the prayer of Moses—when he cried to God— and of those with him overthrew. . . . [2] But if, according to Celsus' supposition, all the Romans were to be persuaded, they will by praying overcome their enemies ; or (rather) they will not make war at all, being guarded by the Divine Power, which promised to save five whole cities for the sake of fifty righteous. For the men of God are the salt that preserves the earthly order of the world ; and earthly things hold together (only) as long as the salt is not corrupted." [3] The next chapter is an

[1] Orig *Cels* viii. 68.
[2] Orig *Cels* viii. 69. He goes on to explain that God had not always fought for the Hebrews, because they had not always fulfilled the conditions of receiving such help by observing His law.
[3] Orig *Cels* viii. 70. On the strength of this thought of the protective providence of God, he says that the Christians look forward calmly to the possible recrudescence of persecution.

obscure one. Origenes quotes Celsus as saying to the Christian the following : " It is absolutely intolerable that thou shouldst say that, if those who now reign over us, having been persuaded by thee, should be taken captive, thou wilt persuade those who reign after (them, and) then others, if they should be taken captive, and others again, (and so on), until, when all who have been persuaded by thee have been taken captive, some one ruler who is prudent and foresees what is happening shall altogether destroy you, before he himself is destroyed." Origenes replies that no Christian talks like this, and attributes it to the nonsensical invention of Celsus himself; and unfortunately we cannot get any further with it.[1] He then proceeds : " After this, he utters a sort of prayer : ' Would that it were possible for the Greeks and barbarians that occupy Asia and Europe and Libya unto the ends (of the earth) to agree (to come) under one law '; (but) judging this to be impossible, he adds : ' He who thinks this (possible) knows nothing.' If it is necessary to speak of this, a few (words) shall be said on the subject, though it needs much investigation and discussion, in order that what was said about the whole rational (creation) agreeing (to come) under one law might appear to be not only possible but certain. Now the Stoics (say) that, when the strongest of the elements prevails, the conflagration will occur, all things being changed into fire : but we say that the Word (will) one day master the whole rational creation and transform every soul into his own

[1] Orig *Cels* viii. 71. Harnack (*ME* i. 264 n) says : " I do not understand, any more than Origen did, the political twaddle which Celsus (lxxi) professes to have heard from a Christian. It can hardly have come from a Christian, and it is impossible nowadays to ascertain what underlay it. I therefore pass it by."

perfection. . . . For the Word is stronger than all the evils in a soul, and the healing that is in him leads it (the soul) forward for each man according to the will of God : and the end of things is the destruction of evil." He then has a long passage on the Christian anticipation of the complete destruction of evil, and concludes : " This I thought it reasonable to say, without exact statement (of details), in answer to Celsus' remark, that he thought it impossible for the Greeks and barbarians inhabiting Asia and Europe and Libya to agree. And perhaps such (an agreement) is really impossible to those still in bodies, but not impossible to those who have been released from them." [1]

He then turns to the concrete appeal of Celsus that the Christians should serve in the army and take part in the business of government. "Celsus next urges us to help the Emperor with all (our) strength, and to labour with him (in maintaining) justice, and to fight for him and serve as soldiers with him, if he require (it), and to share military command (with him). To this it has to be said that we do help the Emperors as occasion (requires) with a help that is, so to say, divine, and putting on 'the whole armour of God.' And this we do in obedience to the apostolic voice which says : ' I therefore exhort you firstly that supplications, prayers, intercessions, thanksgivings, be made for all men, for Emperors and all who are in high station ' ; and the more pious one is, so much the more effectual is he in helping the Emperors than (are) the soldiers who go forth in battle-array and kill as many as they can of the enemy. And then we should say this to those who are strangers to the faith and who

---

[1] Orig *Cels* viii. 72.

ask us to serve as soldiers on behalf of the community
and to kill men : that among you the priests of certain
statues and the temple-wardens of those whom ye
regard as gods keep their right-hand(s) unstained for
the sake of the sacrifices, in order that they may offer
the appointed sacrifices to those whom ye call gods,
with hands unstained by (human) blood and pure from
acts of slaughter ; and whenever war comes, ye do not
make the priests also serve. If then it is reasonable to
do this, how much more (reasonable is it, that), when
others are serving in the army, these (Christians) should
do their military service as priests and servants of God,
keeping their right-hands pure and striving by prayers
to God on behalf of those who are righteously serving
as soldiers and of him who is reigning righteously, in
order that all things opposed and hostile to those that
act righteously may be put down ? And we, (in) putting
down by our prayers all demons—those who stir up
warlike feelings, and prompt the violation of oaths, and
disturb the peace, help the Emperors more than those
who to all appearance serve as soldiers. We labour
with (him) in the public affairs—(we) who offer up
prayers with righteousness, with exercises and practices
that teach (us) to despise pleasures and not to be led
away by them. And we fight for the Emperor more
(than others do): and we do not serve as soldiers *with
him*, even though he require (it) ; but we do serve as
soldiers *on his behalf*, training a private army of piety
by means of intercessions to the Deity.[1] And if Celsus
wishes us to exercise military command on behalf of
(our) country, let him know that we do this also, not in
order to be seen by men and to obtain empty glory in

[1] Orig *Cels* viii. 73.

their eyes by doing so : for in secret (and) under the
control of our inner reason are our prayers, sent up as
from priests on behalf of those in our country. And
Christians benefit the(ir) countries more than do the
rest of men, educating the citizens and teaching them to
be devout towards the God of the State, and taking up
into a sort of divine and heavenly State those who have
lived well in the smallest states. . . .[1] But Celsus urges
us also to (take part in) govern(ing) the country, seeing
that this has to be done for the sake of the safety of
the laws and of piety. But we, knowing in each state
another organization of a ' country '—(an organization)
founded by the Word of God—exhort those who are
powerful in speech and who lead a wholesome (moral)
life to rule over churches, not accepting those who are
fond of ruling, but constraining those who through
(their) great modesty are unwilling rashly to accept the
public charge of the Church of God. . . . And (it is) not
(for the sake of) escaping from the public services of life
that Christians shun such things, but (because they are)
reserving themselves for a diviner and more necessary
service, (namely that) of (the) Church of God, both
necessarily and rightly taking the lead for the salvation
of men, and having taken charge of all—of those within
(the Church), in order that they may daily live better
(lives), and of those who are apparently without, in
order that they may become (engaged) in the serious
words and works of piety, and thus, truly worshipping
God and training as many as they have power to, may
be mingled with the Word of God and the divine Law
and may thus be united to the God who is over all
through the Son of God—Word and Wisdom and

[1] Orig *Cels* viii. 74.

Truth and Righteousness—who unites to Him every one who is bent on living in all things according to (the will of) God." [1]

There are several points in the teaching set forth in these passages which call for special comment.

1. It will have been noticed that Origenes speaks of the Emperor as 'reigning righteously' and of his soldiers as 'righteously rendering military service,' that as a Christian he was prepared to pray for their victory in a righteous conflict,[2] and that he recognized the right of the ancient Jews to fight against their enemies.[3] Elsewhere he speaks of "people everywhere being compelled to serve as soldiers and to make war on behalf of the(ir) countries" in the times before Augustus, "when there was need that there should be war, for instance, between Peloponnesians and Athenians, and similarly between others." [4] He also says that "the wars of the bees perhaps constitute a lesson for the conduct of just and orderly wars among men, if ever there should be need (for them)." [5] All these passages but the last explicitly refer to the warfare of some set of non-Christians: and in the last there is no indication that Origenes has Christians in mind. When the fact is once clearly grasped that his allusions to justifiable wars are always, either explicitly or implicitly, to wars waged by non-Christians, many of the criticisms levelled at his teaching will be seen to rest on a misapprehension.[6]

---

[1] Orig *Cels* viii. 75. [2] Orig *Cels* viii. 73 (p. 135).
[3] Orig *Cels* iii. 7, vii. 26 (p. 130).
[4] Orig *Cels* ii. 30 (see below, p. 207).
[5] Orig *Cels* iv. 82. In the following chapter he rebukes Celsus for his attempt to depreciate the political institutions and defensive wars of men (see below, p. 207).
[6] The question is more fully discussed below, pp. 211 ff.

2. His candid recognition of the temporary place and value of what was good in pagan and Mosaic ethics must not be taken as stultifying or cancelling his equally candid declaration that Christians ought not to and would not take part in war. Several modern writers have fallen into this fallacy. Thus Grotius says that Origenes and Tertullianus are not consistent, and he quotes in regard to the former the passage about the bees.[1] Guizot, in a note on Gibbon,[2] says: "Origen, in truth, appears to have maintained a more rigid opinion (Cont. Cels. l. viii); but he has often renounced this exaggerated severity, perhaps necessary to produce great results, and he speaks of the profession of arms as an honourable one (l. iv. c. [83] 218 . . .)." Professor Bethune-Baker writes: "From all these passages together it is perhaps fair to conclude that Origen considered the Christian ideal incompatible with war, but would in practice have permitted Christians to engage in war. It is clear he regarded it as a Christian duty to pray for 'those that are warring justly.' Further, as it is quite certain that there were many Christians in the armies at the time when Origen was writing, it is not improbable that in his specific answer he is thinking particularly of the Christian clergy. Several of his phrases suggest this limited application."[3] This guardedly expressed, but nevertheless quite erroneous, suggestion is invested by Archdeacon Cunningham with dogmatic certainty: "It is clear that the Great Alexandrian did not regard War as a thing in which the Christian was wrong to take

---

[1] Grotius, *De Jure*, etc., I ii. ix, 2.
[2] Wm. Smith's edition of the *Decline and Fall*, ii. 189.
[3] B.-Baker *ICW* 30.

part."[1] Guignebert remarks: "But already Origenes seems to admit at least defensive war"[2]: and similarly Bigelmair : "Even Origenes at times gave a less rigorous judgment," for he meets a point brought forward by Celsus "with the remark—which contrasts curiously with his position elsewhere—that the wars of the bees were a pattern for the righteous and orderly wars of men."[3] All this misses the point. Origenes' view of the Christian's duty in regard to war is put as clearly as words could make it: and though he compares the intercessions of the Christians to the sacrifices of the pagan priesthood and speaks about the duty of the Christian clergy in training and governing others, the supposition that he meant to limit the abstention from bloodshed to the clergy is quite out of keeping with his actual statements. It is abundantly clear that he regarded the acceptance of Christianity as incompatible with the use of arms ; and his relative justification of the wars of non-Christians cannot be made a ground either for doubting that his rigorism was seriously meant, or for accusing him of inconsistency in maintaining it.[4]

3. Origenes accepts as true the charge implied in the appeal made by Celsus seventy years before, that Christians did as a body refuse to serve in the army and to hold magistracies. "We do not serve as soldiers with the Emperor, even though he require (it). . . . Christians avoid such things " (i.e. public offices).[5]

---

[1] *Christianity and Politics*, p. 252.
[2] Guignebert p. 196 : a note refers to Orig *Cels* iv. 82 f.
[3] Bigelmair 180 f. The same view is suggested by Schmidt (284).
[4] Barbèyrac (*Morale des Pères*, p. 104 f n) recognizes that Origenes does not contradict himself in this matter.
[5] Orig. *Cels* viii. 73, 75 (see pp. 135 f).

He speaks as if he was not aware that Christians ever took any other line[1]: and though this cannot be construed as showing that none of them ever did so—for there is evidence to prove that many did— or that Origenes dishonestly concealed what he knew to be a fact—for the dishonesty would have been so patent as to serve no purpose, yet it proves that even at this date, the middle of the third century, the predominant opinion among Christians was that their religion forbade them to serve in the legions.[2]

4. It is often urged that the early Christian disapproval of all violence has to be read in the light of early Christian eschatology. For if you could assume that within the near future, possibly almost immediately, the existing world-order was going to fall to pieces with a crash, the wicked were going to be rooted out and punished, and the reign of righteousness set up—all by the exercise of a special Divine intervention—then obviously there would not be much difficulty in proving all fighting, and indeed all judicial procedure, to be useless. Now whatever weight must be assigned to this consideration in criticizing the views of primitive Christians, or even of a man like Tertullianus, it is highly significant that the most gifted thinker of the early Church, the man who maintained the Gospel-principle of non-resistance as earnestly and explicitly as any, was unique also in this other excellence—that

[1] Neumann (241) is surely mistaken in supposing that Origenes' reference to soldiers as opponents of Christianity implies the presence of Christians in the army.

[2] De Jong 15: "Considering that Origenes is here defending, not only his own opinion, but Christendom in general, we must assume that also in his time . . . the great majority of Christians was opposed to military service, and that principally out of aversion to bloodshed, and that only a small number took part in it—a conclusion to which in fact the archaeological data, negative on this point, also lead us."

his mind was not fettered by the crude obsessions of orthodox Christian eschatology : he had little or nothing to say of a bodily return of Christ, or of an end of the world due to occur in the near future ; he contemplated an indefinite prolongation of human history under the divine control ; he had his eyes open to the needs of society, and, though keen on the spiritual side of things, suffered from no blind 'otherworldliness '— from none of what Weinel aptly calls 'Jenseitsfanatismus.' Eschatology, it is urged, invalidates the early Christian witness in regard to war : it cannot however invalidate the witness given by Origenes, for he did not share even the weakened eschatological beliefs of his Christian contemporaries. Yet none gave a clearer or more intelligent witness on the subject of Christian gentleness than he.

5. Note further that fear of idolatrous contamination had nothing to do with Origenes' disapproval of military service. He does indeed once mention 'impiety towards God' as a means of currying favour with kings, but never as a bar to service in the army. His view was based—as his analogy with the pagan priesthood, as well as many other passages, clearly shows—on the Christians' determination to keep their hands free from the stain of blood. Yet the late Dr. Gwatkin, in his criticism of Origenes' reply to the charge of disloyalty,[1] altogether ignores this aspect of the case, and speaks as if squeamishness on the subject of idolatry were the only difficulty that had to be considered. Even Troeltsch, as we have seen,[2] says that, if it had not been for this difficulty, Origenes would have acquiesced in Christians serving as soldiers.

[1] Gwatkin, *Early Church History*, i. 191 (cf 236).   [2] Above, p. 115.

6. Origenes happily lays great stress on the positive service which the Christians render to the State, a service which he claims is diviner, more needful, and more effective than that of the soldier or magistrate. " We do help the Emperors as occasion (requires) . . . We labour with (him) in the public affairs . . . we fight for the Emperor more (than others do) . . . Christians benefit the(ir) countries more than the rest of men," and so on.[1] Of this service he specifies two forms. (*a*) Intercessory prayer, which he rightly regards as exceedingly effective when coming from Christians : this prayer is that the Emperor and those associated with him may be successful in their efforts, in so far as their purposes are righteous, " in order that all things opposed and hostile to those that act righteously may be put down" ($\kappa\alpha\theta\alpha\iota\rho\epsilon\theta\tilde{\eta}$). It assumes that the Emperor has a standard of righteousness which is valid relative to his own sub-Christian condition, and it does not commit the Christian who offers it to an approval of the same standard for himself. The Christians, moreover, by their prayers, put down the demons who rouse warlike passions and disturb the peace. (*b*) Influence for good over others by the activities of the Church and the power of Christian life, " educating the citizens and teaching them to be devout towards the God of the State," taking charge of those within and those without the Church, and working effectually for their moral and spiritual salvation. No criticism of Origenes, which does not give full weight to this positive side of his plea, is either fair to him or worthy of a Christian critic. The words of the late Dr. Gwatkin unfortunately fail in this respect. " Even Origen only quib-

[1] Orig. *Cels* viii. 73 f (pp. 134–136).

bles," he says, "in his answer that they do not serve in the army because they support the emperor with their prayers, that they fight for their country by educating their fellow-citizens in true piety, that they help to govern it by devoting themselves to the nobler and more needful service of the church of God. All this evades the point—that men have no right to renounce at pleasure their duties to their country."[1] Now the party guilty of evading the point in this case is not the ancient apologist, but the late lamented historian himself; for in speaking of military service as a duty to one's country, he is, of course, simply assuming without argument the very point under debate : he has not a word to say on the very serious question as to how slaughter in war is to be reconciled with the teaching of Jesus. Not only does he assume that military service is a duty, but he calls the Christian refusal of it a renunciation of duty *at pleasure*. He does not realize that the early Christian, in refusing the use of arms, more than compensated for his withdrawal from the army by the moral and spiritual power for good which he exercised as a Christian, that he did—as Origenes claimed—really and literally help the Emperor in the maintenance of peace and justice, and really did benefit his country more than the rest of men.

7. This brings us to our last point, namely the question whether the Christian ethic as interpreted by Origenes can be safely advocated as a practical policy, or whether it is open to the fatal charge of anarchy. What is going to happen, Celsus had asked, as people are asking now, if this sort of thing spreads? Will not civilization become the prey of barbarians and savages?

[1] Gwatkin, l.c.

On the score of the results which, it is assumed, would
follow from the adoption of his teaching, the political
views expressed by him have been criticized as extravagant.[1] The criticism is in my judgment unwarranted.
To foresee accurately the future history of Christianity
is under no conditions and at no period an easy task,
even when one is emancipated—as Origenes happily
was—from the crude obsessions of orthodox eschatology.
It is therefore not to be wondered at that he should
hesitate to affirm positively that all the inhabitants of
the world would be able, while still in the body, to come
together under one law, though he does not rule out
this contingency as impossible, just as, in repudiating
the extravagant utterance attributed by Celsus to a
Christian, he does not rule out absolutely the possibility
of an Emperor's conversion.[2] His task was to show that
a Christianity, which sets its adherents to work in the
varied external and internal activities of the Church,
which endows them with moral purity and energy and
spiritual power, and which forbids them to participate
in the penal bloodshed and violence which pagan society
finds necessary for its own preservation and well-being
—that such a Christianity can be allowed to spread
indefinitely among mankind, without any fear of a

[1] Lecky ii. 39 ("The opinions of the Christians of the first three centuries were usually formed without any regard to the necessities of civil or
political life"); Harnack *ME* i. 263 f ("How extravagant (hochfliegend)
are his ideas!" Yet Harnack recognizes Origenes as "a great and sensible
statesman"—"ein grosser und einsichtiger Politiker"); Troeltsch 123 f
("With such presuppositions [as those of Origenes] every venture in regard
to social possibilities (and) every idea of the Christian criticism of society
having to be also an organic reformation of it, were out of the question.
God would take care that society held together. The cutting-off of the
forbidden callings suffices; the rest will remain standing. . . . Elsewhere
there are not wanting compromises and compositions which recognize the
necessity of these callings for the social system, and therefore enjoin here
too continuance in the calling").   [2] See above, pp. 133 f.

disastrous breakdown of civilization being occasioned by its expansion. That task he performs with admirable common-sense and insight. He does not desire or advocate or expect a sudden and wholesale abandonment by society of its usual methods of dealing with internal and external enemies, without any of those compensating safeguards and improvements which the gradual and steady growth of Christianity would ensure. And it is as a gradual growth that he thinks of the expansion of Christianity—as a growth consisting of the accretion of one individual after another, " the Word ever taking possession of more (and more) souls " until it has mastered the whole rational creation,[1] as a growth going on, not only among the civilized inhabitants of the Empire, but also among the uncivilized barbarians beyond its borders,[2] not only among the virtuous, but also among the sinful and criminal people, and therefore as removing steadily the wrongdoing which evokes wars and calls for penalties, while supplying steadily pari passu a more effectual cure for that wrongdoing in the shape of the mighty spiritual and moral influence of the Church. His programme thus consists of two gradual processes going on side by side as the result of the spread of Christianity : firstly, the gradual diminution of crime and the risk of foreign aggression, and secondly, the gradual substitution of spiritual influence for physical coercion, i.e. of a more for a less effective remedy for crime and aggression.[3] What ground does such a

[1] Orig *Cels* viii. 68 fin, 72 (see pp. 132–134).

[2] Orig *Cels* i. 53, viii. 4, 68.

[3] As furnishing a modern instance of the soundness of this plea, I transcribe the following passage from W. T. Stead's *Progress of the World* in the *Review of Reviews* for August 1890 (p. 104) : " The enthusiastic Americans who constituted the driving force of the Universal Peace Congress which met at Westminster in July, were provided with a very

programme give for the charge of anarchy? Celsus
actually made such a charge, but had to contradict
himself in doing so. He first professed to posit the
conversion of *all* to Christianity—in itself a legitimate
supposition—but immediately had to make an exception
of the barbarians in order to manufacture some sort of
a bogey. Origenes had no difficulty in pointing out
that Celsus' assumption of *all* doing the same as the
Christian presupposed the conversion of the barbarians
as well as the subjects of the Empire. Some modern
writers have pointed to the attacks later made on the
Empire by Christianized barbarians as if they proved
the shortsightedness of Origenes [1] : but they do nothing
of the sort, for the Christianity given to these barbarians
was not the same article as that for which Origenes was
bargaining; it was the Christianity of a Church that
had made a compact with the powers that be and was
accordingly obliged to sanction for its adherents the

---

striking illustration of the fashion in which the practical impunity with
which the individual can kill has told for peace in the Far West. For
years the Modoc Indians, thanks to their occupancy of the lava beds, a
natural stronghold where a handful of men could hold an army at bay,
defied the utmost efforts of the United States army. The Modocs,
although only a few hundred strong, baffled all the efforts to subdue them.
The war cost millions. Only twelve Modocs were killed, but General
Canby was slain and 160 of his men. After all, the war seemed no nearer
an end than it was at the beginning. In their despair the Americans
abandoned the bullet and took to the Bible. Then, according to Mr.
Wood, the Secretary of the American Christian and Arbitration Society,
in the providence of God one little Quaker woman, " ' believing in the
Lord Jesus Christ's power, and in non-resistent principles, has converted
the whole Modoc tribe to non-resistent Quakers, and they are now most
harmless, self-supporting farmers and preachers of the Gospel of Christ.' "
The story of the transformation effected in the relations between the Red-
skins and the United States Government by substituting Christian for
military principles is one of the strangest of the true stories of our day.
It is not surprising that the men who have found the Gospel a talisman for
civilising a Modoc and an Apache should cross the Atlantic full of faith
that it would be equally efficacious in staying the blood-feud of the
Germans and the French.   [1] Neumann 240; cf Bigelmair 177.

use of the sword at a ruler's bidding. It was the Church's failure to remain true to the full Christian ethic advocated by Origenes, which made possible the scene of Christian barbarians invading the Empire. The extraordinary supposition—which forms part of Origenes' apologia—of a united and converted Empire holding its barbarian foes at bay by the power of prayer, was no part of his own programme: it concludes his reply to the illogical challenge of his opponent. Extravagant as that challenge was, he shows himself fully equal to meeting it, by a grand profession of the Christian's confidence in God—a confidence not so foolish as it sounds to worldly ears, as the history of many a mission-field would be amply sufficient to prove.

The position of Cyprianus, bishop of Carthago, a universally respected and highly influential Churchman, is somewhat uncertain. On the one hand, he includes in his general complaint over the degeneracy and calamities of the time the fact that the numbers and efficiency of the soldiers were decreasing,[1] and never says in so many terms that a Christian ought not to serve in the legions, even when he has occasion to refer to two who had done so.[2] On the other hand, he says some

---

[1] Cypr *Demetr* 3 (decrescit ac deficit in 'aruis agricola, in mari nauta, miles in castris), 17 (deminutione castrorum).

[2] Referring to a certain Celerinus, who had suffered in the persecution of Decius (250 A.D.), he says (*Ep* 39 (33) 3): " His paternal and maternal uncles, Laurentinus and Egnatius, themselves at one time serving as soldiers in the secular camp, but (being) true and spiritual soldiers of God, in overthrowing the devil by the confession of Christ, earned by their famous passion the Lord's palms and crowns." We shall have to refer to this passage later ; but here we may note that it is at least possible that Laurentinus and Egnatius suffered because they wished to leave the service on the ground either of idolatry or bloodshed or both. We shall meet several similar instances later on.

remarkably strong things about war, which more than overbalance his casual and rhetorical allusion to the deficiency of soldiers. He speaks of the "wars scattered everywhere with the bloody horror of camps. The world is wet with mutual blood(shed): and homicide is a crime when individuals commit it, (but) it is called a virtue, when it is carried on publicly. Not the reason of innocence, but the magnitude of savagery, demands impunity for crimes."[1] "God wished iron to be for the cultivation of the earth, and for that reason acts of homicide ought not to be committed."[2] "Adultery, fraud, homicide is mortal sin (mortale crimen) . . . after celebrating the eucharist, the hand is not (i.e. ought not to be) spotted with (the use of) the sword and with blood."[3] Further than that, his immense respect for his fellow-countryman Tertullianus, whom he called his 'master' and whose ardent antipathy to secular things in general he evidently shared, creates a very strong presumption that he agreed with him as to the illegitimacy of military service for Christians. This presumption is supported by the fact that the body of Maximilianus, who was martyred at Teveste in Numidia in 295 A.D. for refusing to allow himself to be enrolled as a soldier, was conveyed by a Christian matron to Carthago, and buried near Cyprianus' tomb.[4]

The Neoplatonic philosopher Plotinos, writing about 268 A.D., said: "God Himself ought not to fight on behalf of the unwarlike; for the law says that (men) ought to be brought safe out of wars by being courageous, but not by praying. For it is not those who pray, but those who attend to the earth, that

---

[1] Cypr *Donat* 6.   [2] Cypr *Hab Virg* 11.
[3] Cypr *Bon Pat* 14.   [4] Ruinart 342.

(ought to) reap its produce."[1] When we consider the connections of Plotinos with Egypt and Alexandria, the fact that both he and Origenes had been pupils of the philosopher Ammonios Sakkas, the reputation of Origenes in philosophic circles, and the standing hostility of the Neoplatonists to Christianity, we can hardly doubt that the passage just quoted is an allusion to the closing chapters of Origenes' *Contra Celsum*, where the author defends the Christians for refusing military service on the ground of the intercessory prayers they offer. Such an allusion would be somewhat pointless, unless Plotinos believed that the position he was criticizing was at least fairly widespread among Christians.

In 295 A.D. occurred the famous and oft-told martyrdom of Maximilianus, to which allusion has just been made. He was a young Numidian Christian, just over twenty-one years old, and was brought before Dion the proconsul of Africa, as fit for military service. He refused to serve, or to accept the soldier's badge, saying repeatedly that he could not do so, because he was a Christian and served Christ. Dion tried again and again to overcome his objections, but without success. It is fairly clear from the martyr's own words that his objection was largely, if not solely, to the business of fighting. The question of sacrificing to idols or to the Emperor is not mentioned by either party. "I cannot serve as a soldier," said Maximilianus; "I cannot do evil; I am a Christian." Dion told him: "In the sacred retinue of our lords Diocletianus and Maximianus, Constantius and Maximus, there are Christian

---

[1] Plotinos, *Ennead* III ii. 8 (Teubner i. 237). I owe this reference to De Jong (16).

soldiers, and they serve." Maximilianus replied : " They
know what is fitting for them : but I am a Christian,
and I cannot do evil." "What evil do they do who
serve?" asked the proconsul. "Thou knowest what
they do," was the reply.[1] Nothing more could be done,
and Maximilianus was sentenced to and suffered the
death-penalty. His body, as has been stated, was taken
to Carthago and buried near the tomb of Cyprianus ; his
father returned home thanking God that he had sent
forward such a gift to the Lord [2]; the story of his trial
and death were speedily committed to writing ; and he
was ultimately received among the saints of the Church.
All this shows what a large measure of sympathy and
approval was evoked by the stand he took, among the
Christians of his own and the immediately succeeding
period.[3] There are, as far as I know, no grounds for

[1] Ruinart (341), to whom we are indebted for an edition of the *Acta
Sancti Maximiliani Martyris*, tells us that this last question and answer
are absent ' in editis,' the reason for the omission apparently being that the
words contradict the traditional Roman Catholic view of war. Ruinart
inserts the words, but suggests that they mean that Maximilianus "did not
reject military service as if it were evil in itself, but on account of the
opportunities of sinning which soldiers often meet with." This is clearly
insufficient to account for the language used ; and the Roman Catholics
remain faced with the awkward fact that one of the canonized saints of the
Church died as a conscientious objector ! It is significant that Bigelmair,
throughout his full treatment of the Christian attitude to military service,
makes no mention of Maximilianus at all. He is certainly an awkward
martyr for a Romanist to deal with, but doubly so for one who is both a
Romanist and a German.

[2] Maximilianus' father, Fabius Victor, is somewhat of an enigma : though
he refused at Dion's bidding to persuade his son to give way and rejoiced
over the latter's witness, yet as ' temonarius' (? = person responsible for
finding a recruit) he had himself presented Maximilianus before the proconsul, and had got him a new coat in anticipation of his enlistment. The
exact situation is a little obscure : but I do not know what grounds Harnack
(*MC* 85) has for assuming that Fabius Victor was himself a soldier and
remained so after his son's death. The ' temonarius,' as far as I can discover, was not necessarily a soldier : De Jong (19 f) discusses the meaning
of the word at length.

[3] The genuineness of the *Acta Maximiliani* is generally admitted
(Gibbon, ch xvi, note 146 (ii. 120, ed. Bury) ; Harnack *C* ii. 473, *MC* 84
n 2). Harnack reprints them (*MC* 114 ff) from Ruinart.

supposing that Maximilianus had come more under the influence of Tertullianus than other Christians of northern Africa, or that Christians who refused to serve belonged for the most part to Montanistic sects.[1] It is probably true that such instances of refusal were sufficiently numerous to have helped to bring about that imperial suspicion and dislike, out of which sprang the great persecution of 303 A.D.[2]

In the latter part of the third century, the difficulty over idolatry, etc., in the army became acute. Regulations had long been in existence which forbade any who would not sacrifice to the Emperors to hold a commission in the army. While these regulations had been allowed by the authorities to fall into desuetude, the fact that they were still technically in force made it possible for any one to appeal to them, if a favourable opportunity arose ; and when that was done, they had to be enforced. It is possible that the two soldier-martyrs mentioned by Cyprianus were the victims of some such occurrence.[3] However that may be, a clear instance occurred at Caesarea in 260 A.D., when, after the cessation of persecution, a distinguished military officer named Marinus was about to be promoted to the rank of centurion, but, being denounced as a Christian by the next claimant to the vacancy and declared ineligible for promotion in view of the ancient laws, was given three hours for reflection,

---

[1] These are Guignebert's suggestions (199).

[2] Gibbon, ch xvi (ii. 120 f, ed. Bury); Lecky i. 460; Gwatkin, *Early Church History*, ii. 328 f.

[3] See p. 147, n 2. It is also just possible that the martyrs to whom he says (*Laps* 2) : " (Your) forehead, pure with God's sign, could not bear the devil's crown, (but) kept itself for the Lord's crown," were soldiers who had refused some pagan rite (so apparently B.-Baker *ICW* 31) ; but more probably the phrase is simply metaphorical.

returned at the end of that time from an interview with his bishop (who told him he must choose between his sword and the Gospels), reaffirmed his Christianity, was sentenced to death, led away, and beheaded.[1] Marinus waited for the occasion of conflict to arise, and when it arose he seems neither to have had nor to have sought a chance of retiring from the service. But Marcellus the centurion, who was martyred at Tingi (Western Mauretania) in 298 A.D., took the initiative himself, and insisted on resigning his office. On the occasion of the Emperor's birthday, he cast off his military belt before the standards, and called out: "I serve (milito) Jesus Christ, the eternal king." Then he threw down his vine-staff and arms, and added: "I cease from this military service of your Emperors, and I scorn to adore your gods of stone and wood, which are deaf and dumb idols. If such is the position of those who render military service, that they should be compelled to sacrifice to gods and emperors, then I cast down my vine-staff and belt, I renounce the standards, and I refuse to serve as a soldier." While the objection to sacrifice thus appears as the main ground for the bold step Marcellus took, it is clear that he was also exercised over the nature of military service as such: for his last words to the judge were: "I threw down (my arms); for it was not seemly that a Christian man, who renders military service to the Lord Christ, should render it (also) by (inflicting) earthly injuries."[2] When

---

[1] Eus *HE* VII xv. Cf the remarks of Harnack *ME* ii. 58 f, *MC* 78 ff.
[2] Ruinart 344 (Projeci. Non enim decebat Christianum hominem molestiis saecularibus militare, qui Christo Domino militat) ; cf 345 (cum Marcellus . . . proclamaret, summa auctoritate constantiae molestiis saecularibus militare non posse).

he was sentenced to death, Cassianus, the clerk of the court, loudly protested, and flung his writing-materials on the ground, declaring that the sentence was unjust : he suffered death a few days after Marcellus.[1]

In the years preceding and following the outbreak of persecution in 303 A.D., we come across several cases of Christian soldiers leaving the army or suffering martyrdom, either on the ground of a general sense of the incompatibility of their official functions with their religious duty, or else on the specific ground of refusing to offer heathen sacrifices. The doubtful 'Acts of Typasius' tells us that he was a soldier of Mauretania, who had served with credit, but, desiring to devote himself wholly to religion, refused a royal donative, and shortly after obtained from Maximianus an honourable discharge. Some years afterwards (305 A.D. or later) he was recalled to the ranks, but as he refused to re-enter the service, he suffered martyrdom.[2] Seleukos, a stalwart Cappadocian, who held a distinguished position in the army, at the beginning of the persecution had to endure scourging, but then obtained his discharge.[3] Tarakhos of Cilicia also obtained his discharge on the outbreak of persecution : at his subsequent trial at Tarsus, he told the governor that he had been a soldier, " but because I was a Christian, I have now chosen to be a civilian "[4] —words which suggest rather more than a mere objection to offer pagan sacrifices. The martyrdom of Nereus and Achilleus at Rome also probably falls to

---

[1] See the *Passio S. Cassiani* in Ruinart 345.
[2] *Anal Bolland* ix. 116 ff. The historical reliability of the story is very doubtful ; cf Harnack *C* ii. 481 f, *MC* 83 n 4.
[3] Eus *Mart* xi. 20–22.   [4] *Acta Tarachi*, etc., in Ruinart 452.

be included here. Pope Damasus (366–384 A.D.), who took a great interest in the records and tombs of the martyrs, put up an epitaph (which has since been discovered) to two praetorian soldiers, Nereus and Achilleus, who, he says, "had given (their) name(s) to military service, and were carrying on (their) cruel duty," but "suddenly laid aside (their) madness, turned round (and) fled ; they leave the general's impious camp, cast down (their) shields, helmets, and bloodstained weapons ; they confess, and bear (along) with joy the triumph of Christ" : they were put to death with the sword. Uncertain as we are of the date of their martyrdom, the most reasonable supposition is that it fell in or shortly before the time of the persecution of Diocletianus—a supposition which is confirmed by the various other cases of a similar kind which we have just noticed. The references to the 'impious camp' and the 'bloodstained weapons' remind us both of the offence of idolatry and also of that of bloodshed.[1]

The office of the judge and magistrate, though it shares with that of the soldier the infliction of bodily damage and death upon other men, yet exhibits this infliction in a less wholesale and indiscriminate, a less objectionable and shocking, form. Further than that, it resembles far more closely than the soldier's position does those numerous and useful public services which involve nothing in the way of violence to others. While the element common to the law-court and the

---

[1] See Achelis in *Texte und Untersuchungen* XI 2 (esp. pp. 44 f), for a full study of the fictitious Acta of these martyrs, as well as of the historic groundwork. Harnack (*MC* 83) says : "The Acts of Nereus and Achilleus . . . are to be left on one side"—but the same need not be said of Damasus' epitaph.

army made Christians sensitive in regard to the former as well as to the latter, the dissimilarity between them caused the objections to the one to be far more strong and definite than the objections to the other. The views of Christians in the latter part of the third century in regard to law-courts, magistracies, death-penalties, and so on, would form an interesting supplement to their views on military service. The evidence unfortunately is more scanty than we could wish. Two passages, however, of some interest may be quoted. The Didaskalia definitely forbids the Christian to sue a wrongdoer in a pagan court. " It is very high praise for a Christian to have no evil dispute with anyone : but if, through the work of an enemy, temptation arises against anyone,[1] let him try earnestly to be freed from him, even though he has to suffer some harm ; only let him not go to the judgment of the gentiles. . . . Let not the gentiles know of your legal disputes ; and do not accept evidence from them against yourselves : nor in your turn prefer suits in their courts." [2] We have seen that the Canons of Hippolutos in their original form forbade the admission to the Church of a magistrate who wielded the power of the sword. We do not know how long this original regulation remained unmodified. Very probably the modifications took place at different times and rates in different places. We know that in the latter part of the third century it was certainly not universally observed ; for in the times preceding 303 A.D., there were Christian governors of provinces [3] : at Alexandria

---

[1] I omit the words " eique fit iudicium," which follow here in Funk's Latin version : they are out of keeping with the context, do not appear in the parallel Greek of the Apostolic Constitutions, and are clearly a gloss.

[2] *Didask* II xlv. 1, xlvi. 1.   [3] Eus *HE* VIII i. 2.

there was a Christian official who daily administered justice attended by a guard of soldiers [1] : in Spain there were Christian magistrates. But a regulation may remain in existence a long time after people have begun to break it, as the long survival of the Eastern Church-Orders proves ; and even where it was felt that such a rule, however desirable as an ideal, could not be enforced in practice and ought not therefore to be authoritatively laid down, the sentiment of repulsion towards the penal and bloody side of a magistrate's work still made itself felt. One of the Canons of the Synod of Illiberis (Elvira, in the south of Spain), which apparently met about 300 A.D., ran : " Resolved, that it be laid down that a (Christian) magistrate, during the one year in which he holds the office of duumvir, should keep himself away from the church." [2] Hefele regards the patronage of idolatry connected with the office as the ground of this decision,[3] but Dale rightly views this as insufficient. " Tertullian," says Dale, " enumerates acts which, though part of the common experience of all magistrates and rulers during that age, were inadmissible in the true servant of Christ. " As to the duties of civil power," he says, " the Christian must not decide on any one's life or honour—about money it is permissible ; he must bind no one, nor imprison and torture any." It was considerations of this nature, rather than the idolatrous associations connected with the office, which led the Synod to exclude the official, during his year of tenure, from communion with the

---

[1] Eus *HE* VIII ix. 7.
[2] *Can Illib* 56. The duumvir in a provincial town was roughly what the consul was at Rome, viz. the chief magistrate. The same Synod penalized Christians who acted as ' informers ' (*Can Illib* 73).
[3] Hefele 161.

Church : for to sentence even a slave to death, to imprison the debtor, or to put the household of a suspected criminal to the rack, though the duty of a magistrate, would in the Christian be a sin." [1] The sense of the incongruity of Christianity and political life in general, more particularly on its punitive and coercive side, expressed itself in the strong disapproval that was felt—even down to mediaeval and modern times—to the direct participation of the Christian clergy in any activities of this kind.[2]

We conclude our study of this section of the subject with a few passages from two Christian authors who flourished towards the close of our period, viz. Arnobius and Lactantius. Arnobius speaks as if abstention from warfare had been the traditional Christian policy ever since the advent of Christ. The amount of war had been diminished, he said, not increased, since Christ came. "For since we—so large a force of men—have received (it) from his teachings and laws, that evil ought not to be repaid with evil, that it is better to endure a wrong than to inflict (it), to shed one's own (blood) rather than stain one's hands and conscience with the blood of another, the ungrateful world has long been receiving a benefit from Christ, through whom the madness of savagery has been softened, and has begun to withhold its hostile hands from the blood of a kindred creature. But if absolutely all . . . were willing to lend an ear for a little while to his healthful and peaceful

---

[1] A. W. W. Dale, *The Synod of Elvira*, 234 f. The Synod of Arelate (Arles, 314 A.D.) provided that Christian magistrates, who " begin to act contrary to the discipline, then at last should be excluded from communion ; and similarly with those who wish to take up political life " (*Can Arel* 7).

[2] Cf Cypr *Laps* 6 for an early expression of this sentiment.

decrees, and would not, swollen with pride and arrogance, trust to their own senses rather than to his admonitions, the whole world would long ago have turned the uses of iron to milder works and be living in the softest tranquillity, and would have come together in healthy concord without breaking the sanctions of treaties."[1]

Lactantius is still more definite and uncompromising. He explicitly rules out both military service and capital charges on the ground that, involving homicide, they are a violation of justice. We may recall a few salient passages. Referring to some indefinite earlier time, he says: "Fire and water used to be forbidden to exiles; for up till then it was thought a wrong to inflict the punishment of death on (those who,) though (they were) evil, (were) yet men."[2] "If God alone were worshipped, there would not be dissensions and wars; for men would know that they are sons of the one God, and so joined together by the sacred and inviolable bond of divine kinship; there would be no plots, for they would know what sort of punishments God has prepared for those who kill living beings."[3] Latterly the gentiles had banished justice from their midst by persecuting the good; but even "if they slew the evil only, they would not deserve that justice should come to them; for justice had no other reason for leaving the earth than the shedding of human blood."[4] "Someone will say here: 'What, therefore, or where, or of what sort is piety?' Assuredly it is among those who are ignorant of wars, who keep concord with all, who are friends even to their enemies, who love all men

[1] Arnob i. 6: see above, pp. 65 f.   [2] Lact *Inst* II ix. 23.
[3] Lact *Inst* V viii. 6.   [4] Lact *Inst* V ix. 2.

as brothers, who know how to restrain (their) anger, and to soothe all fury of mind by quiet control." [1] In controverting the argument that the just man is foolish, for, to save his own life, he will not in warfare take a horse away from a wounded man, Lactantius answers that, for one thing, the just man will never be faced with these circumstances. "For . . . why should he wage war, and mix himself up in other people's passions—he in whose mind dwells perpetual peace with men? He . . . who regards it as wrong, not only to inflict slaughter himself, but even to be present with those who inflict it and to look on, will forsooth be delighted with . . . human blood!" [2] In criticizing patriotic wars, he says: "In the first place, the connection of human society is taken away; innocence is taken away; abstention from what is another's is taken away; in fact, justice itself is taken away, for justice cannot bear the cutting asunder of the human race, and, wherever arms glitter, she must be put to flight and banished. . . . For how can he be just who injures, hates, despoils, kills? And those who strive to be of advantage to their country do all these things." [3] "Whoever reckons it a pleasure that a man, though deservedly condemned, should be slain in his sight, defiles his own conscience, just as if he were to become spectator and sharer of a murder which is committed in secret." [4] "When God prohibits killing, He not only

[1] Lact *Inst* V x. 10.
[2] Lact *Inst* V xvii. 12 f. The gaps in my quotation deal with the parallel case of the just man who in a wreck will not take a plank from a drowning companion. Lactantius absurdly argues that the just man will never need to take a voyage, being content with what he has. Though in this point he allows his rhetoric to get the better of his common sense, it does not follow that his argument on the other point, ill-adapted as it was to the immediate purpose in hand, was equally frivolous.
[3] Lact *Inst* VI vi. 20,22.   [4] Lact *Inst* VI xx. 10.

forbids us to commit brigandage, which is not allowed even by the public laws; but He warns (us) that not even those things which are regarded as legal among men are to be done. And so it will not be lawful for a just man to serve as a soldier—for justice itself is his military service—nor to accuse anyone of a capital offence, because it makes no difference whether thou kill with a sword or with a word, since killing itself is forbidden. And so, in this commandment of God, no exception at all ought to be made (to the rule) that it is always wrong to kill a man, whom God has wished to be (regarded as) a sacrosanct creature." [1] Lactantius does not either claim or suggest that there were no Christians in the army when he wrote; and his language may perhaps be held to imply that he is counteracting the opinions of other Christians: but he could hardly have written as he did, if his views were merely those of an inconsiderable handful of extremists. One would rather gather that he must have been conscious of having at his back a very large body of Christian sentiment and conviction.

[1] Lact *Inst* VI xx. 15–17.

PART III

FORMS OF THE EARLY CHRISTIAN ACCEPTANCE OF WAR

HITHERTO we have concentrated our attention on the various ways in which the Christian abhorrence and disapproval of war expressed itself. We have now to study the reverse side of the picture—the various conditions and connections in which war was thought of by Christian people without that association of reproach which so frequently attached to it. The contents of this reverse side of the picture are very heterogeneous, ranging from the use of military metaphors and similes up to the actual service of Christians in the legions. It will be our task to examine each phase of this side of the subject candidly and carefully, and to attempt an estimate of the precise value of each in its relation to that strong antipathy towards war, the various manifestations of which we have just been reviewing. We begin with

THE CHRISTIAN USE OF MILITARY TERMS AND PHRASES TO ILLUSTRATE THE RELIGIOUS LIFE.—It was apparently Paul who introduced this custom of drawing from the military world metaphors and similes illustrative of different aspects of Christian, particularly apostolic, life. He urged the Thessalonians to put on the breastplate of faith and love, and to take the hope of salvation as a helmet.[1]   He supported his right to subsist at the expense of the Church by asking : " Who ever engages in military service at his own expense ? "[2] He spoke of his spiritual and disciplinary powers in the Church in the language of one holding a military command and suppressing a mutiny.[3]   He spoke of his weapons of righteousness on the right hand and on the left, i.e. for attack and defence.[4]   He called Epaphroditos and Arkhippos his fellow-soldiers and others his fellow-captives.[5]   In a detailed enumeration of the items that make up the offensive and defensive equipment of a soldier, he elaborated the parallel between human warfare and the Christian's struggle against evil angelic powers.[6]   Further use of military metaphors is made in the Pastoral Epistles.   There the author bids Timotheos join him in bearing hardship as a good soldier of Jesus Christ.   " No one going on military service gets entangled in the affairs of (civil) life, (for his aim is) to please him who enrolled him."[7]   It is important to notice that Paul, as if aware of the liability of such language to misconstruction, twice went out of

[1] 1 Thess v. 8.   [2] 1 Cor ix. 7 ; cf 2 Cor xi. 8.   [3] 2 Cor x. 3–6.
[4] 2 Cor vi. 7 ; cf, for other military expressions, Rom vi. 13, 23, xiii. 12.
[5] Phil ii. 25, Philemon 2, 23, Rom xvi. 7, Col iv. 10.
[6] Eph vi. 12–18.
[7] 2 Tim ii. 3 f ; cf 1 Tim i. 18.   It is to be observed that the language of 1 Tim vi. 12, 2 Tim iv. 7, from which we get the familiar phrases about ' fighting the good fight,' is drawn, not from the battle-field, but from the race-course (cf 1 Cor ix. 25, Heb xii. 1).   Harnack discusses these NT military metaphors in great detail (*MC* 12–18).   He finds their origin " in the pictures of the Old Testament prophets " (12), having apparently in mind such passages as Isa xi. 4 f, xlix. 2, lix. 17, Hosea vi. 5.   He observes that while every Christian has to fight, it is not usually the ordinary Christian who is described as a soldier, but only the apostle and missionary. He points out that the analogy became more than a mere analogy, when it was used to prove that the missionary should be supported by the Church, and should not engage in the business of civil life.

his way to remind his readers that in using it he was not referring to earthly warfare. "Though we walk in the flesh, we do not serve as soldiers according to the flesh; for the weapons of our military service are not those of the flesh, but powerful through God for the demolition of strongholds, demolishing theories and every rampart thrown up against the knowledge of God, and taking prisoner every project (to bring it) into obedience to Christ," and so on.[1] Again, "Our struggle is not against flesh and blood, but against the (angelic) rulers, against the (angelic) authorities, against the world-potentates of this darkness, against the spiritual (forces) of wickedness in the heavenly (regions). Wherefore take up the armour of God," and so on.[2]

The Gospel of Luke preserves for us the one explicitly military parable of Jesus, that of the two kings preparing for war.[3] Clemens of Rome says to the Corinthians: "Let us render service then, brothers, as strenuously as we can, under His faultless orders. Let us consider those who serve our governors as soldiers, in what an orderly, obedient, and submissive way they carry out their instructions. For all are not prefects or chiliarchs or centurions or captains of fifty, and so on; but each one in his own rank carries out what is ordered by the Emperor and the governors. The great cannot exist without the lower, nor the lower without the great. There is a union among all, and that is why they are (so) useful" (καὶ ἐν τούτοις χρῆσις).[4] Ignatius writes: "Please Him whom ye serve as soldiers, and from whom ye receive wages. Let no

---

[1] 2 Cor x. 3–5.   [2] Eph vi. 12 f.
[3] Lk xiv. 31–33: see above, p. 38, and cf Mt xi. 12 f (= Lk xvi. 16), xxii. 7.   [4] 1 Clem xxxvii. 1–4.

one of you be found (to be) a deserter. Let your baptism abide as (your) weapons, faith as a helmet, love as a spear, patience as armour. Let your works be your deposits, in order that ye may receive the recompense due to you."[1] It will be seen that, while Ignatius does not do more than use military metaphors, Clemens goes a good deal further. In two respects his allusion to military life is a novelty. Firstly, he draws from his illustration the lesson of subordination of Christians to Church-leaders; and secondly, he unquestionably feels a real admiration for the Roman army as such. We shall have occasion to refer later to this second point.

Justinus uses the military analogy in rather a striking way. "It would be a ridiculous thing," he says to the Emperors, "that the soldiers engaged and enrolled by you should respect their agreement with you in preference to their own life and parents and country and all their friends, though ye can offer them nothing incorruptible, and that we, loving incorruptibility, should not endure all things for the sake of receiving what we long for from Him who is able to give (it)."[2] In the apocryphal 'Martyrdom of Paul,' both the author himself and the characters he introduces speak of Christians as soldiers in the service of God[3]: similar language is put into Peter's mouth in his apocryphal 'Martyrdom.'[4] In the Gnostic 'Excerpts from Theodotos,' it is said: "(We) must be armed with the Lord's weapons, keeping the body and the soul unwounded."[5] Eirenaios refers, chiefly in Scriptural language, to the achievements of Christ under the figure of military

---

[1] Ig *P* vi. 2 : cf *S* i. 2. We may remember that Ignatius was, at the time of writing, in the charge of a squad of ten soldiers.
[2] Just 1 *Ap.* xxxix. 5.   [3] *M Paul* 2-4, 6 (i. 108–116 ; Pick 44–48).
[4] *M Petr* 7 = *Act Petr* 36 (i. 90 ; Pick 116).   [5] *Excerp Theod* 85.

exploits.[1] Clemens of Alexandria has a large number of military expressions and comparisons designating various features in the Christian life.[2] The pugnacious Tertullianus, despite his aversion to military service in actual life, was especially fond of using language of this sort.[3] It was adopted in fact far more readily and extensively in the Western than in the Eastern Church. The use of the one Latin word ' sacramentum ' for the soldier's oath and for certain important Christian observances facilitated the introduction of the military conception of Christianity. While nothing was further from Tertullianus' real meaning than that Christians should actually take arms on behalf of their religion, yet the thought of Christians as soldiers was sufficiently vivid and real to him to enable him to play with the idea of an actual revolt.[4]

Origenes found the idea of the Christian life as a spiritual warfare of great value in that it furnished a key to much in the Old Testament that would have been repugnant to him, had he felt obliged to accept it in its literal meaning. Military metaphors appear in his best-known works, but are naturally most fully worked out in his Homilies on the books of Numbers, Joshua, and Judges. In the Homilies on Joshua, he

---

[1] Eiren IV xx. 11 (ii. 223) (quotation of Ap xix. 11–17), xxxiii. 11 (ii. 265) (quotation of Ps xlv. 4 f), *frag* 21 (ii. 490) (the armed angel that met Balaam was the Word): cf II ii. 3 (i. 255) (world to be referred to God as victory to the king who planned it).

[2] Clem *Protr* x. 93, 100 fin, 110, xi. 116, *Paed* I vii. 54, viii. 65, *Strom* I xi. 51, xxiv. 159 ff, II xx. 110, 120, IV iv. 14, 16, viii. 60, xiii. 91, xxii. 141, VI xii. 103, xiv. 112, VII iii. 21, xi. 66, xiii. 83, xvi. 100 f, *Quis Dives* 25, 34 f.

[3] Tert *Mart* 1, 3, *Apol* 50 init, *Nat* ii. 5 (i. 592 f), *Spect* 24 fin, *Cul* ii. 5, *Paen* 6, *Orat* 19, *Jud* 7, *Praescr* 12, 41, *Cast* 12 init, *Marc* v. 5 (ii. 480), *Fug* 10 f, *Res* 3, *Scorp* 4 fin, *Pudic* 22 fin, *Jejun* 10, 17.

[4] Tert *Apol* 37 (i. 463) (see above, p. 107). Harnack treats the whole subject with great thoroughness in *MC* 32–40.

says : "If those carnal wars did not carry a figure of spiritual wars, the books of Jewish history would, I believe, never have been handed down by the apostles (as) fit to be read in the churches by the disciples of Christ, who came to teach peace."[1]

Other writings of the first half of the third century containing military phrases and illustrations are Hippolutos' treatise against Noetos,[2] the apocryphal 'Acts of Thomas,'[3] the Pseudo-Cyprianic 'De Pascha Computus,'[4] and the 'Octavius' of Minucius Felix, which has a fine rhetorical comparison of the steadfast martyr to a victorious soldier.[5]

From the middle of the third century onwards the frequency with which military language is used to describe phases of Christian life and experience becomes very noticeable, particularly in Latin writers. Christians are spoken of as Christ's soldiers ; Christ is the imperator ; the Church is his camp ; baptism is the sacramentum ; heretics and schismatics are rebels and deserters, and so on. A multitude of military phrases occur in the portrayal of Christian trials and achievements, particularly in connection with persecution. A detailed analysis of the passages would tell us very little in regard to our main enquiry : some of them are simply edifying rhetoric ; in some the parallel is carried

---

[1] Orig *Hom in Jos* xv init (Migne *PG* xii. 897). Cf also Orig *Princ* III ii. 5 (milites Christi), IV 14 (see below, p. 175), 24, *Orat* xiii. 3 f, xxiv. 4, *Cels* vii. 21 f. Harnack collects the passages from Origenes' exegetical works in *MC* 26–31, 99–104. Westcott says of the Homilies on Joshua : "The parallel between the leader of the Old Church and the Leader of the New is drawn with great ingenuity and care. The spiritual interpretation of the conquest of Canaan, as an image of the Christian life, never flags " (*DCB* iv. 107b).

[2] Hipp. *Noet* 15 (quotation of Ap xix. 11–13).

[3] *Acts of Thomas* 39, 126 (iii. 157, 234 ; Pick 260 f, 328).

[4] Ps-Cypr *Pasch* 10.   [5] Minuc xxxvii. 1–3.

out in great detail; in others it consists of a bare illustrative analogy.[1] We observe that the military metaphor
commended itself most strongly to Cyprianus and those
who corresponded with him,[2] Commodianus,[3] and the
authors of the martyr-acts,[4] that it was on the whole
more popular with the Latin or Western[5] than with the
Eastern[6] writers; and that fondness for it was greatly
stimulated by persecution.[7] The way in which the
word 'paganus,' which originally meant civilian as distinct from soldier — a sense which it kept till after
300 A.D., came eventually to mean non-Christian,
indicates how strongly the idea of the Christian as
the soldier par excellence permeated the mind of
Latin Christianity.[8]

Most of the passages in which military metaphors
and similes are used are obviously quite non-committal
as to the writer's attitude to earthly warfare, though
there are certainly some in which the analogy is put in

[1] Cf Harnack *MC* 40–43.

[2] Cypr *Test* ii. 16, iii. 117, *Donat* 15 init, *Laud* 10, 19, 26, *Ep* 10 (8) 1,
5, 37 (15) 1, 28 (24) 1, 31 (25) 5, 30 (30) 2, 6, 38 (32) 1, 39 (33) 2 f, 46 (43),
54 (50) 1, 55 (51) 4, 17, 19, 56 (52) 2, 57 (53) 1–5, 59 (54) 17, 58 (55) 1–4,
6, 8 f, 11, 60 (56) 2, 61 (57) 2 f, 65 (63) 1, 73 (72) 10, 22, 74 (73) 8 f,
77 (77) 2, 78 (78) 1, 80 (81) 2, *Laps* 2 (see above p. 151 n 3), 36, *Dom
Orat* 15, *Mort* 2, 4, 9, 12, 15, *Bon Pat* 12, *Zel Liv* 2 f, *Fort* pref 1 f, 4,
treatise 13.

[3] Commod *Instr* i. 34, ii. 9–13, 20, 22, *Carm* 77 : cf Scullard, 259.

[4] *Passio Mariani et Jacobi* i. 3, iii. 4, viii. 4, x. 3 (Gebhardt 134 ff);
Acta Fructuosi 3 (Ruinart 266); *Passio Montani et Lucii* iv. 6, xiv. 5
(Gebhardt 147 ff); *Acts of Codratius* (Conybeare 195, 202, 206); *Passio
Quirini* 2 init (Ruinart 522); *Acta Marcelli* 1 f, 4 (Ruinart 343 f); *Passio
Typasii* 2 (*Anal Bolland* ix. 118).

[5] Pont *Vit Cypr* 8, 10 ; Ps-Cypr *Rebapt* 16 fin, *Jud* i, 7 ; Arnob ii. 5, 8 ;
Lact *Inst* I iii. 19, III xxiii. 2, V xix. 25, xxii. 17, VI iv. 15–19, xx. 16,
VII xix. 5 f, *Mort Pers* xvi. 4–11.

[6] Dion Alex *De Natura* (Feltoe 142), and in Eus *HE* VI xli. 16 ;
Didask II vi. 10 f; *Clem Ep Jas* 4 ; *Clem Hom* ix. 21, *Recog* iv. 33, vii. 24 ;
Eus *PE* 15c, 16b, 165b, 663b.

[7] Cf Harnack *ME* i. 414–418.

[8] See Harnack's interesting note in *ME* i. 416–418, *MC* 122.

such a way as to suggest that the writer accepts the rightness of war. Thus Cyprianus says: " It is a good soldier's (business) to defend the camp of his commander against rebels and enemies : it is the business of a proud general to keep the standards entrusted to him," and he goes on to plead accordingly for the re-baptism of heretics.[1] Or again : " If it is a glorious thing for earthly soldiers to return in triumph to their country after conquering the enemy, how much more excellent and great is the glory of returning in triumph to Paradise after conquering the devil ! "[2] Lactantius reinforces a strong appeal to the reader to enter upon the toilsome spiritual warfare against the devil by drawing an elaborate parallel between the demands of that conflict and the wisdom of enduring, for the sake of peace and security in the future, the bother of having to prepare to defend oneself and one's home against an earthly foe.[3] But despite appearances, passages like these cannot be taken as more than mere illustrations. For the purpose of pointing an argument or decorating a lesson, a writer will sometimes use rhetorical analogies which seem likely to carry weight, but which do not represent his own considered opinions on that from which the analogy is drawn. We know, for instance, that Lactantius, despite these glowing words on the obvious need of self-defence, as a matter of fact totally disapproved of all bloodshed, including capital punishment and military service: and it seems practically certain that Cyprianus did the same.[4]

At the same time, the frequent and unrestricted use of military metaphors was not without its dangers.

---

[1] Cypr *Ep* 73 (72) 10.
[2] Cypr *Fort* 13.
[3] Lact *Inst* VI iv. 15 fl.
[4] See above pp. 147 f, 159 f.

Harnack remarks : " When the forms of military life are taken over into the higher religions, the military element appears at first to be thereby converted into its exact opposite, or to be changed into a mere symbol. But the form too has a logic of its own and its own 'necessitates consequentiae.' At first imperceptibly, but soon more and more clearly, the military element, which was received as a symbol, introduces also the thing itself, and the 'spiritual weapons of knighthood' become the worldly (weapons). But even where it does not get as far as that, there enters in a warlike disposition which threatens the rule of meekness and peace."[1] And again later, of the Latin Christianity of the third century : " A tone that was on the one hand fanatical and on the other hand bombastic entered into the literature of edification in the West. The Christian threatened to become a 'miles gloriosus.' Even though it might all through be a question of spiritual warfare, (yet) an earthly delight in battle and strife, in plunder and victory in the ordinary sense, could (quite easily) develop itself in this fashion. Military speech was not by any means justified by the actual circumstances, apart from the intermittent persecutions : it (just) became the fashion. The martyr-acts that were written in the great persecution under Diocletian and his colleagues, and still more those that were written later, are often enough lacking in the peace and prudence which was prescribed to the Christians in their classic documents—except the Apocalypse. But who can criticize the attitude of people who were handed over to the executioner and went to meet a dreadful death ? Their biographers only are open to criticism."[2] We may say therefore, with

[1] Harnack *MC* 8.   [2] *Op cit* 42 f.

regard to this first department of Christian thought in which war stood for something good, that while it lent itself to abuse and misconstruction, particularly in the case of the cruder minds and harsher spirits in the Church, it dealt strictly speaking only with warfare in its purely spiritual sense, and comprised nothing that was necessarily at variance with the most rigid abstention from the use of arms.

THE WARS OF THE OLD TESTAMENT AND OF HEBREW HISTORY.—The broad fact that meets us here is the ease with which the early Christian was able, whenever necessary, to keep his own ethic and that of the Old Testament in different compartments of his mind, without being seriously disturbed by—and even without noticing—the discrepancies between them. The Scriptures were for him divinely inspired; the history they recorded had been divinely controlled; whatever was narrated and approved by the Biblical authors was regarded as sacred, and as such not a proper subject for human criticism—it was accepted with child-like and unquestioning reverence. The reader had no trained historical sense with which to discern development in man's knowledge of God's Will: hence he lacked, not only the inclination, but also the means, of properly relating the ethic of his own faith to that of a long distant foretime. The soundness of his own moral intuitions saved him from presuming to follow indiscriminately the example of those great ones of old, of whom he read and spoke with such genuine reverence and admiration. No greater mistake could be made than to suppose that the early Christian would have permitted himself or his fellow-Christians to do whatever he could peruse without censure or even with approval in the pages of Scripture. An instance will suffice to make this point clear. Concubinage and prostitution were practices which early Christian sentiment strongly condemned as sinful. Whatever might be the frailty of his flesh, no early Christian ever seriously thought of advocating or even defending such practices in his own day—least of all from the pages of Scripture. Yet we find Paul referring to the concubinage of Abraham without a hint that it was sinful,[1] and James and the author of Hebrews alluding to Rahab the harlot, not only without censure, but even in terms of high praise.[2] Similarly with the subject of war. For the early Christian the warlike habits of 'the great of old' and his own peaceful principles formed two separate realms, both of which he recognized without attempting—or feeling any need to attempt—to harmonize them. He could recall with complacency, and even with a devout admiration, the wars of the ancient Israelites, totally unconscious of any problem presented to him by their horrors, and without in any way committing himself to a belief in the propriety of similar action on his part. Thus it was that Stephen and Paul both recalled with a glow of patriotic enthusiasm how God had subdued and destroyed the Canaanites before their ancestors under Joshua,[3] and the author of Hebrews spoke proudly of Abraham returning from the slaughter of the kings, reminded his readers how "by faith the walls of Jericho fell down, . . . by faith Rahab the harlot was not destroyed with the disobedient, because she had received the spies in peace," and mentioned in his catalogue of the heroes

[1] Gal iv. 22 ff.   [2] Jas ii. 25 ; Heb xi. 31.   [3] Ac vii. 45, xiii. 19.

of faith "Gideon, Barak, Samson, Jephthah, David, Samuel, and the prophets, who by means of faith subdued kingdoms, . . . escaped the edge of the sword, out of weakness were made strong, became mighty in war, routed armies of foreigners."[1] Clemens of Rome tells in detail the story of Rahab and the spies, making the scarlet thread she bound in the window a type of the Lord's redeeming blood.[2] 'Barnabas' finds a type of the cross in the hands of Moses extended above the battle between Israel and Amalek, and a type of Jesus himself in Joshua, whom Moses ordered to record God's determination to destroy Amalek.[3] Justinus quotes to Truphon the words of Moses: "The Lord thy God, who goeth before thy face, He shall destroy the nations," and says: "Ye, who derive your origin from Shem, came, according to the judgment of God, upon the land of Canaan, and took possession of it"[4]: he reminds him how the angel of the Lord slew 185,000 Assyrians before Jerusalem in Hezekiah's time.[5] Like the other writers just mentioned, he sees types of Christ, the cross, etc., in military incidents, objects, and persons that appear in the Old Testament, in Joshua, in Moses' outstretched arms, and the stone he sat on, in Rahab's scarlet thread, and in the horns with which Joseph would push the nations (Deut. xxxiii. 17).[6]

While the juxtaposition of the discrepant standards of Scripture and of the Christian life created no difficulty

---

[1] Heb vii. 1, xi. 30–34. It is quite a mistake to use this passage, as Professor B.-Baker does (*ICW* 6, 18), in support of his view that "war is sanctioned . . . by the teaching and practice of Christ and of His immediate disciples," if by that is meant that war is something in which the follower of Jesus was permitted to take part.

[2] 1 Clem xii. 　　　　　　　　　　　　　[3] Barn xii. 2, 9.

[4] Just *Dial* 126 (772), 139 (796). 　　　[5] *Op cit* 83 (672).

[6] *Op cit* 90 f (692 f), 111 (732), 113 (736 f), 115 (741, 744), 131 (781).

for the childlike mind of the first generations of Christians, yet it was obviously bound sooner or later to attract attention. As soon as the Church began to develop her thinking powers and to face the tangled and perplexing problems of practical life, the antinomy had to be reckoned with. That the sanction of war in the Old Testament had some influence on Christian practice by the time of Tertullianus, we know; though we cannot say how soon that influence began to make itself felt. In the realm of theology, however, the difficulty came to a head in the heresy and schism of Markion, about the middle of the second century. Markion's theory was that all divinely ordained wars, judgments, penalties, and so on, were to be referred, not to the Supreme Being, the good God who was the Father of Jesus, but to an inferior Deity, the just God of the Jews. This dualism the orthodox Christians rejected and resisted with horror, and indeed it was as easy to find disproof of it, as support for it, in Scripture. Neither Markion nor his opponents had the modern key, viz. the theory of the progressive revelation of the Divine character to men; and the orthodox, in meeting his arguments, were driven to seek for warlike features in the God of the New Testament, and thereby gravely imperilled one of the most essential features of the Christian gospel.[1]

---

[1] Harnack says (*MC* 26): " Marcion's grasp of the Christian idea of God was without doubt essentially accurate. But the thought of a development of the Jewish conception of God into the Christian was as remote from him as from his opponents; so that he had to break with the historical antecedents of Christianity, and his Catholic opponents had to adulterate the Christian idea of God with what was out-of-date. Both fell into error, for there was no other way out. It will however always remain a credit to the Marcionite Church, which long maintained itself, that it preferred to reject the Old Testament, than to tarnish the picture of the Father of Jesus Christ by the intermixture of traces of a warlike God."

Forty or fifty years later, the situation had developed. We find indeed, as before, many allusions to the ancient Hebrew wars without any question being raised as to their incompatibility with Christian usage. Joshua continues to be represented as a type of Jesus, and the massacres he is said to have perpetrated are complacently referred to. Moses is praised as a great general, his outstretched arms are taken as a sign of the cross, the Maccabees' decision to fight on the Sabbath is quoted, and so on.[1] But the importance and urgency of the question raised by Markion were more than ever realized, for his church was still strong and flourishing. Lengthy exposures of his errors were penned by Eirenaios, Tertullianus. and Hippolutos. More significant for our immediate purpose—for these replies to Markion deal only incidentally with the question of wars—is the fact revealed by Tertullianus, that the Old Testament was now being used by certain Christians in order to justify themselves for bearing arms. The plea does not seem to have been always very intelligently framed, for we are told that these Christians appealed not only to the wars of Joshua and the Israelites, but also to Moses' rod, Aaron's buckle, and John the Baptist's leather girdle![2] How utterly and seriously misleading this reverence for the Old Testament could be for simpleminded Christians— particularly of the less scrupulous and puritanical sort —we gather from a treatise belonging to about the

---

[1] The reader who cares to study these allusions in detail will find them in Eiren III xvi. 4, xvii. 3, IV xxiv. 1, *frags* 18 f, 44 (ii. 86, 93, 232, 488 f, 509), *Demonstr* 20 (11), 27 (16), 29 (17) ; Clem *Strom* I xxiv. 158–164, II xviii. 82, 88 ; Tert *Jud* 4, 9 f (ii. 606, 622 f, 627 f), *Marc* iii. 16 (ii. 343), 18 (ii. 347), iv. 36 (ii. 451), *Monog* 6 fin, *Jejun* 7, 10 ; Hipp *Dan* I viii. 3, III xxiv. 8, IV xliv.   [2] Tert *Idol* 19 (i. 690) : see above, p. 109.

middle of the third century, and probably written by Novatianus, in which certain Christians are referred to who justified themselves for attendance at the public shows in the amphitheatre on the ground that David had danced before the ark and Elijah had been the charioteer of Israel.[1] But even among the more intelligent and sincere Christians, who lived in the times when participation in warfare had become a Christian problem, the fact that the Old Testament wars were traditionally justified had some effect in preventing a unanimous decision against such participation.[2]

One way out of the difficulty was to regard the Old Testament wars as parables, allegories, and types, descriptive of the spiritual life. Many Christians, we are told, regarded these difficult narratives as types, though they were not quite clear as to what they were types of.[3] It needs a special insight, Origenes contends, to enable one to interpret these passages aright : " strangely enough, by means of the history of wars and of conquerors and of (the) conquered, certain mysteries are made clear to those that are able to test them." [4] What large use Origenes himself made of this method of interpretation we have already seen. We may note that, great as was his confidence in it, his historical sense prevented him from applying it completely ; and not having the one clue to the problem, he had eventually to leave the discrepancy between the two dispensations unresolved. Thus, when Celsus pointed out the contradiction ,between the Old Testament promises of wealth and dominion and precepts for the conduct of

---

[1] Novat *Spect* 2 : ubi, inquiunt, scripta sunt ista, ubi prohibita ? alioquin et auriga est Israel Helias et ante arcam Dauid ipse saltauit.
[2] Cf Harnack *MC* 11 f.   [3] Orig *Princ* IV i. 9 fin.
[4] Orig *Princ* IV 14.

war, on the one hand, and the teaching of Jesus on the other, Origenes argued that the former are to be taken in a spiritual sense, as the Jews themselves eventually took them, the literal sense being in many cases obviously impossible. The promises of the Law were never literally fulfilled; the Jews therefore would not have remained so zealous for the Law, had they understood it—as Celsus does—literally. At the same time, Origenes recognizes that the Law had a literal, as well as a spiritual, meaning, that the Jews understood the laws permitting them to punish offenders and to fight against their enemies literally and not spiritually, and that they were allowed to do so, as otherwise they would have perished as a nation. Yet he also argues that the promise that the Jews should slay their enemies cannot be taken literally, and points out that the destruction of Jerusalem proved that God did not wish the Jewish State to stand any longer.[1] It is easy enough to see the unresolved contradiction in Origenes' position— indeed, one can hardly believe that he himself could have been quite satisfied with it: but further advance was impossible without the more modern ideas of the part played by man's subjective conditions in the deter- mination of human duty and the consequent necessity of a progressive, i.e. a changing, revelation of the divine Will. A further point along this very line was reached by a Christian writer (the author of the 'Dialogus de Recta Fidei') of the early years of the fourth century, in connection with the closely allied problem of the contradiction between the Mosaic Law of Retaliation and the Sermon on the Mount. That problem, how- ever, is still more closely connected with the question

[1] Orig *Cels* iii. 7, vii. 18–26.

the teaching of Jesus), and that it involved the subtle fallacy of supposing that what God permits or enjoins for men in one stage of development, He equally permits or enjoins for men in quite a different stage.

APOCALYPTIC WARS.—But Scripture spoke of other wars than those of past history. The Jews looked forward to an approaching cataclysm, a great intervention of God in human affairs, involving a general resurrection and judgment, the reward of the righteous, the punishment of sinners, and the establishment of a divine kingdom under the regency of the Messiah. It seems to have been generally expected that the occurrence of terrific wars, involving the overthrow and slaughter of the enemies of the Chosen People and their Messiah, would form a part of this series of events, though there was no unanimity as to the details of the programme. The Christian Church practically took over the Jewish apocalyptic beliefs en masse: hence we find war entering into their hopes and expectations of the future. Mark includes in the apocalyptic discourse of Jesus the following passage : " When ye hear (of) wars and rumours of wars, be not amazed : (this) must happen, but the end is not yet. For nation shall rise against nation, and kingdom against kingdom; there shall be earthquakes in divers places ; there shall be famines. These things (are the) beginning of (the Messianic) birth-pangs." Matthew and Luke report the same or similar words.[1] Luke represents Jesus in the Parable of the Pounds as describing the king on his return summoning into his presence for execution those who

---

[1] Mk xiii. 7 f ‖s. According to ' The Vision of Isaiah,' the war continues incessantly from the Creation to the Parousia (see above, pp. 49 f).

did not wish him to reign over them.[1]　Paul says that the Lord Jesus will destroy the Lawless One (i.e. Antichrist) with the breath of his mouth, and bring him to nought by the manifestation of his coming.[2]　This theme of Messianic warfare appears in a multitude of different shapes in the Apocalypse.　The openings of the first, second, and fourth seals usher in disastrous wars.[3]　Christ is represented as a conqueror,[4] having a sharp two-edged sword issuing from his mouth[5]: he threatens to make war with it upon the Nikolaitans,[6] and to slay Jezebel's children.[7]　A tremendous conflict is about to come, in which he will conquer the Beast and the kings of the earth with terrific slaughter.[8] After his millennial reign, there will be further wars against Gog and Magog.[9]　The Book of Elkesai, written apparently during the reign of Trajanus, prophesied that, when three more years of that reign had elapsed, war would break out among the ungodly angels of the north, and a convulsion of all ungodly kingdoms would ensue.[10]　Justinus quotes several passages from the Old Testament, speaking of a warlike triumph on the part of God or of the Messianic King.[11]　In the apocryphal 'Acts of Paul,' the apostle tells Nero that Christ "is going one day to make war upon the world

---

[1] Lk xix. 27, cf 11.　　　　[2] 2 Th ii. 8.
[3] Ap vi. 1–8.　　　　[4] Ap iii. 21, v. 5 : cf John xvi. 33.
[5] Ap i. 16, ii. 12, xix. 15.　[6] Ap ii. 16.　　[7] Ap ii. 23.
[8] Ap xiv. 14–20, xvi. 13 f, 16, xix. 11–21.　　[9] Ap xx. 7–10.
[10] Brandt in Hastings' *Encyclopaedia of Religion and Ethics*, v. 263b.
[11] Isa lxiii. 1–6 (the one in dyed garments from Bosrah) is quoted by Justinus in *Dial* 26 (532), Dan vii. 11 (destruction of the Beast) and 26 (overthrow of the Horn) in *Dial* 31 (540 f), Ps xlv. 5 (arrows in the heart of the king's enemies) in *Dial* 38 (557), Ps cx. 1 ("until I make thine enemies thy footstool," etc.) and 5 (kings crushed in the day of God's wrath) in *Dial* 32 (545).　From *Dial* 32 (544) we gather that Justinus regarded the putting of Christ's enemies under his feet as a process going on from the time of the Ascension.

with fire." [1]   In the Gnostic 'Excerpts from Theodotos,' we read of a great battle going on between the rebel 'powers' and the angels, the former fighting against, the latter—like soldiers—for, the Christians : God rescues the Christians from the revolt and the battle and gives them peace.[2]   The Montanist prophetess Maximilla foretold wars and anarchy.[3]   Tertullianus, in his Apology, assures the pagans that the events going on around them—" wars, bringing external and internal convulsions, the collision of kingdoms with kingdoms, famines, and pestilences, and local massacres "—had all been foretold in Scripture [4]; and in his reply to Markion he quotes Jesus' announcement of eschatological wars, etc., as demonstrating his connection with the severe and terrible Creator, inasmuch as he says that they must come to pass, and does not concern himself to frustrate them, as he would have done had they not been his own decrees.[5]   Hippolutos quotes the passage in Daniel where Michael is said to have been sent to make war on the prince of Persia [6] ; he speaks in some detail of the warlike character and doings of Antichrist,[7] and refers generally to the wars that are to be the prelude of the Last Things.[8] The Didaskalia quotes for the guidance of the Christian bishop the passage in Ezekiel, where the watchman is bidden warn the people when God is bringing a sword upon the earth, and adds: " So the sword is the judgment, the trumpet is the gospel, the watchman is the bishop appointed over the Church." [9]

---

[1] *M Paul* 3 (i. 110 ff ; Pick 45).
[2] *Excerp Theod* 72.
[3] Eus *HE* V xvi. 18 f.
[4] Tert *Apol* 20 (ii. 389 f).
[5] Tert *Marc* iv. 39 (ii. 455 f, 458 f).
[6] Hipp *Dan* IV xl. 3 (Dan x. 13, 20 f).
Hipp *Dan* IV xvii. 8 f.
[7] Hipp *Dan* IV xlix. 1, 4.
[9] *Didask* II vi. 6–11.

Cyprianus told his people that the wars and other calamities, which had been foretold as due to occur in the Last Times, were then actually occurring, showing that the Kingdom of God was nigh.[1] Victorinus of Petavium, in his Commentary on the Apocalypse, said: "Now the white horse and (the One) sitting on it shows our Lord coming with a heavenly army to reign; and at his coming all the nations will be gathered together and will fall by the sword. But the other (nations), that were more noble, will be kept for the service of the saints, and they themselves also will have to be slain at the last time when the reign of the saints is over, before the judgment, when the Devil has been again sent away. Concerning all these things the prophets uttered predictions in like manner."[2] Lactantius refers to the wars and troubles of the Last Times, particularly those of the time of Antichrist,[3] and quotes in connection with them a passage from the Hermetic writings, which says that God, "having recalled the wandering and purged away the wickedness, partly (by) flooding (it) with much water, partly (by) burning (it) up with sharpest fire, sometimes casting (it) out by wars and pestilences, led his own world (back) to (its) ancient (state) and restored it."[4]

The vague idea of a victorious war to be waged by the Messiah against the wicked was thus taken over from Jewish apocalyptic and seems to have become a fairly regular element in Christian belief. With the Jews, who had a land and a Holy City of their

---

[1] Cypr *Mort* 2.
[2] Victorinus in Haussleiter, *Theologisches Literaturblatt*, April, 1895, col. 195.
[3] Lact *Inst* VII xv. 10 f, xvi. 1–5, 12–14, xvii. 6 ff, xix.
[4] Lact *Inst* VII xviii. 4.

own, and whose Messianism was consequently of a materialistic and political kind, such a belief might at any time take practical form in the proclamation of a holy war against the enemies of God's Chosen People. When however it was transplanted to Christian soil, the risk of an attempt to anticipate by force of arms the Messiah's final triumph virtually disappeared. It was not until the time of Constantinus that the success of Christianity appeared to be bound up with a military victory—and not till long after that that a 'holy war' was proclaimed in Christendom. The Christian took no part as an earthly warrior in fighting for Messiah's victories. Those victories were expected to be won with armies of angels, or better still were interpreted in a spiritual sense. Tertullianus went out of his way several times to explain that the military character ascribed to Christ in Scripture was to be understood spiritually and figuratively, not literally : war, literally understood, he said, would produce deceit, and harshness, and injustice, results the very reverse of what was foretold as the work of Christ.[1] The expectation, therefore, of the quasi-military triumph of Christ, like the respectful view taken of the Old Testament wars, was not likely to encourage the Christian to take arms on behalf of his faith, except perhaps in the case of crude intellects that had barely grasped the essentials of Christianity, and here and there in the earliest times when the Church had hardly emancipated herself from the sway of the apocalyptic and Jewish political spirit. "One must not forget the psychological fact that the

---

[1] Tert *Marc* iii. 13 init (ii. 337 f) (a ridiculous picture of the infant Immanuel acting as warrior), 14 (ii. 340) (see above, p. 51), iv. 20 (ii. 406 f), v. 18 (ii. 516 f), *Res* 20 (ii. 821).

world of imagination and the world of actual life are separate, and that under (certain) conditions a very quiet and very peaceable man can at times give himself up to extravagant imaginations, without their actually influencing his own inner attitude. History proves that the military Jesus Christus redivivus of apocalyptic never in the (course of the) first three centuries turned the Christians into warlike revolutionaries." [1] Nevertheless, this belief in a warrior-Christ who would conquer his enemies, played a certain part in preventing a unanimous and uncompromising rejection of warfare as a permissible element in Christian life. [2]

THE JEWISH WAR OF 67–71 A.D. was itself the fulfilment of certain apocalyptic prophecies which Jesus was believed to have uttered, and as such it got separated off from the general body of Messianic wars (which were regarded in the main as yet to come) and invited the formation of a special judgment concerning itself. The Gospel of Mark, as we have seen, represented Jesus as announcing the devastation of Judaea, the siege and capture of Jerusalem, and the destruction of the Temple, in connection with the "wars and rumours of wars," the rising of nation against nation and kingdom against kingdom, which formed part of the "birth-pangs" that were to usher in the coming of the Son of Man. [3] The unanimous verdict of Christians who wrote after 70 A.D. was that the disastrous war culminating in the fall of Jerusalem that year—in which, it will be remembered, the Christians had refused to take a part [4]—was a divinely ordained

[1] Harnack *MC* 10: he discusses the whole question very fully (8–12 : cf 43 f).   [2] Harnack *MC* 11 f (see below, pp. 193 f).
[3] Mk xiii (see above, pp. 35, 179).   [4] See above, pp. 98 f.

punishment inflicted on the Jewish nation for its sin in rejecting and crucifying Christ. Luke and Matthew, in their versions of the apocalyptic discourses and other sayings of Jesus, represent the matter pretty clearly in this light.[1] 'Barnabas' says that the Temple of the Jews was destroyed because they went to war with their enemies.[2] A Christian interpolation in the Sibulline Oracles represents the destruction of the Temple as a punishment for the murders and ungodliness of which the Jews were guilty.[3] The Gospel of Peter pictures the Jews, immediately after the burial of Jesus, as "knowing what evil they had done to themselves" and lamenting and saying: "Woe (to us) for our sins: for the judgment and the end of Jerusalem has drawn nigh."[4] Justinus tells Truphon the Jew: "If ye were defeated in war and cast out, ye suffered these things justly, as all the Scriptures testify.[5] . . . And that the sons of Japheth came upon you by the judgment of God and took away from you your land and possessed it, is apparent."[6] The Christians of Celsus' time said "that the Jews having punished Jesus . . . drew upon themselves wrath from God."[7] Theophilos mentions God's threat to the Israelites that they should be delivered into subjection to all the kingdoms of the earth, if they did not repent, and adds: "And that this has already happened to them is manifest."[8] Tertullianus tells the Romans that Judaea would never have been beneath their sway, "but for their culminating sin against

---

[1] Mt xxiv. 1 f, 6–8, 15–22 (cf x. 14 f, xi. 20–24, xiii. 40–42, xxi. 41–46, xxiii. 34–39); Lk xvii. 31–37, xix. 41–44, xxi. 5 f, 9–11, 20–24.
[2] Barn xvi. 4.　　　　[3] *Sibulline Oracles* iv. 115–118, 125–127.
[4] Robinson and James, p. 22.
[5] Just *Dial* 110 (732): the prophecies are quoted in I *Ap* xlvii.
[6] Just *Dial* 139 (796).　　[7] Orig *Cels* iv. 22.　　[8] Theoph iii. 11.

Christ "[1]; and in the course of his argument against the Markionites, he bids them "recollect that end of theirs, which they (i.e. the Jews) were predicted as about to bring (on themselves) after (the time of) Christ, for the impiety wherewith they both despised and slew him . . . (many prophecies quoted). Likewise also the conditional threat of the sword: 'If ye refuse and hear me not, the sword shall devour you,' has proved that it was Christ, for not hearing whom they have perished," and more to the same effect.[2] Hippolutos has several allusions to the matter: for instance, in his Commentary on Daniel he says: "The Lord having come to them and not being acknowledged by them, they were scattered throughout the whole world, having been cast out of their own land; and having been defeated by their enemies, they were thrust out of the city of Jerusalem, having become a source of hostile rejoicing to all the nations."[3] The main burden of the surviving fragment of Hippolutos' 'Demonstration against the Jews' is the awful sufferings they had drawn on themselves from God in return for their treatment of Christ.[4] Minucius Felix makes Octavius say to his pagan interlocutor about the Jews: "For their own wickedness they deserved this (mis)fortune, and nothing happened (to them) but what was previously foretold for them if they should continue in (their) contumacy. So thou wilt understand that they forsook before they were forsaken, and that they were not, as thou impiously sayest,

---

[1] Tert *Apol* 26 fin (ii. 432).
[2] Tert *Marc* iii. 23 (ii. 353 f), cf *Jud* 13.
[3] Hipp *Dan* IV lviii. 3. In *De Antichristo* 30, he quotes Isaiah's prophecies about the desolation of Jerusalem as being now fulfilled, and mentions the martyrdom of Isaiah and the crucifixion of Christ in connection with them.
[4] *ANCL* ixb. 41, 43–45: cf Krüger 331 f.

captured with their God, but were given up by God
as deserters from (His) discipline." [1] In the Pseudo-
Cyprianic ' De Pascha Computus ' it is said that the
Temple at Jerusalem, " with the state itself, was again
in the time of Vespasianus destroyed (exterminatum)
by our Lord himself on account of the unbelief of the
Jews." [2] Origenes says repeatedly in the course of his
reply to Celsus and elsewhere that the calamities which
had overtaken the Jewish nation were a punishment for
their sins in general and for their treatment of Christ
in particular. I select three passages for translation.
" One of the (things) which prove that Jesus was something divine and sacred is the fact that (calamities of)
such greatness and such quality have on his account
befallen the Jews now for a long time. And we say
boldly that they (the Jews) will not be restored. For
they committed a crime the most unhallowed of all,
(in) plotting against the Saviour of the race of men in
the city where they offered to God the appointed sym-
bols of great mysteries. It was needful, therefore, that
that city, where Jesus suffered these things, should be
altogether destroyed, and that the race of Jews should
be overthrown, and that God's invitation to happiness
should be transferred to others," etc.[3] " If the Jews,
then, after treating Jesus in the way they dared, were
destroyed with (all their) youth, and had their city
burned, they did not suffer this as the result of any
other wrath than that which they had stored up for
themselves, God's judgment against them having been
passed by God's appointment, (and) being named
wrath according to a certain ancestral custom of (the)

[1] Minuc xxxiii. 4.   [2] Ps-Cypr *Pasch* 15.
[3] Orig *Cels* iv. 22.

Hebrews."[1] "The city, in which the people of the Jews asked that Jesus should be crucified, saying : 'Crucify, crucify him '—for they preferred that the robber who had been cast into prison for sedition and murder should be released, but that Jesus, who had been handed over through envy, should be crucified—after no long time was attacked, and was besieged for a long time in such a sort that it was overthrown from the foundations and laid waste, God judging those who inhabited that place unworthy of civic life (τῆς κοινοτέρας ζωῆς). And—though it seems a strange thing to say (ἵνα παραδόξως εἴπω)—(when God) handed them over to the(ir) enemies, (He was) sparing them, for He saw (καὶ ὁρῶν) that they were incurable so far as (any) change for the better was concerned and that they were daily increasing in the(ir) outpour of evil. And this happened because by their design the blood of Jesus was shed upon their land, which was (consequently) no longer able to bear those who had dared (to commit) such a crime against Jesus."[2] It is interesting to notice that Origenes says elsewhere that we must guard against interpreting scriptural references to the wrath of God and His punishment of offenders in a literal or materialistic way : we must seek, he says, for the spiritual meaning, that our feelings and thoughts about Him may be worthy.[3] He explains on another occasion that God's wrath is not a human passion, but a stern disciplinary measure, and though He may make use of the wicked in His administration of the world, the wicked are no less censurable for that.[4] The

---

[1] Orig *Cels* iv. 73.

[2] Orig *Cels* viii. 42. Cf also *op cit* i. 47, ii. 8, 13 fin, 34, 78, iv. 32, v. 43, vii. 26, viii. 47, 69, *Orat* xxxi. 7.

[3] Orig *Princ* II iv. 4.　　[4] Orig *Cels* iv. 70 (see below, pp. 215 f), 72,

martyr Pionios at Smyrna (250 A.D.) speaks of "the whole Judaean land . . . testifying up to the present day the wrath of God which came upon it on account of the sins which its inhabitants committed, killing (and) expelling foreigners (and) acting violently."[1] The Pseudo-Cyprianic treatise, ' Quod Idola Dii non sint,' speaks in a general way of the calamities that had overtaken the Jews on account of their sins and in particular their rejection and crucifixion of Jesus.[2] Another Pseudo-Cyprianic work, 'Adversus Judaeos,' says : "Christ, being repudiated by the people, sent (them) the tyrant they wished for, who overthrew their cities and condemned their population to captivity and took plunder and reduced their country to the desolation of Sodom," depicts the exile, misery, and beggary of Israel, and adds : "This is the punishment in Israel('s case) and the situation in Jerusalem."[3] The Didaskalia says : "Our Lord and Saviour, when he came, . . . taught the things that save, and destroyed the things that are of no advantage, and abolished the things that do not save, not only (by) teaching (the truth) himself, but also (by) working through the Romans[4]; and he put down the Temple, causing the altar to cease (to be), and destroying the sacrifices and destroying all the bonds which had been enjoined in the ceremonial law."[5] Lactantius mentions that it had been foretold "that after a short time God would send a king, who should conquer the Jews and level their cities with the ground and besiege them (till they were) consumed with hunger and thirst; that then they

---

[1] *M Pionii* iv. 18 (Gebhardt 99).
[2] Ps-Cypr *Quod Idola* 10, cf 12 f.   [3] Ps-Cypr *Jud* 6–8.
[4] per Romanos operans ; a variant reading gives inspirans for operans (cf Harnack C ii. 496 n 2).   [5] *Didask* VI xix. 1.

should feed on the bodies of their own (people) and consume one another; lastly that they should come (as) captives into the enemies' hands and should see their wives bitterly maltreated in their very sight, (their) maidens violated and prostituted, their sons torn in pieces, their little ones dashed (to the ground), everything finally laid waste with fire and sword, the captives banished for ever from their lands—because they had exulted over the most loving and most approved Son of God." After quoting this prophecy, Lactantius adds: "And so, after their death" (i.e. Peter's and Paul's), "when Nero had slain them, Vespasianus destroyed the name and nation of the Jews, and did everything that they had foretold would happen."[1] Eusebios says that the Hebrew Prophets foretold "the unbelief and contradiction which the race of Jews would display towards him (Christ) and the things done by them to him and the calamities which immediately and not long after came upon them for this—I mean the last siege of their royal metropolis and the entire destruction of the(ir) kingdom and their dispersion throughout all the nations and their enslavement to the(ir) enemies and foes," etc.[2] Finally, we read in the 'Dialogus de Recta Fidei': "At last, after Christ stretched his hands over Jerusalem, that people, who did not believe him, was overthrown together with the temple itself and the city; and anyone who by chance survived was exiled from his country and led away as a captive."[3]

---

[1] Lact *Inst* IV xxi: the prophecy was contained in the so-called 'Preaching of Peter and Paul,' which may be as early as the first decade or so of the second century (see Krüger 61 f).
[2] Eus *PE* 8d, 9a.   [3] *Adamant* i. 11.

WAR AS AN INSTRUMENT OF DIVINE JUSTICE.—
The destruction of Jerusalem in 70 A.D., while from the
point of view of the Gospels at least it partook of the
nature of an apocalyptic event, was perhaps even more
accurately regarded as an instance of the divine use of
war as a chastisement or punishment for human sin.[1]
Besides the allusions, just quoted, to the special exemplification of this principle in the case of Jerusalem, we
come across several allusions to the general theory.
Clemens of Rome speaks of God as the champion and
defender (ὑπέρμαχος καὶ ὑπερασπιστής) of those who serve
Him, and quotes the Isaianic threat: "If ye are unwilling
and will not hear me, the sword shall devour you."[2]
Theophilos quotes with tacit approval a Sibulline
oracle, in which God is said to raise up against the
wicked wrath and war and pestilence and other woes.[3]
Eirenaios, referring apparently to the conquest of
Canaan by the Israelites, says that the posterity of
cursed Ham was mown down by God,[4] and, referring
to the parable of the King's marriage-feast, says of God:
" He requites most fairly according to (their) desert(s
those who are) ungrateful and do not realize His
kindness : He repays with entire justice : and accordingly it says : 'Sending His armies, He destroyed
those murderers, and burned their city.' Now it says
' His armies,' because all men are God's."[5]   Tertullianus
assumes the idea of war being a chastisement sent by
the Creator as a doctrine common to himself and the

---

[1] Dr. Forsyth makes great use of this argument, in his *Christian Ethic
of War* (10, 30 f, 40, 87 f, 138, etc.).
[2] I Clem xlv. 7, viii. 4.   [3] Theoph ii. 36.   [4] Eiren *Demonstr* 20 (11).
[5] Eiren IV xxxvi. 6 (ii. 282 f)—Eirenaios goes on to quote Rom xiii.
1b–6, about the magistrate's sword, an aspect of the case which we shall
deal with later.   Cf Eiren *frag* 44 (ii. 509) (Balaam deservedly slain).

Markionites, and presses in opposition to them the saying that Christ had come to send a sword[1] : he refers to a number of incidents in early Hebrew history in which those who had offended against God were punished with slaughter, and concludes : "And thus, throughout almost all the annals of the judges and of the kings who succeeded them, the strength of the surrounding nations being preserved, He meted out wrath to Israel by war and captivity and a foreign yoke, as often as they turned aside from Him, especially to idolatry."[2]   Origenes says that Jesus "had no need of the use of whips and bonds and torture against men in the fashion of the former dispensation."[3]   Cyprianus, in answer to the pagan complaint that the frequency of wars, famines, plagues, droughts, etc., was due to the Christians, urges that "those (calamities) happen, not because your gods are not worshipped by us, but because God is not worshipped by you."[4]   When, early in the fourth century, the persecuting colleagues and successors of Diocletianus were overthrown in war by Licinius and Constantinus, the Christians regarded the defeat of the former as a divine chastisement for the sufferings they had inflicted on the Church.[5]

It perhaps hardly needs to be pointed out that a belief in the use of war for the divine chastisement of the Jews and of others who have been guilty of great offences, whatever theological problems it may raise, certainly does not involve the believer in the view that

---

[1] Tert *Marc* i. 24 (ii. 275) (nec fulminibus tantum, aut bellis, et pestibus, aliisque plagis Creatoris, sed et scorpiis ejus objectus—speaking of the Markionite's flesh), iv. 29 (ii. 435).

[2] Tert *Scorp* 3 (ii. 129).   [3] Orig *Cels* iv. 9.   [4] Cypr *Demetr* 2, 5.

[5] Lact *Inst* I i. 15, VII xxvi. 13 f, *Mort Pers* lii. 3 ; Eus *HE* IX xi. 9, X i. 1, 7, etc., *Vit Const* i. 3, etc.

it is right or permissible for him to take a part in inflicting such penalties. While Christians agreed that the fall of Jerusalem and its accompanying calamities were a divine chastisement, no one thought of inferring from that that the Roman army was blameless or virtuous in the bloodthirsty and savage cruelty it displayed in the siege. And in regard to the more general view of war as a divine chastisement, if it could be inferred from the fact of its being so that a Christian might lawfully help to inflict it, it would follow that he might also under certain conditions help to cause and spread a plague or to inflict persecution on his fellow-Christians—for both plagues and persecutions were regarded as divine chastisements just as war was. The obvious absurdity of this conclusion ought to be enough to convince us that the Christian idea of war being used by God to punish sin certainly does not mean that the Christian may take part in it with an easy conscience: on the contrary, the analogy of pestilence, famine, persecution, etc., which are often coupled with war, strongly suggests that participation in it could not possibly be a Christian duty. And there can be no doubt that the vast majority of early Christians acted in conformity with that view, whether or not they theorized philosophically about it. At the same time, just as to-day a superficial view prompts some people to leap at conclusions in this matter which their premises do not justify, so probably in those days there were some who allowed their conduct and thought to be unduly swayed by the fact that there were sundry departments of their minds in which war could be thought of without reproach. " A total rejection of war could not follow—for this reason, that God himself, according to the view of the earliest Christians, brings about and conducts wars. He has done it in earlier times through Joshua and David; He has done it in the present through the overthrow of the Jewish people and the destruction of Jerusalem; and He will do it in the future through the returning Christ. How therefore can one reject wars in every sense and universally, when God Himself provokes and leads them? Apparently there exist necessary and righteous wars! and such a war will be the war at the end of the day. If that is certain—even supposing it was forbidden to the Christian to go on service—the attitude towards war could no longer be an unbroken one. . . . Thus, apocalyptic," and, we may add, the Old Testament, and the Christian philosophy of history generally, each "contributed in its (own) measure to the (result) that the Christians did not shut themselves off altogether against war." [1]

THE FUNCTIONS OF THE STATE.—All the connections, hitherto studied, in which war received some sort of recognition from the early Christians, lay within ideal realms of thought remote from the concrete and practical duties of the times in which they lived. The Christian warfare was a purely spiritual struggle; the wars of the Old Testament belonged to a far-distant past; the fall of Jerusalem in A.D. 70 soon receded into the background; the apocalyptic wars lay in the indefinite, even though possibly the near, future, and would be waged, so far as the Messiah's side was concerned, with armies of angels, not of men; even the idea of war being a divine chas-

[1] Harnack *MC* 11 f.

tisement was simply a general abstraction and a pious conviction. But there was yet another connection in which the early Christians gave a quasi-recognition to war, a connection which was more nearly concerned than any of the foregoing with the practical affairs of their own day,—I mean the functions of the State in the maintenance of order and the suppression of crime. Though the severity of persecution (among other causes) led some to take up a position of uncompromising hostility towards the Roman Empire as a Satanic Beast-power,[1] the Church as a whole adopted the view that the State was a useful and necessary institution, ordained by God for the security of life and property, the preservation of peace, and the prevention and punishment of the grosser forms of human sin.[2] The general adoption of this view was largely owing to the immense authority of the Apostle Paul In writing to the Christians at Rome, Paul had occasion to warn them against an anarchical unwillingness to submit to the government and to pay their taxes. His specific reference to taxation suggests that he was enlarging on the Gospel precept : " Render unto Caesar the things that are Caesar's." He drove his point home by insisting on the divine origin of civil government. " There is no authority," he said, " except (that given) by God ; and those that exist have been constituted by God . . . the rulers are not a terror to

---

[1] This attitude appears mainly in the Apocalypse and in Hippolutos' *Commentary on Daniel.* Cf also *P. Scill* 112 : ego imperium huius seculi non cognosco.

[2] An inscription is preserved in which the (pagan) tenants of certain of the imperial estates in Africa express their appreciation of their landlord, the Emperor Hadrianus : they speak of " the sleepless vigilance with which he watches over the welfare of mankind " (H. Stuart Jones, *The Roman Empire* (' Story of the Nations ' Series), p. 189).

good work, but to evil. Dost thou wish not to be afraid of the magistracy (ἐξουσίαν)? do what is good, and thou shalt have praise from it : for he is to thee the servant of God for good. But if thou doest evil, be afraid, for he bears not the sword for nothing ; for he is God's servant, for the infliction of (His) wrath as a punishment (ἔκδικος εἰς ὀργήν) upon him who does evil. . . . They are God's officers, subsisting for this very (purpose)." [1] The view of Peter is substantially similar, though he calls the state a human, not a divine, institution. " Be submissive to every human institution (κτίσει) for the Lord's sake, whether to the Emperor as supreme, or to governors as (men) sent by him for (the) punishment of evil-doers and (the) praise of those who do well. . . . Honour the Emperor." [2] The author of the Pastoral Epistles enjoins prayer " for Emperors and all who are in authority, in order that we may lead a quiet and peaceful life with all piety and gravity." [3]

The history of the Pauline theory of civil government as an arrangement instituted by God is one of fascinating interest, but a full study of it would take us far astray from our immediate enquiry. It is worth while, however, to note the fact that it appears, in a more or less definite form, in most of the representative writers of our period, viz. Clemens of Rome, the Fourth Gospel,[4] Polukarpos, Athenagoras, the apocryphal Acts of John, Theophilos, the Acts of Apollonius, Eirenaios, Tertullianus, Hippolutos,[5] Minucius Felix,

---

[1] Rom xiii. 1b, 3 f, 6b.   [2] 1 Pet ii. 13 f, 17.
[3] 1 Tim ii. 1 f.   [4] John xix. 11.
[5] Mostly with reference to Nebuchadnezzar, but also generally. The idea is not so incompatible with Hippolutos' view of the Empire as a Satanic Beast-power, as appears at first sight. Weinel (24) has pointed out that Satan could be thought of as the servant of God.

Origenes, Dionusios of Alexandria, the Didaskalia, the Clementine Recognitions, Lactantius, and Eusebios.[1] It is absent from Cyprianus and Arnobius.[2]

Such a view carried with it a recognition of the rightfulness of judicial penalties ; and Christian writers, despite the non-resistance principles of their faith, are on the whole very frank in the way they express this recognition. Paul, as we have seen, connects the punitive functions of government with the Divine wrath against sin. The magistrate is " God's servant, for the infliction of (His) wrath as a punishment on him who does evil." Peter enjoins respectful submission to the Emperor's governors " as (men) sent by him for the punishment of evil-doers." The Christian belief in the future punishment of the wicked in eternal fire undoubtedly did something to facilitate this justification of judicial penalties. Thus Justinus, in reply to the criticisms levelled at the doctrine of eternal punishment, says that, if eternal punishment is unjust, then " lawgivers unjustly punish those who transgress the(ir) good ordinances. But since those (lawgivers) are not unjust, and neither is their Father, who teaches them by the Word to do the same (as Himself),[3] those who agree with them are not unjust."[4] Athenagoras speaks

---

[1] In regard to Constantinus.

[2] In Arnobius (i. 2) and the Pseudo-Cyprianic *Quod Idola Dii non sint* (4 f), we find a theory of the establishment of empires by chance or lot (cf Tert *Pall* 1 (ii. 1031) (At cum saecularium sortium variavit urna, et Romanis Deus maluit, . . .) ; Lact *Inst* VII xv. 13 ; Scullard 96 f). For a modern opinion on the Divine appointment of the State, see Horace Bushnell, *Nature and the Supernatural*, p. 12.

[3] Or possibly, " who teaches (men) by the Word to do the same as they (i.e. the lawgivers) (do) " (τὰ αὐτὰ αὐτοῖς [Otto : αὐτῷ] πράττειν διὰ τοῦ Λόγου διδάσκων).

[4] Just 2 *Ap* ix. 1 f. He goes on to say that the Logos had shown that some human laws were bad and some good.

about a man being put to death justly.[1] Theophilos calls the Emperor "a man appointed by God . . . for the purpose of judging justly : for he has in a way been entrusted by God with a stewardship. . . . (My) son," he says, quoting Proverbs, "honour God and (the) Emperor, and be not disobedient to either of them ; for they will speedily punish their enemies."[2] Eirenaios says that the devil, in claiming to have the control of the kingdoms of the world, was a liar and was claiming what did not belong to him. He reaffirms the doctrine of the divine appointment of rulers,[3] and continues : "Since man, (by) departing from God, grew so savage as to reckon even a kinsman his enemy, and to engage without fear in every (sort of) disturbance and murder and avarice, God imposed upon him the fear of man— for they did not know the fear of God—so that, being subjected to the power of men and restrained by their law, they might attain to some (measure) of justice and exercise mutual forbearance, in dread of the sword openly held forth, as the Apostle says : ' For not without cause does he bear the sword : for he is God's servant, an avenger for wrath to him who does evil.' And for this reason, too, the magistrates themselves, wearing the laws as a garment of justice, shall not be questioned or punished for what they do justly and lawfully. But whatever they do for the overthrow of justice, unfairly and impiously and illegally and in a tyrannical fashion, in these things they shall perish, the just judgment of God coming upon all equally and failing in nothing. For the benefit of the gentiles,

---

[1] Athenag *Legat* 35 (969) : see below, p. 214.
[2] Theoph i. 11 : cf Prov xxiv. 21 f.
[3] Eiren V xxiv. 1 (ii. 388 f).

therefore, was earthly rule established by God—but not by the devil, who is never quiet, nay, who does not wish even the (heathen) nations to live in tranquillity—in order that, fearing the rule of men, men might not consume one another like fishes, but by the establishment of laws they might smite down the manifold wrongdoing of the gentiles. And accordingly, those who exact tribute from us are 'God's servants,' 'serving for this very purpose.'[1] 'The powers that are have been ordained by God': it is clear that the devil lies when he says: 'They have been handed over to me, and to whomsoever I will, I give them.' For by the order of Him, by whose order men are born, are kings also appointed, fitted for those who are ruled over by them at that time. For some of them are given for the correction and benefit of (their) subjects and the preservation of justice, but some for fear and punishment and rebuke, and some for deception and disgrace and pride, according as they (the subjects) deserve, the just judgment of God, as we have already said, coming upon all equally."[2]

Tertullianus, in protesting against Christians being tortured in order to make them deny their faith, says to the Roman rulers: "This (imperial) government whose servants ye are is the rule of a citizen, not of a tyrant. For with tyrants, torture is applied also as a penalty: with you it is confined solely to (extorting) evidence. Keep (to) your own law in (using) it (only) until confession (is obtained); and if it is anticipated by confession, there will be no occasion for it. There is need of sentence (being passed); the wrongdoer has to be marked off for the (penalty which is his) due, not

[1] Eiren V xxiv. 2 (ii. 389).   [2] Eiren V xxiv. 3 (ii. 389 f).

to be released. No one is agitating for his acquittal ; it is not lawful to desire that, and so no one is compelled to deny (his crime)." [1]   In attacking the gladiatorial fights, he makes the concession : " It is a good thing when evil-doers are punished. Who but an evil-doer will deny this ? " [2]   He refers elsewhere to " the justice of the world, which even the Apostle testifies is not armed with the sword in vain, which in being severe (saeviendo) on man's behalf is a religious (justice)." [3] He quotes the words of Paul in Rom xiii, and says that the Apostle "bids thee be subject to the magistrates (potestatibus) . . . in consideration of their being as it were assistants of justice, as it were servants of the divine judgment, which here also judges of wrongdoers in advance." [4]   The Pseudo-Melitonian apologist tells Caracalla : " It is a shameful thing that a king, however badly he may conduct himself, should judge and condemn those who do amiss " [5]—implying apparently that he would be perfectly right in doing so, if he lived uprightly.

In his Commentary on Romans, Origenes says, à propos of the question whether a persecuting government is included in the phrase ' There is no power except from God,' that persecution is a culpable misuse of a power which, like all powers, e.g. those of sight, hearing, etc., is given by God for a good purpose, in this case " for the punishment of evil men, and the praise of good men." [6]   Discussing the question of the sense in which the earthly judge is God's servant, he observes that the Apostolic Decree in Acts xv. 23 f,

---

[1] Tert *Apol* 2 (i. 276 f).   [2] Tert *Spect* 19 (i. 651).
[3] Tert *Anim* 33 (ii. 706).   [4] Tert *Scorp* 14 (ii. 150).
[5] Ps-Mel 10 (*ANCL* xxiib. 121).
[6] Orig *Comm in Rom* t ix. 26 (Migne *PG* xiv. 1226 f).

28 f, does not forbid murder, adultery, theft, sodomy, and so forth : it might seem therefore that these are permitted. "But behold the ordinance of the Holy Spirit ! Since indeed other crimes are punished by secular laws, and it seemed superfluous that those which are sufficiently embraced by human law should now be forbidden by a divine law, He decrees those alone concerning which the human law had said nothing and which seem to pertain to religion. Whence it appears that the earthly judge fulfils a very large part of the law of God. For all the crimes which God wishes to be punished, He wished to be punished not by the leaders and rulers of the churches, but by the earthly judge; and Paul, knowing this, rightly names him God's servant and an avenger against him who does what is evil. . . . We have shown that the Holy Spirit has given a place in many things to human law."[1] Later, in his reply to Celsus, Origenes quotes Romans xiii. 1, 2a against Celsus' contention that kings were appointed by demons : he touches on the problem presented by the existence of evil kings, but passes it by, referring the reader to the Commentary on Romans.[2] He also says that the proceedings taken by bees against drones offer no fair comparison "with the judgments and punishments inflicted on the idle and evil in the cities."[3] He broaches the question whether evil demons may not have been appointed by the Logos "like the executioners in the cities and those who are appointed for gloomy but needful public duties."[4]

---

[1] Orig *Comm in Rom* t ix. 28 (Migne *PG* xiv. 1227 f).
[2] Orig *Cels* viii. 65.   [3] Orig *Cels* iv. 82.
[4] Orig. *Cels* vii. 70.

Many of the complaints made about the maladministration of justice, in persecution and otherwise, voice the Christian recognition of the need and value of good administration. Achatius said to the Prefect: "The public law punishes the fornicator, the adulterer, the thief, the corruptor of males, the evil-doer, and the murderer. If I am guilty of these, I condemn myself before (thou utterest) thy voice: but if I am led to punishment because I worship Him who is the true God, I am condemned by the will, not of the law, but of the judge." [1] Cyprianus complained that, not only are the innocent often condemned in the law-courts, but the guilty do not even perish with them.[2] "A crime is committed by a wrongdoer, and no innocent man is found who will avenge it. There is no fear of accuser or judge: bad men secure impunity, while modest (men) are silent, accomplices are afraid, (and) those who are to judge (the case) are open to bribes." [3] According to the Clementines, man has received wisdom to enable him to administer justice.[4] "Who is there among men," asks Clemens, "who does not covet his neighbour's goods? And yet he is restrained and acts with more self-control through fear of the punishment which is prescribed by the laws." [5] Methodios says that adulterers ought to be tortured and punished.[6] Arnobius says that as the images of the gods do not deter men from crime, "recourse is had to the sanctions of laws, that from them there might be a most certain fear and a fixed and settled condemnation." [7] Lactantius re-echoes the sentiment of Cicero, who

---

[1] *Acta Disput Achat* iii. 2 (Gebhardt 117)
[2] Cypr *Donat* 10.　　[3] Cypr *Demetr* 11.　　[4] *Clem Hom* iii. 36.
[5] *Clem Recog* ix. 15.　　　　　　　　　　[6] Method *Symp* ii. 5.
[7] Arnob vi. 26 : cf iv. 34, vii. 39 ff, appx (punishment of a slave).

" prefers to the teachers of philosophy the statesmen, who control public affairs, . . . who preserve the safety and liberty of citizens either by good laws or sound advice or weighty judgments (grauibus iudiciis)." [1] " Not from our number," he says, " but from theirs " (i.e. the pagan persecutors) " always arise those . . . who, if they sit (as) judges, are corrupted by a bribe, and either destroy the innocent or discharge the guilty without punishment." [2] He speaks of a man being condemned to death on account of his deserts.[3] He tells Constantinus that it is his task " to correct misdeeds " and to remove the evil men themselves from the State.[4] He comes much closer to the theory of the subject in his treatise ' On the Anger of God ': " They are deceived by no small error," he says, " who defame censure, whether human or divine, with the name of bitterness and wickedness, thinking that he who visits wrongdoers with punishment ought to be called a wrongdoer. But if so, we have wrongful laws, which ordain punishments for sinners, and wrongful judges, who visit those convicted of crime with ' capital ' punishment.[5] But if the law is just, which repays to the wrongdoer what he deserves, and (if) the judge is called upright and good, when he punishes evil deeds — for he who punishes evil men guards the safety of the good—therefore God, when He opposes evil men, is not a wrongdoer ; but he is a wrongdoer, who either wrongs an innocent man, or spares a wrongdoer so that

---

[1] Lact *Inst* III xvi. 2. [2] Lact *Inst* V ix. 15, 17.
[3] Lact *Inst* VI xx. 10 (see p. 159).
[4] Lact *Inst* VII xxvi. 12 : cf I i. 13 : taeterrimum aliorum facinus expiasti.
[5] ' Capital' punishment, in ancient times, did not necessarily mean the death-penalty, though it might do so. It meant the complete loss of one's status as a citizen, either by death, or exile, or enslavement.

he may wrong many.[1] . . . The public laws condemn those who are manifestly guilty ; but there are many whose sins are hidden, many who restrain the accuser either by prayers or by a bribe, many who elude judgment by favour or influence.[2] . . . Unless fear guards this earthly kingdom and empire, it is dissolved. Take away anger from a king, (and) not only will no one obey him, but he will even be cast down from his high rank."[3] Eusebios accounts for the moral blindness with which primitive man glorified vices, by pointing out that " at that time laws were not yet being administered among men, nor did punishment threaten offenders." [4] He speaks of the hierophants and others, who confessed their impostures under torture in the Roman court at Antioch and were put to death by Licinius with torture, as " paying the just penalty of their pernicious deception."[5] The doctrine of Fate, he urges, " would upset the laws, which are made for men's advantage. For what must one enjoin or forbid to those who are held down by another constraint ? Nor will one be obliged to punish offenders who have done no wrong against the same cause, nor to assign honours to those who act excellently—though each of these has furnished a cause for the repression of injustice and for the encouragement of well-doing (respectively)." [6]

If the view that the government was an institution ordained by God implied the rightfulness, in some sense, of judicial penalties, it also implied the rightfulness, in some sense, of war. The fact that the police and the military were not distinguished, that the characteristic

---

[1] Lact *Ira Dei* xvii. 6 f.
[2] Lact *Ira Dei* xx. 7.
[3] Lact *Ira Dei* xxiii. 10 : cf xvii. 16, xviii. 1 f.
[4] Eus *PE* 73cd.
[5] Eus *PE* 135cd, cf *HE* IX xi. 5 f.
[6] Eus *PE* 244d.

work of each was done with the 'sword,' made it easy
for ideas concerning the one to be transferred in the
minds of Christians to the other. The eulogistic terms
in which Clemens of Rome spoke of the imperial armies
and the discipline that made them so useful [1] are probably to be connected with his clear and repeated statements that the Emperors had been given their authority
by God.[2] Eirenaios mentions 'the military arts'
among human activities generally recognized as useful,[3]
and says that God "requites most fairly according to
(their) desert(s those who are) ungrateful and do not
realize His kindness : He repays with entire justice :
and accordingly it says : 'Sending His armies, He
destroyed those murderers, and burned their city.'
Now it says 'His armies,' because all men are God's
. . . and for this reason the Apostle Paul . . . says :
'There is no power except from God'"—then follows
a full quotation of Rom xiii. 1b–6, about the divinely
ordained function of the magistrate in repressing evil.[4]
Clemens of Alexandria deals at some length with
generalship as being, like legislation and the administration of justice, one of the usual departments of the
royal office, and in particular with the military genius
of Moses, from whom, he says, Miltiades and Thrasu-
boulos borrowed their tactics.[5] Some of his military
illustrations are more than mere illustrations, e.g. " (It
is) not only the athletic warriors, (who) wage the
contest of freedom in wars, but those who have been
anointed by the Word (wage it) at banquets and in

---

[1] 1 Clem xxxvii. 1–4 (καὶ ἐν τούτοις χρῆσις) : see p. 163.
[2] 1 Clem lxi. 1, 2.   Guignebert (191 n 4), Harnack (*MC* 18 f, 52 f), and
Weinel (26) have interesting remarks on Clemens' view of the Roman army.
[3] Eiren II xxxii. 2 (i. 373).   [4] Eiren IV xxxvi. 6 (ii. 282 f).
[5] Clem *Strom* I xxiv. 158–163, xxvi. 168.

bed and in the courts, being ashamed to become captives of pleasure." [1]   Tertullianus speaks scornfully of
the unwarlike habits of Puthagoras, "who avoided the
battles that were then going on in Greece." [2]   In trying
to prove that the body as well as the soul can be
morally guilty, he draws a contrast between the way
in which "a sword drunk with acts of brigandage"
would be shunned as guilty, and the way in which
"a sword (which is) honourably bloodstained in war,
and is a worthier slayer of men" (than the brigand's
weapon) would receive praise and consecration.[3]

Julius Africanus dedicated to the Emperor Alexander
Severus an encyclopaedia of all the natural sciences,
and gave it the title of Κεστοί ('Embroidered Girdles') :
he included in it a section on military science, in which
he treated frankly of the different means of destroying
the enemy, and even included instructions for poisoning
food, wine, wells, and air.[4]   But Africanus is merely

[1] Clem *Strom* VI xiv. 112 : cf also *Paed* III iii. 24 f, *Strom* I xxiii. 157,
IV iv. 14, 16.

[2] Tert *Anim* 31 (ii. 701) : Ecce . . . Pythagoram vero tam residem et
imbellem, ut praelia tunc Graeciae vitans, Italiae maluerit quietem.

[3] Tert *Res* 16 (ii. 815) : . . . gladius bene de bello cruentus et melior
homicida laudem suam consecratione pensabit.   Passing reference will
suffice to the allusions in Tert *Nat* ii. 17 (i. 608) to the part played by war
in the rise and fall of States under the control of Providence, in *Pall* 1
(ii. 1031) to the exemplification of this in the wars between Rome and
Carthago, in *Pall* 2 (ii. 1036) to the repulse of the barbarians as a sign of
God's favour to the Emperors, and in *Anim* 30 (ii. 700) to the useful
purpose served by wars, pestilences, etc., as remedies for overpopulation.

[4] The section on military tactics is to be found in *Veterum Mathe-
maticorum . . . Opera*, Paris, 1693, pp. 227-303.   A summary and
partial translation of it into French was published at Berlin in 1774 by
Charles Guischard, a Prussian infantry colonel, in a work entitled *Mémoires
critiques et historiques sur plusieurs points d'antiquités militaires*.   He
censures Julius Africanus for his barbarity as well as for his superstition :
"The Christian religion in its birth did not always cure men of their errors
in point of morals," he says, " nor of this leaning which they then had to
superstition. . . . Julius Africanus therefore could be orthodox, could
compose commentaries on the Bible, and at the same time a book of magic
charms, and could teach the art of poisoning wells " (p. 400).

an individual curiosity in this matter, and represents no one but himself. Only the fact that he was nominally a Christian entitles him to be mentioned here. How little the ethical side of Christianity had touched him is clear from the fact that his Κεστοί included a section on aphrodisiac secrets, which was full of obscenities.[1]

We have already had occasion to allude by way of anticipation to Origenes' relative justification of war[2]; and it remains for us in this place to put together the relevant passages. Referring to the timely unification of all kingdoms in the Empire of Augustus, he says: "The existence of many kingdoms would have been an obstacle to the extension of Jesus' teaching to the whole world, . . . on account of people everywhere being compelled (διὰ τὸ ἀναγκάζεσθαι) to serve as soldiers and to make war for the(ir) countries: and this (was what) happened before the time of Augustus and still earlier, when there was need (ὅτε γε χρεία ἦν) that there should be war, for instance, between Peloponnesians and Athenians, and similarly between others."[3] He concedes to Celsus that "the so-called wars of the bees perhaps constitute a lesson for the conduct of just and orderly wars among men, if there should ever be need (for them)."[4] He mentions in a tone of protest that Celsus tries to "depreciate as far as he can not only our—(the) Christians'—but all men's, cities and constitutions and sovereignties and governments and wars for fatherlands."[5] He speaks of the

[1] On Africanus, cf *DCB* i. 57a, Harnack *MC* 73 n 3; Bardenhewer *Patrologie*, 163.　　　　　　　　　　　　　[2] See above, p. 137.
[3] Orig *Cels* ii. 30. I pass over the casual allusion in i. 59 to stars portending revolutions, wars, or other events.
[4] Orig *Cels* iv. 82 (εἴ ποτε δέοι).
[5] Orig *Cels* iv. 83. It hardly perhaps needs to be said that Origenes does not here imply the existence of Christian patriotic wars, as a less

Emperor's soldiers as "those who render military service righteously." [1]

Cyprianus reckons it among the calamities of the time that the numbers and efficiency of the soldiers are decreasing.[2] The Clementine Recognitions speak of the obedience of armies as an instance of the beneficial effect of fear.[3] Methodios says that kings, rulers, generals, and various other classes of people, are useful to themselves and the community, if they are temperate.[4] Lactantius says that God made man naked and ·unarmed, because he could be armed by his talent and clothed by his reason [5] : he censures Epikouros for his policy of being all things to all men, by virtue of which he forbade the timid man to serve as a soldier [6] : he criticizes Maximinus Daza as ignorant of military affairs,[7] while he eulogizes Constantinus for having endeared himself to his soldiers by his personal attractions and character and his "diligence in military matters." [8] He describes with satisfaction and gratitude to God the victories of

rigidly literal translation in better English would more strongly suggest. Such an idea is indeed impossible in view of what he says elsewhere, not to mention the obvious facts of the situation. The phrase is nothing more than a loosely worded enumeration of the standing institutions of Church and State.

[1] Orig *Cels* viii. 73. His references in 69 f to the Romans praying to the one God and so being able to conquer their enemies more effectively (see above, p. 132) must not be pressed. He is dealing with an imaginary situation and omits for the moment to make allowance for that introduction of the Christian ethic which his hypothesis strictly required. In 70 he immediately corrects the omission : " . . . or (rather) they will not fight at all," etc.

[2] Cypr *Demetr* 3 (decrescit ac deficit in aruis agricola, in mari nauta, miles in castris), 17 (ruinis rerum, iacturis opum, dispendio militum, deminutione castrorum). [3] *Clem Recog* ix. 15. [4] Method *Symp* viii. 16.
[5] Lact *Opif Dei* ii. 6 : cf *Inst* VII iv. 14. [6] Lact *Inst* III xvii. 3.
[7] Lact *Mort Pers* xix. 6. The loss of military discipline is mentioned in *Inst* VII xvii. 9 as one of the disasters of the time of Antichrist.
[8] Lact *Mort Pers* xviii. 10.

Constantinus and Licinius over Maxentius and Daza respectively,[1] mentions how Licinius prescribed a form of prayer for his soldiers to use before the battle,[2] tells us how Constantinus, in obedience to a dream, had the sacred monogram inscribed on his soldiers' shields,[3] and warmly congratulates him on his triumph.[4] Eusebios writes in a very similar strain. He criticizes Daza for rendering his soldiers wanton, rapacious, and effeminate,[5] and says that his death was not like "the brave endurance of a glorious end, such as often befalls generals who act bravely in war on behalf of virtue and friends."[6] The closing chapters of his Church History and the whole of his later Life of Constantinus abound in grateful and even fulsome eulogies of the sovereign who had overthrown the persecutors by force of arms and thereby secured peace for the Church.

It was quite in keeping with the foregoing view of the imperial armies that the Christians, who habitually prayed for the Emperor and his subordinates, not only as enemies and persecutors,[7] but also (and usually) as the guardians of law and order,[8] should pray also for the efficiency and success of his soldiers who helped him keep out the barbarian invader and administer justice throughout the Empire.[9] While prayer for

---

[1] Lact *Mort Pers* xliv–xlviii.
[2] Lact *Mort Pers* xlvi : cf Harnack *MC* 89 f.
[3] Lact *Mort Pers* xliv. 5 f.   [4] Lact *Inst* I i. 13–16, VII xxvi. 11–17.
[5] Eus *HE* VIII xiv. 11. Cf Harnack *ME* ii. 55 n 2 (" Eusebius's feelings thus are those of a loyal citizen of the empire "), *MC* 73.
[6] Eus *HE* IX x. 14.   [7] e.g. Pol xii. 3.   [8] 1 Tim ii. 1 f.
[9] Harnack *ME* ii. 53 n. ". . . The emperor, even from the apocalyptic standpoint, had a certain divine right of existence as a bulwark against anarchy and the barbarian hordes ; for the " pax terrena " was a relative good, even from the strictest Christian standpoint. . . . Now the emperor needed soldiers to maintain this "pax terrena." They were part and parcel of the "sword" which (Rom xiii. 4) is recognized as a divine attribute of authority, and which no church-father ever dared to deny, in so many words, to the emperor." Similarly *MC* 123.

rulers in general appears at a very early point in Christian literature, prayers specifically for the army are not mentioned, as far as I have been able to discover, before the time of Tertullianus. This writer however refers to it as a standing Christian usage. "(We are) all (of us) always praying for all emperors, that their life may be prolonged, (their) rule secure, (their) household (kept) in safety, (their) armies strong, the senate faithful, the people upright, the world quiet, and whatever (else his) wishes are (as) man and (as) Caesar."[1]   Origenes says that it is the special province of Christians, who do not themselves fight, to "strive by prayers to God on behalf of those who render military service righteously and on behalf of him who is reigning righteously, in order that all things opposed and hostile to those that act righteously may be put down."[2]   Achatius said to the judge in the Decian persecution : " Our prayer for him (the Emperor) is persistent and constant, that he may spend a long time in this life and rule the peoples with just power and pass the time of his reign in peace, then for the safety of the soldiers and the stability of the world."[3] " We always ask," says Cyprianus, " and pour (out our) prayers for the repulse of enemies, for the obtaining of rain, and for the removal or moderation of troubles ; and we beg constantly and urgently for your (the pagans') peace and safety, propitiating and appeasing God night and day."[4]   "Why have our meetings deserved to be cruelly broken up," asks Arnobius, " seeing that in them the Supreme God is prayed to,

---

[1] Tert *Apol* 30 (i. 443).
[2] Orig *Cels* viii. 73 : for the context, see pp. 134 f.
[3] *Acta Disput Achat* i. 3 : deinde pro salute militum et pro statu mundi et orbis (Gebhardt 115).   [4] Cypr *Demetr* 20.

peace and pardon are asked for all—magistrates, armies, kings, friends, enemies ? " [1]

In estimating the meaning and value of the foregoing teaching in regard to the State, some allowance must be made for the immense authority of Paul's words, for the fact that they were written before the outbreak of imperial persecution in 64 A.D. and in order to counteract a strong tendency towards rebellious and aggressive anarchy in the Christian Church, particularly at Rome,[2] for immaturity of reflection in some of the writers we have quoted, and also for the natural habit, in controverting an opponent, of speaking ad hominem in a way that one would not speak if simply delivering a personal view. But all this takes us only a short way towards accounting for the language used. We are brought here to the very heart of the Christian problem of the State. Nothing could be more clear and explicit than the declarations as to the origin and purpose of civil government. It is an institution ordained by God for the purpose of restraining, by means of coercion and penalty, the grosser forms of human sin. If this view was a fixed datum in Christian political theory, the rule that a Christian must never inflict an injury on his neighhour, however wicked that neighbour may be, was also a fixed datum in Christian ethical theory : and the problem consists in reconciling these two apparently conflicting data. One thing is clear—that the fact of being appointed by God for a certain work or permitted by God to do it, did not, in the Christian view, guarantee the righteousness of

[1] Arnob iv. 36.
[2] Carlyle, *Mediaeval Political Theory in the West*, vol. i. 91–97.

the agent or of his doings.   The Apocalypse says that
'it was given' to the Beast to have authority over all
peoples and to make war upon the saints, that is to
say, he was in some sense allowed or authorized by
God to do it, for the achievement of some good end,
such as the chastisement or discipline of the Church.[1]
But this did not mean that the Beast was righteous or
that his persecution of the saints was not blameworthy.
Eirenaios makes it fairly clear that he could as easily
think of wicked rulers being appointed by God as he
could of good ones.[2]   God uses the wickedness of
some as a chastisement for others.   But even this does
not get to the bottom of the matter, for it refers
only to the crimes of rulers, not to the just legal
penalties they inflict.   The key to the problem is
simply this, that the just ruler who as the servant of
God enforces the laws, punishes wrongdoers, and wages
war against the unrighteous aggressor, is, in the thought
of Paul and the early Fathers, always a *pagan* ruler,
and therefore, though eligible for conversion, is yet, quâ
pagan, not to be expected to obey the distinctively
Christian laws of conduct or to exercise the distinctively
Christian restraint upon wrongdoing.   Not all the
servants of God are necessarily Christians.   God has a
use for those in the sub-christian stage of moral
development, as well as for those who enjoy the full
light of the Gospel.   Paul evidently had a genuine
respect for the nobler elements in the gentile mind,[3]

[1] Ap xiii. 2, 4, 5, 7, 14, 15 : see Moffatt's note on 7 in *Expositor's Greek Test.* ("The beast's world-wide authority goes back to the dragon's commission (2) but ultimately to the divine permission (so in 5).   There is a providence higher even than the beast ").

[2] Eiren IV xxxvi. 6 (ii. 282 f) (quoted on p. 205), V xxiv. 3 (ii. 389) (quoted above p. 199).   [3] Rom ii. 14 f ; cf i. 19 f.

including that sense of responsibility for the peace and
well-being of society, that love of law and order, that
appreciation of the elements of justice, which—with
whatever admixture of baser motives and whatever
crudity of unloving restrictive method—formed the
fundamental principles of the Roman Empire. In other
words, the Christian justification of coercive government and of war, though real and sincere, was only a
relative justification : it was relative to the non-christian condition of the agents concerned. It therefore
furnished no model for Christian conduct and no justification for any departure on the part of the Christian
from the gentler ethics characteristic of the religion of
Jesus. That the matter in its various bearings was
always fully understood in this light by Christian
authors, I do not argue. Indeed, from the slowness of
the modern mind to grasp the relativity of all moral
acts to the subjective conditions of the agent concerned,
one can easily understand how it was that this view of
the divine appointment of rulers was by the end of our
period widely understood to carry with it the Christian's
right to participate in the violence and bloodshed of
the State. But I do maintain that this doctrine in its
strict and proper meaning is perfectly consistent with
the practice and advocacy of the completest abstention on the part of the Christian from such participation,
and that the explanation of it which I have offered
furnishes the key to a good many paradoxes in
Christian literature. It explains, for instance, how
Paul himself can forbid Christians to avenge themselves,
telling them to stand aside and leave room for the
wrath of God, to whom vengeance belongs, and to
conquer evil with good by feeding the hungry enemy,

and so forth, and then a few verses lower speak of the pagan magistrate as the servant of God for the infliction of His wrath as a punishment on the wrongdoer.[1] It explains how Hermas can speak of the persecuting command of the Emperor to the Christians : " Either keep my laws or go out of my country," as a *just* command.[2] It explains how Athenagoras can say that Christians cannot endure to see a man killed, *even iustly*, and à fortiori cannot kill him.[3] It explains how Origenes can maintain that it is never right for a Christian to kill a man, and defend the Christian refusal to serve in the legions, and yet speak of the legionaries as "rendering military service righteously," can refer to the "just and orderly wars of men" as being sometimes necessary, can speak with approval of Judith's act in murdering Holofernes,[4] and can even argue for the right of the Christians to contravene the laws of the State on the analogy that it is right to conspire against and assassinate a tyrant.[5]

---

[1] Rom xii. 17–xiii. 6 : cf. especially the words of xii. 19 (μὴ) ἑαυτοὺς ἐ κ δ ι κ ο ῦ ν τ ε ς, ἀγαπητοί, ἀλλὰ δότε τόπον τῇ ὀ ρ γ ῇ· γέγραπται γάρ Ἐμοὶ ἐ κ δ ί κ η σ ι ς, ἐγὼ ἀνταποδώσω, λέγει Κύριος) with those of xiii. 4 (Θεοῦ γὰρ διάκονός ἐστιν, ἔ κ δ ι κ ο ς ε ἰ ς ὀ ρ γ ὴ ν τῷ τὸ κακὸν πράσσοντι).

[2] Herm *S* I 4 : λέγει γάρ σοι δ ι κ α ί ω ς ὁ κύριος τῆς χώρας ταύτης· Ἡ τοῖς νόμοις μου χρῶ, ἢ ἐκχώρει ἐκ τῆς χώρας μου.

[3] Athenag *Legat* 35 (969) Οὓς γὰρ ἴσασιν οὐδ' ἰδεῖν κ ἂ ν δ ι κ α ί ω ς φονευόμενον ὑπομένοντας, τούτων τίς ἂν κατείποι ἢ ἀνδροφονίαν ἢ ἀνθρωποβορίαν ; . . . ἀλλ' ἡμεῖς πλησίον εἶναι τὸ ἰδεῖν τὸν φονευόμενον τοῦ ἀποκτεῖναι νομίζοντες, ἀπηγορεύσαμεν τὰς τοιαύτας θέας (i.e. the gladiatorial shows). [4] Orig *Orat* xiii. 2 f.

[5] Orig *Cels* i. 1. It is a complete mistake to assume, as is apparently done by Bestmann (ii. 295) and Bigelmair (110), that Origenes meant that a Christian might justifiably conspire against and assassinate a tyrant. In the ordinary ethical code of historical Greece, to slay a tyrant was an act of the most laudable heroism (Grote, *History of Greece*, iii. 26 f) ; and Origenes simply accepts, for the purpose of his argument, this backward moral sentiment as admitted by his opponent and as relatively valid, without thereby implying that the act would be justified in the case of one on whom the full light of Christianity has come. Origenes also assumed the rightness of exempting pagan priests from military service in

While it may be confidently asserted that the relative justification accorded by Christians to the use of the sword by the pagan magistrate and soldier cannot logically be made to justify the use of it by themselves, we are still left with ultimate questions unsettled, viz. how to relate God's use of the pagan sword to the gentle love that He shows through Jesus, and how to harmonize the justice of it when regarded as a divine ordinance with the evil of it when looked at from the Christian point of view. These questions were never finally answered, but one or two things that were said in connection with them are interesting as bringing out the Christian attitude still more clearly.

We have already seen that Origenes broached the question whether the evil demons may not have been appointed by the Logos "like the executioners and those in the cities who are appointed for gloomy but needful public duties."[1] It is clear from this comparison that it is to the normal execution of justice—not to the maladministration of it—that Origenes attaches a quasi-demonic stigma. He expresses this view at greater length when replying to Celsus' contention that the Christian's opinion of what is evil is not necessarily true, for he does not know what is of advantage to himself or his neighbour or the world. Origenes replies that this argument " suggests that the nature of evil (things) is not absolutely wicked, for that which is regarded as evil in individual cases may be admitted to be of advantage to the whole (community). But lest anyone, misconstruing what has been said,

order that they might offer sacrifices (see above, p. 135): yet how absurd would it be to infer from this that he would have approved of Christians becoming pagan priests and offering sacrifices !

[1] Orig *Cels* vii. 70 : see p. 201.

should find (in it) an incentive to violence, on the ground that his wickedness is an advantage to the whole (community) or may possibly be an advantage, it has to be said that, although God, without prejudice to the freewill of each of us, may use the wrongdoing of the wicked for the administration of the whole (community), appointing them for the service of the whole (community), nevertheless such a man is blameable, and, as blameable, has been appointed to a service (which is) abominable for an individual, but useful to the whole (community); just as in the cities one would say that a man who had committed certain crimes, and because of th(os)e crimes had been condemned to certain public works useful to the whole (community), was doing something useful to the whole city, but was himself engaged in an abominable task and (one) in which no one of moderate intelligence would wish to be engaged." [1] Origenes does not explicitly mention the secular power in this connection, but there can be little doubt that he had it at the back of his mind; for on what other topic would his declared views have so obviously compelled him to admit that an act might be wrong for an individual but useful to the community as a whole? [2]

In the Clementine Homilies a quasi-manichaean view of the world is set forth. "God appointed two kingdoms and established two ages. . . . Two kingdoms have been appointed, the one (the kingdom) of what

---

[1] Orig *Cels* iv. 70.

[2] Yet Origenes was unable to do full justice to the relativity of morality (see *Cels* v. 28, where he insists overmuch on the absolute nature of what is right, and denies that differing customs and usages can be right for different nations): hence his attitude to governmental coercion lacks something to make it entirely sound.

are called the heavens, and the other (the kingdom) of those who now reign upon earth. And two kings have been established, one of whom is chosen to reign by law over the present and temporary world, who has also been composed (so as) to rejoice over the destruction of (the) wicked ; but the other, being king of the age to come, loves the whole nature of man.[1] . . . Of these two, the one acts violently to the other, God having bidden (him). But each man has power to obey whichever of them he wishes for the doing of good or evil. . . . If anyone does evil, he becomes the servant of the present evil (king), who, having by a just judgment received the power against him on account of (his) sins, and wishing to use it before the coming age, rejoices (in) inflicting punishment in the present life, and by thus indulging his own passion accomplishes the Will of God. . . . But these two governors are the swift hands of God, eager to anticipate the accomplishment of His Will : that this is so has been said in the Law . . . 'I will kill, and I will make alive ; I will strike, and I will heal.' For truly He kills, and brings to life. He kills by means of the left hand, that is, by means of the Evil One, who has been composed (so as) to rejoice over the evil treatment of the impious. But He saves and benefits by means of the right hand. . . . These do not have their beings outside of God ; for there is no other source (of being besides God) ; nor are they cast forth from God like animals, for they were of the same mind with Him. . . . The wicked one, therefore, having served God blamelessly to the end of the present age, inasmuch as he is not of the one essence which is solely inclined to evil, can, by a change in his composition,

[1] *Clem Hom* xx. 2.

become good. For not even now does he do evil, though he is evil, having received power to do evil lawfully (νομίμως κακουχεῖν)."[1] This view, despite its crudity, is interesting as an apparent attempt to explain how it is that an act like the punishment of a criminal may be right and lawful when done by an imperfect creature of God, and might lead to good and useful consequences, and yet might have to be put right outside the pale of Christianity, and therefore be wrong if performed by Christian hands.

The problem of how to reconcile the Christian ethic with the Christian justification of the State was virtually the same as the problem of how to reconcile the former with the Christian reverence for the Mosaic Law as divinely inspired. Of the many things said on this question, by far the most important is a suggestion made by the unknown author of the 'Dialogus de Recta Fidei' (a work of the early years of the fourth century). He shows us Adamantios, who is apparently meant to be Origenes, in discussion with a Markionite. The latter argues from the discrepancy between the Old and New Testaments that there must be more than one God. Adamantios points out traces of gentleness, love, etc., in the Old Testament, and of severity and vengeance in the New, and thus upsets his opponent without really solving the problem. At one point, however, he puts his finger for a moment on the real key to it. "I do not think it will seem absurd," he says, "if we use an illustration, in order that the sense of what we are saying may become clearer. Does not a woman, when she has borne a son, first nourish him with milk, and afterwards, when he has grown up, with more solid

[1] *Clem Hom* xx. 3.

foods? And I do not think the woman is on this account reckoned by anyone to act inconsistently, because she first gave her breasts to the baby with milk, (and) afterwards, when he had grown up, provided (him with) stronger foods. The Apostle Paul, too, knew how to promulgate laws to men according to their several progress, when he says : ' I gave you milk to drink, not food, for ye were not yet able (to take it); but not even yet are ye able, for ye are still carnal.' In the same way, therefore, God also gave laws to men according to the progress of their minds. To Adam he gave a law in one way as to a little child, but in another way to Noah, in another way to Abraham, in another way to the people of Israel through Moses. Through the Gospel also, according to the further progress of the world, the law-giving is different. Why therefore does God seem inconsistent, seeing that, in the same way as (He might treat) a man from (his) birth on to old age, He has so treated the whole world, which began from its first childhood, then after that, growing and progressing, came to middle age, and thence hastened to the maturity and perfection of old age, (and treated) each age of it with apt and adequate laws? But lest ye should think that I affirm this without evidence, I (will) show that this is written, how one and the same God commands different things. God bids Abraham sacrifice his own son : afterwards by Moses, He forbids a man to be slain at all, but orders him who is caught in this act to be punished. Because therefore He orders at one time a son to be slain, but at another the slayer to be punished, do we say that there are two Gods contrary to one another ? " Here Eutropios, the pagan arbiter of the discussion, asks : " Does He Himself order (a man) to be killed, and (yet) say : ' Thou shalt not kill ' ? " Adamantios replies : " Precisely. And not only is it found so in this, but also in many other things. For sometimes He orders sacrifices to be offered to Himself, and then again He forbids it. . . ." [1] The passage is unique in early Christian literature for the place it gives to the differing subjective conditions of men in the determination of the content of the moral law.

We cannot pursue further the question of the early Christian view of the State ; but enough has been said to show that there was nothing in the relative justification which Christians accorded to the ordinary functions of government, including even its punitive and coercive activities, which logically involved them in departing from the ethics of the Sermon on the Mount and personally participating in those activities. If a modern reader be disposed to reject this doctrine as one which selfishly leaves the dirty work of society to non-Christians, it is right to remind him, firstly, that, so far as the endurance of hardship and danger went, the early Christians were far worse off than the magistrates, executioners, and soldiers ; for not only had they to take their share as civilians in ordinary and special risks to which people are exposed alike in peace and war, but they had also to endure all the troubles and disabilities and persecutions which public odium heaped upon them ; and secondly, that they had their own method of repressing crime, more thorough and effective than the method of the State, and that

---

[1] *Adamant* i. 9 : the discussion on the point occupies i. 9–16, 18 (cf ii. 15). For Tertullianus' view of the gradual development of righteousness, see above, p. 177, n 3.

their power to remove occasions for the use of the sword increased directly in proportion to their numbers and their zeal.

None therefore of the various forms in which Christians may be said to have 'accepted' war necessarily committed them to participation in it. It cannot, however, be maintained that this fact was always adequately appreciated by them, or that their words and conduct were always consistent with the avowed ethics of their faith. We shall see in a later section how numbers of them came after a time to serve in the army ; but, short of this, there are several cases of real or apparent compromise on which a word may be said. Some of these lie so near the borderline between the permissible and the impermissible as to be patient of different interpretations. The sudden death of Ananias and Sappheira, for instance, when their deceit was exposed by Peter, was not the execution of a death-sentence, but the natural consequence of a well-merited rebuke, and was doubtless looked upon as a divine visitation.[1] Paul on the whole has a firm grasp of the real principles of Christian conduct, but his Roman citizenship, his legal type of mind, and his preoccupation with other aspects of Christian truth, led him at times into expressions and actions which are not easily harmonized with his words at the end of Rom. xii. His demand for the recognition of his legal rights, his readiness to plead his cause in a court of law, and his appeal to Caesar,[2] are not to be numbered amongst these; for they concerned simply his own immunity from injustice, and did not involve the

[1] Ac v. 1–11.
[2] Ac xvi. 35–39, xxii. 23–29, xxiv. 10 ff, xxv. 6–12.

punishment of his accusers or enemies. But his sentence
of blindness on Elymas the sorcerer,[1] which reminds us
of the case of Ananias and Sappheira, his apparent
silence on the unchristian character of the Philippian
gaoler's calling,[2] which again recalls the similar silence
of Peter in the case of the centurion Cornelius,[3] his wish
that the Judaizing errorists would castrate themselves,[4]
his consignment of the incestuous Corinthian to Satan
for the destruction of his flesh that his spirit might be
saved on the day of the Lord Jesus,[5] the one-sidedness
of the terms in which his doctrine of the State is set
forth,[6] and his communication to the military commander of the plot against his life,[7]—are cases so near
the border-line that much discussion would be needed
to enable us to measure what degree of inconsistency,
if any, was involved in each of them.

Many instances occur throughout our period of
Christians pleading, protesting, appealing, etc., to
pagan magistrates, and this has often been taken
as showing that they were allowed by the Church
to sue their enemies in pagan courts in order to get
them punished. So Bigelmair : " In disputes between
Christians and non-christians, the legal protection of the
heathen courts, which was not denied to the Christians,
had to be appealed to. . . . Recourse to heathen courts
was never contested." [8]   Similarly Bestmann.[9]   But the
cases quoted by Bigelmair prove nothing of the kind,
for in all of them the Christians were the defendants,
not the plaintiffs, and did not ask for the punishment of

---

[1] Ac xiii. 9–11.
[2] Ac xvi. 29–34.
[3] Ac x, xi.
[4] Gal v. 12.
[5] 1 Cor v. 1–5.
[6] Rom xiii. 1–6.
[7] Ac xxiii. 12–24.
[8] Bigelmair 94 f.
[9] Bestmann i. 403–405.

their enemies. Justinus, indeed, sadly compromises the Christian position when, in his eagerness to disavow the wrongdoings of pseudo-Christians, he asks the Emperors to punish those who were Christians only in name, but who were not living in conformity with Christ's teachings.[1] Origenes has been criticized for his willingness to pray for the victory of the Emperor's soldiers, when he would not fight along with them.[2] But one who thinks it wrong to fight may well recognize that one of two warring parties is better than the other and may wish that, while neither is acting in a Christian way, one may prevail rather than the other : and if the wish is legitimate, so too may be the prayer for the fulfilment of that wish. Lactantius could have justified a good deal of what he said about the justice of anger, and so on, had he made allowance for the partial relativity of all morality to subjective conditions ; but even so he would have had to find a larger place for love, expressing itself through non-resistance and gentleness and suffering, as the characteristically Christian policy for overcoming sin in others.

We are without exact information as to the extent to which Christians entered on political life in general, held office as magistrates, and brought suits to the pagan courts. There may have been a few cases of such action in the very early times. But broadly speaking, such cases were very rare before the middle of the third century. Athenagoras, Clemens of Alexandria, Tertullianus, and the Didaskalia, all regard it as forbidden to Christians to sue wrongdoers in the pagan courts. Origenes wrote in 248 A.D. as if Christians

---

[1] Just I *Ap* xvi. 14.
[2] Backhouse and Tylor, *Early Church History*, p. 130.

generally refused public office. But Christian feeling and practice grew laxer from that time onwards. The Clementines relate how the friends of Peter, being alarmed at the indignation which Simon of Samaria had excited against him at Antioch, sent for the Roman centurion Cornelius, who happened to be there with a message from the Emperor to the Governor of the province, and asked for his assistance. Cornelius offered to give it out that the Emperor had ordered sorcerers to be sought for and slain at Rome and in the provinces, that many had already been so dealt with, and that he (Cornelius) had been secretly sent by the Emperor to seize and punish Simon. This news being conveyed to Simon by Peter's spies, the former speedily departed in accordance with the Apostle's desire.[1] This amusing piece of fiction sheds an interesting sidelight on the author's view of the Christian's relations with the State and the army; but too much of course must not be made of it. In 272 A.D. a synod of Christian bishops appealed to the Emperor Aurelianus to eject from the cathedral house and church of Antioch the bishop, Paulus of Samosata, who had been condemned for heresy and deposed some years earlier, but had kept his place under the protection of Zenobia, Queen of Palmyra. The Emperor's decision was in favour of the appellants. "Thus," says Eusebios, "the aforesaid man was expelled from the church by the secular government with the utmost disgrace."[2] Under Diocletianus, before the persecution, Christians were appointed to the governorships of provinces,[3] which of course involved judicial and military duties. One of the martyrs in the

---

[1] *Clem Hom* xx. 13, *Recog* x. 54 f.   [2] Eus *HE* VII xxx. 19.
[3] Eus *HE* VIII i. 2.

persecution was Philoromos, who " had been appointed to no mean office in the imperial administration of Alexandria, and daily administered justice, attended by soldiers according to his rank and Roman dignity." [1] Another case was that of the governor ($\sigma\tau\rho\alpha\tau\eta\gamma\acute{o}\varsigma$) of the Phrygian town, the population of which was martyred en masse.[2] Constantius, who governed Western Europe, regularly employed Christians as his ministers of state.[3] The Synod of Illiberis provided for Christians who held the annual office of duumvir in Spanish towns and took part in the violence and bloodshed of the law-courts.[4] After the triumph of Constantinus all but a few remaining barriers were swept away. The clergy were not supposed to shed blood in war or to administer justice outside the ecclesiastical courts, and the ascetics and a few like-minded Christian laymen also refrained : but apart from these cases, it came to be taken for granted that the ordinary functions of civil government were as open to the average Christian as they had been to the average pagan.

THE CHRISTIANS' EXPERIENCE OF GOOD IN THE CHARACTER OF SOLDIERS.—Before investigating the actual participation of Christians in military life, it will be well to take note of the favourable impressions received by them on various occasions in regard to non-Christians engaged in it. This study thus forms the counterpart of our earlier sketch of the Christians' experience of bad treatment at the hands of soldiers.[5] The penitent soldiers baptized by John

---

[1] Eus *HE* VIII ix. 7.
[2] Eus *HE* VIII xi. 1 : see above, p. 95. [3] Eus *Vit Const* i. 16 f.
[4] See above, pp. 156 f. [5] See above, pp. 89–96.

the Baptist,[1] the centurion of Capernaum, who built the Jews a synagogue and at whose faith Jesus marvelled,[2] the centurion at the cross who exclaimed at the death of Jesus: ' Truly this man was a son of God,'[3] Cornelius, the centurion of Caesarea, and the ' pious soldier' who waited on him,[4] Sergius Paulus, the proconsul of Cyprus,[5] the man—doubtless a soldier—who, at Agrippa's bidding, led James the son of Zebedee to the judgment-seat, confessed himself a Christian, asked and received the Apostle's pardon as they were led away, and was beheaded with him,[6] the dutiful and officious but otherwise humane gaoler of Philippi,[7] the various military officials who had charge of Paul [8]— more particularly the centurion Julius, who took him to Rome and showed him great kindness on the journey [9] —all these are significant for the impression they made on the minds of Christians in their own day, as well as of the evangelists, etc., who wrote of them later. The apocryphal Acts of John represent the soldiers who had charge of the Apostle as treating him with great kindness.[10] Basileides, a military officer in Egypt at the time of the persecution of Severus, had to lead the maiden Potamiaina to death, and on the way defended her from the insults of the crowd and showed her much pity and sympathy.[11] When Perpetua and her friends suffered at Carthago in the same persecution, the military adjutant Pudens, who was in charge of the prison, was struck with their virtue, allowed many of

---

[1] Lk. iii. 14.
[2] Lk vii. 2–10 ‖.
[3] Mk xv. 39 ‖s.
[4] Ac x. 1–8, 22.
[5] Ac xiii. 7, 12.
[6] Clem Alex in Eus *HE* II ix.
[7] Ac xvi. 24, 27, 33 f.
[8] Ac xxi. 31–40, xxii. 24–29, xxiii. 10, 17–35, xxiv. 22 f, xxviii. 16, 31.
[9] Ac xxvii. 1, 3, 43.
[10] *Acts of John* 6 (ii. 154 ; Pick 129 f).
[11] Eus *HE* VI v. 3 : see more fully below, p. 233.

their friends to visit them, and was ultimately converted; the tribune also was induced to grant them privileges.[1]   Origenes performed his visit to the Emperor's mother Julia Mammaea at Antioch—and doubtless also that to the Governor of Arabia—under a military escort.[2]   Gregorios Thaumatourgos, with his brother and sister, were conducted from his home at Neo-Caesarea in Pontus to Palestine by the soldier who had been sent to bring the last-named to her husband, and to invite her brother to travel with her.[3]   In the Decian persecution, Besas, a soldier of Alexandria, rebuked those who insulted the martyrs, and soon after perished as a Christian.[4]   Imprisoned Christians were often able to procure minor privileges by paying money to the soldiers who had charge of them; and the Didaskalia bade the friends of prisoners send them money for this purpose.[5]   When Cyprianus was waiting to be taken before the proconsul just before his death, a military officer, who had formerly been a Christian, offered him a dry suit of clothes, as the martyr's own garments were soaked with sweat.[6]   Eusebios of Laodicea, while resident at Alexandria at the time of the revolt of Aemilianus (260 or 262 A.D.), was on the friendliest terms with the Roman general, and obtained from him a promise of safety for those who should desert from the besieged quarter of the town.[7]   We may recall here the episode in the Clementines, in which the Apostle Peter and his friends are represented as availing themselves of the friendly help of Cornelius the centurion.[8]

---

[1] *Perpet* 9, 16, 21.
[2] Eus *HE* VI xix. 15, xxi. 3 f.
[3] Greg Thaum *Paneg* v. 67–72.
[4] Dion Alex in Eus *HE* VI xli. 16.
[5] *Didask* V i. 1.
[6] Pont *Vit Cypr* 16.
[7] Eus *HE* VII xxxii. 8 f.
[8] See above, p. 224.

THE PARTICIPATION OF CHRISTIANS IN MILITARY SERVICE.—The purpose of this section is to present the reader with as complete and accurate a statement as possible of the extent to which Christians actually served as soldiers in the pre-Constantinian period. It will thus serve as the complement to the former section dealing with the Christian refusal of service, alongside of which it will naturally be read, and will involve a certain amount of overlapping with what has gone before. Taking first the period of the New Testament, and excluding the converts of John the Baptist, the centurion of Capernaum, and the centurion at the cross, as not being disciples of Jesus at all, Sergius Paulus, the proconsul of Cyprus, as not being a full convert to Christianity in the ordinary sense,[1] and the soldier—if soldier he was—who was executed with James the Apostle, as being relieved by his prompt martyrdom of all necessity of deciding whether he ought to remain in his calling or to resign it,[2] we are left with Cornelius, the one or two soldiers who may have been baptized with him, and the gaoler at Philippi,[3] as the only real cases of Christian soldiers in New Testament times. The New Testament itself and the earliest Christian literature nowhere express disapproval of the continuance of these men—assuming they did continue—in their calling, or of the military calling in general. It is even possible that Luke, who records these cases, as well as the conversation between John the Baptist and the soldiers, may have meant to intimate thereby his view as to the propriety of admitting soldiers to the Church without requiring them to abandon the profession of

[1] See above, pp. 97 f. [2] See above, p. 226.
[3] Ac x. 1 ff, 7 ff, 47 f, xvi. 27–34.

arms[1]: and the existence even of these few cases makes it possible that from the earliest times there *may* have been soldier-converts in the Church.[2] But as a matter of fact there is no trace of the existence of any Christian soldiers between these cases mentioned in Acts and—say—170 A.D. The supposed records of Christian soldiers of the times of Trajanus and Hadrianus are without historical value.[3]

We come however upon an important piece of evidence in the reign of Marcus Aurelius. During one of that Emperor's campaigns against the Quadi, a tribe inhabiting what is now Moravia, in 173 or 174 A.D., the Roman army found itself in serious difficulties owing to lack of water. In the Twelfth Legion, the Legio Fulminata, which was recruited and usually stationed in Melitene, a region in eastern Cappadocia where Christianity was strong, there were a considerable number of Christian soldiers. These prayed for relief from the drought, and at once a shower refreshed the Roman troops, while a storm discomfited the enemy. Such is, in bare outline, the story of what —as far as we can make out—actually happened. It was evidently an incident of some importance, for it was commemorated on the column set up by Marcus Aurelius at Rome, and noticed by a number of writers, both Christian and pagan. The pagan accounts do not mention the Christians in the army at all,[4] and so are of no value for our immediate purpose, beyond confirming the historical background of the story. The earliest Christian witness is Apolinarios, bishop of Hierapolis

---

[1] Harnack *MC* 53.   [2] So Harnack *ME* ii. 52.   [3] See pp. 99-101.
[4] The pagan witnesses are the pillar of Marcus, Dio Cassius (lxxi. 8, 10), and Capitolinus (*Hist. Aug. Life of M. Antoninus Philosophus*, xxiv. 4).

in Phrygia, who gave a simple account of the incident
—probably very soon after its occurrence—perhaps in
the Apology which he addressed to Marcus Aurelius.[1]
As reported by Eusebios, he spoke as if the whole
legion had been Christian, and said that it received
from the Emperor the name of κεραυνοβόλος (i.e.
thundering) in memory of what happened.[2] Now
there is no doubt at all that either Eusebios misunderstood and misreported Apolinarios,[3] or else
Apolinarios himself made a mistake about the name
of the Legion : for the Twelfth Legion was called
Fulminata (thunderstruck) not Fulminatrix (thundering),
and had moreover borne that name since the time of
Augustus or at least that of Nero.[4] In view of
this error, the value of Apolinarios as a witness for
the existence of a whole legion of Christian soldiers
simply disappears; and it is more than doubtful whether
he meant to speak of such a legion at all. The next
witness whom we can date with any confidence is
Tertullianus, who twice mentions the incident,[5] but
without committing himself as to the number of
soldiers. Even the so-called Letter of Marcus Aurelius
to the Senate[6] (which some put before the time of
Tertullianus, some as late as early in the fourth
century,[7] and which is usually regarded as a Christian
forgery,[8] though Harnack regards it as substantially

---

[1] So Harnack (*C* i. 360 f), though the dates are a little difficult to
reconcile.   [2] Eus *HE* V v. 3 f.
[3] So Lightfoot *AF* II i. 491.   [4] *DCB* iv. 1024a.
[5] Tert *Apol* 5 (i. 295) (illam germanicam sitim christianorum forte
militum precationibus impetrato imbri discussam), *Scap* 4 (i. 703) (christianorum militum orationibus ad Deum factis).
[6] Text in Otto's *Justinus* i. 246 ff, Lightfoot *AF* II i. 485 f, Blunt
133 f; ET in *ANCL* ii. 68 f.
[7] Bigelmair 186 n 1.   [8] Lightfoot *AF* II i. 490 ; Blunt 131 f.

genuine, but interpolated [1]), does not claim a whole legion of Christian soldiers—does not in fact mention the legion at all—but contents itself with the vague phrase, 'a great crowd'[2] of 'those who with us are called Christians.' Eusebios seems to have believed that the whole legion was Christian,[3] and was probably unintentionally responsible for the attribution of this view to Apolinarios. The remarks of Xiphilinos[4] are interesting, but much too late to be of any value as evidence. While the Christian versions contain obvious embellishments and exaggerations, and the idea of a whole legion of Christian soldiers must be dismissed,[5] there can be no doubt about the main fact, that, in or about 174 A.D., the Legio Fulminata contained a considerable number of Christian soldiers. This means that the conversion of soldiers to Christianity must have been going on for some little time previously, though for how long we do not know. It is often said that these men were not censured or criticized by their fellow-Christians for their position[6]; but in view of the fact that Celsus's censure of the Christians in general for objecting to military service came within a few years of the incident just described,[7] and in view of the fact that the later decision of the Church would tend to obliterate records of the earlier rigorism, it is not safe to conclude from the absence of any extant criticism of these Christian soldiers that their position passed uncriticized.

---

[1] Harnack *C* i. 702.
[2] πλῆθος καὶ μέγεθος αὐτῶν.
[3] Eus *HE* V v. 1–4.
[4] Dio Cassius lxxi. 9.
[5] So Stokes in *DCB* iv. 1024b.
[6] So Harnack *ME* ii. 55 ("Neither then nor subsequently did any Christian censure these soldiers for their profession "), *MC* 57 ; Bigelmair 189.
[7] See above, p. 104.

Julius Africanus appears to have served as an officer in the expedition of the Emperor Severus against Osrhoene in 195 A.D. [1] : but we have already seen reason for refusing to regard him as in any way a representative Christian.[2] Clemens of Alexandria does not seem ever to have faced the problem of Christianity and war ; and hence, despite his clear grasp of Christian principles in the abstract,[3] he uses expressions which concede the compatibility of military service with the Christian faith. He appeals to the Greek thus : " Be a farmer, we say, if thou art a farmer ; but know God (while thou art) farming : and sail, thou lover of navigation, but (sail) calling upon the heavenly Pilot : has the (true) knowledge taken hold of thee (when) serving as a soldier ? Listen to the General who orders what is righteous." [4] Some years later, when writing for Christian readers, he says : " Barefootedness is very becoming to a man, except when he is on military service " [5] ; and later, criticizing the love of wealth and display : " But even now the soldiers wish to be adorned with gold, not having read that (passage) in the poet : ' He came to the war, wearing gold, like a young girl.' " [6] He says that the divine ' Instructor,' under the heading of for-bearance, " enjoins by John upon those in military service to be content with their wages only." [7] He quotes the Mosaic regulations in regard to the exemption of certain classes of men from military service and of summoning the enemy to come to terms before attacking them, without any intimation that they would

---

[1] Gelzer, *Sextus Julius Africanus und die byzantinische Chrono-graphie*, i. 8.   [2] See above, p. 207.   [3] See pp. 71 f, 78.
[4] Clem *Protr* x. 100.   [5] Clem *Paed* II xi. 117.
[6] Clem *Paed* II xii. 121.   Clem *Paed* III xii. 91.

not be applicable to Christians.[1] He mentions "the soldier's hope and the merchant's gain " along with life, angels, etc., as examples of the "things present" which are powerless to oppose faith.[2]

We have already had occasion to notice the susceptibility to Christian influence of soldiers employed in the horrible work of persecution—a susceptibility which led in many cases to their conversion.[3] One or two cases merit repetition here. The soldier Basileides of Alexandria had, while still a heathen, received instruction under Origenes. During the persecution of 202 A.D., it fell to his lot to conduct the Christian maiden Potamiaina to death, and apparently to preside over the execution, which consisted of boiling pitch being poured over the girl's body from the feet upwards. He showed her what sympathy and kindness he could under the circumstances, and the experience issued—as well it might—in his conversion. This was at first kept a secret, but soon became known through his refusal as a Christian to take an oath when challenged to do so by his fellow-soldiers. He was led to the judge, confessed, and received sentence. He was visited in prison by the Christians, and baptized, and the next day was beheaded. Nothing is said in the extant record as to his conversion leading him to want to resign his post in the army.[4] Somewhat similar was the case of the adjutant Pudens,

[1] Clem *Strom* II xviii. 82, 88.

[2] Clem *Strom* IV xiv. 96. Ramsay (*Cities and Bishoprics of Phrygia*, ii. 718) is mistaken in including Clemens among those who " absolutely forbade that Christians should be soldiers or bear arms."

[3] See above, pp. 226 f. Harnack says (*MC* 75) : " That the soldier who accompanied a Christian to death, in particular the (soldier who acted as) informer, himself became a Christian, gradually became a stereotyped feature in the stories of martyrs, but is not always legendary." For instances in more or less fictitious martyr-acts, see Neumann 288–290.

[4] Eus *HE* VI iii. 13, v.

whose conversion took place at the time of the martyrdom of Perpetua and her companions at Carthago,[1] though we do not know what became of him afterwards.[2]

The information contributed by Tertullianus is important. In 197 A.D. he wrote to the pagans : "Ye cry out that the state is besieged—that there are Christians in the fields, in the fortified towns, in the islands." [3] "We are (people) of yesterday, and we have filled all that belongs to you—cities, islands, fortified towns (?) (castella), country towns, places of assembly, the very camps, the tribes, the decuries, the palace, the senate, the forum." [4] "With you we go on voyages and serve as soldiers and farm and trade : we mix (our) industries (with yours) ; we make our work public for your service." [5] He refers to the incident in the reign of Marcus Aurelius, when the drought afflicting the Roman army was removed "by the shower obtained by the prayers of the Christian soldiers (who were) by chance (serving under him)." [6] A little later, in arguing that no Christian ought to be a soldier, he lets us see that there were Christians who took the opposite view and supported their position by appealing to the examples of Moses, Aaron, Joshua, the Israelites, and even John the Baptist.[7] He himself says that Paul, in "teaching that everyone ought to live by his own labour, had introduced plenty of examples, (those,

---

[1] See above, pp. 226 f.   [2] *DCB* iv. 520b.

[3] Tert *Nat* i. 1 (i. 559) : similar words in *Apol* i (i. 262). The word translated 'fortified towns'—castellis—may mean simply 'villages.'

[4] Tert *Apol* 37 (i. 462 f). The statement is of course an exaggeration, and must be taken with a grain of salt. Tertullianus makes a reference in *Apol* 32 (i. 447) to Christians taking the military oath.

[5] Tert *Apol* 42 (i. 491).   [6] See p. 230 n 5.

[7] Tert *Idol* 19 (i. 690 f) : see above, p. 109.

namely), of soldiers, shepherds, and husbandmen." [1]
Later still (211 A.D.), we have from him an account of
the circumstances which occasioned the composition of
his treatise 'De Corona Militis.' Shortly after the
accession of the Emperors Caracalla and Geta, an
imperial largess was being distributed to the Roman
troops in Numidia, when one Christian soldier made
himself conspicuous by refusing to put on the laurel
garland which everyone else was wearing for the occasion. His fellow-Christians in the army—not to mention the heathen soldiers—and some at least of the
Christian civilians as well, condemned his action on the
ground that it was rash and presumptuous and likely to
provoke persecution, and that nowhere in Scripture are
we forbidden to be crowned. [2] The incident shows that
there were at that time many Christians in the Roman
army in Africa, and that some—possibly a majority—
of the members of the local church raised no objection
to their being there. It does not prove that the whole
of the local church—still less that the Church generally
—had no scruples at all about its members serving as
soldiers. [3]

It is important also to notice that the 'De Idolo-

---

[1] Tert *Marc* v. 7 (ii. 487). I do not know any passage in Paul's letters
justifying this statement about soldiers.

[2] Tert *Cor* 1 (ii. 76 f). He astutely points out the similarity between
the Christian and the pagan criticisms : exinde sententiae super illo,
nescio an Christianorum, non enim aliae ethnicorum, ut de abrupto, etc.,
etc. Harnack has suggested (*ME* i. 418 n, ii. 56, *MC* 68) that this
soldier's object was to secure for his Christian comrades in the army the
same exemption from the semi-idolatrous garland that was enjoyed by the
worshippers of Mithras.

[3] It is therefore a gross exaggeration to say that the fact that the soldier
was condemned " is conclusive proof that the Christian society of the time
found no cause of complaint in the fact of its members serving in the
legions, and that they did not regard such service as incompatible with
their religion " (B.-Baker *ICW* 25).

latria ' and ' De Corona ' of Tertullianus are our oldest pieces of evidence for the existence of Christian soldiers who had joined the army *after* their conversion. In the former, his discussion of the questions 'whether a believer may turn to military service, and whether the military . . . may be admitted to the faith '[1] may be taken to imply that in practice cases had already arisen in which both these questions had been answered in the affirmative. In the ' De Corona' his condemnation of the act of ' transferring (one's) name from the camp of light to the camp of darkness '[2] shows pretty clearly that the thing had been done. Immediately afterwards he speaks of those who had been converted when already in the army as a special class of Christian soldiers[3]; evidently, therefore, there were others who had become soldiers after conversion. These passages, however, are the earliest references we have to Christians becoming soldiers after baptism : all the Christian soldiers mentioned before the period of ' De Idololatria ' (198–202 A.D.) may quite well have been—for all we know to the contrary—converted when already in the army. Such would obviously have been the more normal case.

In the year 217 A.D. the tomb of an imperial official, Marcus Aurelius Prosenes, received a supplementary inscription from his freedman, the Christian Ampelius, who described himself as 'returning from the campaigns.'[4] Another inscription, about the middle of the

---

[1] Tert *Idol* 19 (i. 690) : see pp. 108 f.
[2] Tert *Cor* 11 (ii. 92) : see above, p. 111.   [3] *Ib.* : see above, p. 112.
[4] The inscription runs : Prosenes receptus ad Deum V non [apr]ilis Sa[uro in Camp]ania, Praesente et Extricato II (sc. consulibus). Regrediens in Urbe(m) ab expeditionibus scripsit Ampelius lib(ertus) (De Rossi, *Inscriptiones Urbis Romae*, I 9; Marucchi, *Christian Epigraphy*, 225 : Neumann (84 n) gives a slightly different interpretation).

third century, found at Hodjalar in Phrygia, gives us the epitaph on the family tomb of two Christian soldiers.[1]

Cyprianus tells us that the two uncles of a certain Christian who suffered in the persecution of Decius (250 A.D.) had been soldiers.[2] Dionusios of Alexandria tells us that there were soldiers among the martyrs in that very persecution.[3] At Alexandria during the persecution, a soldier named Besas rebuked the crowd that was insulting the martyrs on their way to execution. He was immediately challenged, arraigned as a Christian, confessed, and was beheaded.[4] On another occasion a squad of five soldiers, attending at the trial of a Christian, attracted attention by making violent gestures of anxiety when the accused threatened to deny his faith, and then rushed before the tribunal and confessed themselves Christians. The governor, as well as his council, was amazed, but seems to have ordered them to execution.[5] We have already spoken

[1] Ramsay, *Cities and Bishoprics of Phrygia*, ii. 717.
[2] See above, p. 147 n 2.
[3] Dion Alex in Eus *HE* VII xi. 20 : the letter of Dionusios here quoted refers to the Decian persecution, though Eusebios erroneously connects it with that of Valerianus (Feltoe 65).
[4] Dion Alex in Eus *HE* VI xli. 16.
[5] Dion Alex in Eus *HE* VI xli. 22 f. Their conversion seems to have been due to a sudden rush of feeling under the affecting circumstances of the hour. Harnack, I think, overlooks the fact that only five men were concerned, assumes that before their public confession they were already virtually Christians ("Christen oder . . . christlich Gesinnten"), and infers that Christianity must have been very widespread in the army in Egypt, as there could have been no idea of picking out Christian soldiers for this particular task (Harnack *ME* ii. 58, *MC* 76 f). This seems to me to be making too much out of the passage. Sudden conversions were not uncommon at scenes of persecution ; and there is no reason to suppose that these five men were in any way definitely Christian before this incident. They may have known about Christianity and been sympathetic towards it, but that does not warrant Harnack's conclusion that Christianity was widespread in the army in Egypt. I pass by the untrustworthy 'Acts of Polueuktes,' the soldier who is said to have been beheaded for refusing to sacrifice in compliance with an edict of 'Decius and Valerian'! (Conybeare 123-146 ; Harnack *ME* ii. 61, *MC* 83).

of the Christian military officer Marinus, who was martyred at Caesarea in 260 A.D.[1] " The number of Christian officers and soldiers in the army gradually increased . . . after the reign of Gallienus ; so much so that the military authorities began to connive at Christianity ; they made allowance for it, and looked on quietly while Christian officers made the sign of the cross at the sacrifices. Moreover they also dispensed silently with their attendance at these sacrifices." [2]　In 295 A.D., on the occasion of the martyrdom of Maximilianus in Numidia, the proconsul of Africa said to him : " In the sacred retinue of our lords Diocletianus and Maximianus, Constantius and Maximus, there are Christian soldiers, and they serve (as such)." [3]　The silence of the Synod of Illiberis on the legitimacy of military service is significant. The Spanish bishops seem to have realized that there was too much to be said on both sides for them to commit themselves to either.[4]　Eusebios tells us that long before the outbreak of the general persecution in 303 A.D., the Emperor Galerius attempted, by means of degradation, abuse, and menace of death, to compel the Christians in the army, beginning with those in his own household, to desert their faith.[5]　We learn from Eusebios and Hieronymus that about 299 A.D. a general named Veturius attempted to purge the troops under him of Christian soldiers ; and a great number of them consequently retired from the service, and a few suffered the

---

[1] See above, pp. 151 f.　　　[2] Harnack *ME* ii. 54 : cf *MC* 81 f.
[3] See above, pp. 149 f.　Fabius Victor, the martyr's father, seems to have been a Christian before the trial, and may have been a soldier (see p. 150 n 2) : anyhow, he had bought his son a new military coat in anticipation of his joining up.
[4] Harnack *MC* 79 n 2 (80).　　　[5] Eus *HE* VIII appendix, 1.

penalty of death. The devil, says Eusebios, thought that if he could first subdue the Christians in the army, he would easily be able to catch the others—a remark which indicates that in Eusebios' belief the Christians in the army at that time were numerous and highly respected.[1] The martyrdom of the Christian centurion Marcellus in Mauretania in 298 A.D. [2] may have been the outcome of a similar movement on the part of the military authorities in that quarter of the Empire. Typasius, another soldier of Mauretania, is said to have obtained his discharge from the army before the persecution broke out.[3] The famous legend of the martyrdom of the whole Thebaic legion (recruited in the Egyptian Thebaid) at the hands of Maximianus at Agaunum near the Lake of Geneva, is variously referred to 286, 297, or 302 A.D. The evidence for it is late, and the story as it stands is impossible. It may be that the actual martyrdom of a few—conceivably a few hundred —Christian soldiers for refusing to sacrifice underlies the legend : more than that cannot be said.[4] In 302 A.D. Diocletianus, alarmed by unfavourable omens, which the priests attributed to the presence of Christians, required his whole retinue to sacrifice on pain of being scourged, and wrote to the commanding officers that soldiers should be required to sacrifice and, if they would not obey, dismissed from the service.[5] The following winter, when Galerius was urging him to undertake a general persecution of the Christians, Diocletianus long persisted "that it would be enough if he forbade that religion only to those at court and to

---

[1] Eus *HE* VIII iv (with McGiffert's note) ; Hieron *Chron ad ann* 2317 ; Harnack *ME* 59 n, *MC* 80.　　[2] See above, p. 152.　　[3] See above, p. 153.
[4] *DCB* iii. 641b–644b ; Bigelmair 194–201 ; Harnack *ME* ii. 61 n 1, *MC* 83 ; De Jong 17 f.　　[5] Lact *Mort Pers* x. 4.

the soldiers." [1]   When the persecution actually began, Christian soldiers were its first victims.[2]   The fact that many of them suffered martyrdom is sufficiently established, and little purpose would be served by adding details concerning all the individual cases known to us. One of them, Julius, who suffered in Moesia, said to the judge : " During the time that I was, as it appears, going astray in the vain service of war (in vana militia), for twenty-seven years I never came before the judge as an offender or a plaintiff (scelestus aut litigiosus).   Seven times did I go out on a campaign (in bello), and I stood behind no one (post neminem retro steti), and I fought as well as any (nec alicuius inferior pugnavi).   The commander never saw me go wrong ; and dost thou think that I, who had been found faithful in the worse things, can now be found unfaithful in the better ? " [3] Other soldier-martyrs were Marcianus and Nicander in Moesia (or Italy),[4] Dasius, also in Moesia,[5] Nereus and Achilleus, apparently at Rome,[6] Tarakhos in Cilicia,[7] Ferreolus, a military tribune, at Vienna in Gaul,[8] Theodorus of Tyrus at Amasia in Pontus,[9] and Seleukos of Cappadocia at Caesarea.[10]   In 303 A.D. a revolt broke

---

[1] Lact *Mort Pers* xi. 3.

[2] Eus *HE* VIII i. 8 ; Epiphanios *Haeres* lxviii. 2 (Migne *PG* xlii. 185) (some of them, like some of the clergy, gave way and sacrificed).

[3] See the *Acta Julii* in *Anal Bolland* x. 50 ff. reprinted by Harnack in *MC* 119-121.   An older edition is given by Ruinart (569 f).   Another Christian soldier had been martyred just before Julius, and when he went to his death, a third was awaiting sentence.

[4] Ruinart 571-573 ; cf Harnack *ME* ii. 62 n 4.

[5] *DCB* i. 789b ; Harnack *ME* ii. 62 n 5, *MC* 83 n 5 ; Bigelmair 192 f.

[6] See above, pp. 153 f.

[7] Ruinart 451 ff ; Harnack *C* ii. 479 f ; *DCB* iv. 781 : see above, p. 153.

[8] Ruinart 489 ff ; *DCB* ii. 506b.   [9] Ruinart 506-511 ; *DCB* iv. 956 f.

[10] Eus *Mart* xi. 20 ff (see above, p. 153).   I pass by the doubtful story of the ' quattuor coronati,' four soldiers who are said to have been flogged to death at Rome for refusing to sacrifice (*DCA* i. 461 f ; *DCB* iv. 702 f ; Bigelmair 328-330, Harnack *C* ii. 478 n 2).   It is just possible that Getulius and Amantius, the husband and brother-in-law of Symphorosa,

out in Melitene and Syria, and Diocletianus suspected that the Christians were at the bottom of it, and it is possible that his suspicions were not altogether without foundation.[1] We know that the Christians of Armenia, when the Emperor Maximinus Daza tried to force them to abandon their Christianity, took up arms and defeated him.[2]

There must have been large numbers of Christians in the armies of Constantinus and Licinius in their campaigns against Maxentius and Maximinus Daza. Pachomius, later famous as a monk, served in the war against Maxentius, and was won to Christianity by the love which his Christian fellow-soldiers showed to himself and others.[3] The Constantinian troops were witnesses of the professed adherence of their great leader to the Christian faith just before the battle of the Milvian Bridge, and actually bore in that battle the sign of the cross upon their shields and in their standards: they took part in the bloodshed of the battle, and doubtless joined in their leader's confident boast that he had conquered by virtue of that same sign.[4] The campaign of Licinius against Daza, after his meeting with Constantinus at Milan, would enlist Christian sympathy as warmly as did that of Constantinus against Maxentius. Both conflicts were regarded, not unnaturally, as

who are said to have been military tribunes under Hadrianus and to have suffered martyrdom for refusing to sacrifice, were really among the soldier-martyrs of the great persecution under Diocletianus (see above, pp. 100 f). It is also barely possible that Albanus, the proto-martyr of Britain, was martyred about this time and was a soldier (Workman, *Persecution in the Early Church*, p. 271 ; *DCB* i. 69 f). Other soldier-martyrs of minor importance and questionable historicity are mentioned by Bigelmair (192–194) and Harnack (*MC* 84 n 3).

[1] Eus *HE* VIII vi. 8.   [2] Eus *HE* IX viii. 2, 4.

[3] *DCB* iv. 170b ; Harnack *ME* ii. 63 n 1, *MC* 85.

[4] Eus *HE* IX ix. 1–12, *Vit Const* i. 26–31, 37–41, iv. 19–21 ; Lact *Mort Pers* xliv.

struggles between Christianity and Paganism. Licinius himself prescribed for his soldiers a form of prayer, which was monotheistic, if not overtly Christian, in tone.[1] His victory would naturally attract additional Christian favour and support.[2] We do not know how far Christian soldiers were implicated in the bloody acts of vengeance—the massacres, tortures, and murders—that marked his triumph.[3] Later in his reign, between 315 and 322 A.D., Licinius relapsed into paganism, and required the soldiers in his army to sacrifice on pain of being degraded and dismissed the service. A number of martyrdoms resulted.[4] The final war between Licinius and Constantinus was again a war between Paganism and Christianity, and ended in a decisive triumph for the latter.[5]

Reserving for Part IV all discussion of the position finally attained through the ascendancy of Constantinus and all attempt to summarize the movements of Christian thought and practice which we have been studying, we may bring this section to a close with a word or two on the question of the numbers of Christians in the army

[1] Lact *Mort Pers* xlvi. Harnack regards this act of Licinius as showing how widespread Christianity must have been in his army (*MC* 89 f).

[2] Eus *HE* IX x. 3.

[3] Eus *HE* IX x. 4 (destruction of Daza's army), xi. 3 (all his favoured partizans slain), 4 (a few examples out of many given), 5 f (torture and death of Theoteknos and others at Antioch, cf *PE* 135cd), 7 f (Daza's children and relatives slain) ; Lact *Mort Pers* xlvii. 2–4 (immense slaughter of Daza's troops), l. 2 f (death of Candidianus, son of Galerius, who had put himself unsuspectingly in Licinius' hands), 4 (Licinius slays Severianus, son of the late Emperor Severus), 6 (he slays Maximus, the eight-year-old son, and the seven-year-old daughter, of Daza, after throwing their mother into the river Orontes), li (Valeria, widow of Galerius, and her mother Prisca, caught at Thessalonica, beheaded, and their bodies cast into the sea). To the commission of such acts as these did those believers who took up arms under this Christian Emperor render themselves liable !

[4] Eus *HE* X viii. 10, *Vit Const* i. 54. It is to this period (320 A.D.) that the legend of the forty soldiers martyred at Sebaste in Armenia belongs (cf *DCB* ii. 556 f; De Jong 33 f).   [5] Eus *Vit Const* ii. 16 f.

during these closing years of our period. In the unfortunate absence of any definite statistics, we have to content ourselves with a few vague statements. It is clear that there were more soldiers in the armies at the end than in the middle of the third century, and that Constantinus' accession to power increased the number still further. We may perhaps conjecture that before the persecution there was a larger percentage of Christians in the army of Constantinus, the tolerant Emperor of the West, than in those of the southern and eastern Emperors, though of this we cannot be sure, and the comparatively larger numbers of Christians in the eastern than in the western empire would tend to put the position the other way round. It is doubtless true that there were 'many' soldiers in the legions of Diocletianus and Galerius round about 300 A.D.; but what does 'many' mean? Figures are, of course, out of our reach; but when we consider that these two emperors endeavoured to purge all the Christians out of their army, we cannot imagine that the percentage of Christians could have been very high. No sovereign readily deprives himself of a tenth, or even of a twentieth part of his military power. Furthermore, as we shall see presently, Christian opinion, even at this date, was still very far from being unanimous as to the propriety of military service for Christians. A good deal of caution is necessary in accepting some of the phrases in which the state of affairs is at times described.[1]

[1] Harnack is on the whole cautious, but is a little inclined to over-estimate the evidence (see his remarks quoted above, p. 237 n 5 and 242 n 1, and cf. *MC* 83, 87). Cf Westermarck, *The Origin and Development of the Moral Ideas*, i. 346 (" the number of Christians enrolled in the army seems not to have been very considerable before the era of Constantine ") ; De Jong 26 (" this is certain, that the Christians in the army were as yet only a small minority ").

PART IV

SUMMARY AND CONCLUSION

An attempt must now be made to gather together the scattered threads of the foregoing records and to present something in the nature of a general summary of the whole question. We saw at the outset that Jesus adopted for himself and enjoined upon his followers principles of conduct which, inasmuch as they ruled out as illicit all use of violence and injury against others, clearly implied the illegitimacy of participation in war, and that it was for this reason that he resisted the temptation to establish the Kingdom of God by the use of arms. We saw that his principles were meant to guide the conduct, not of the whole of unredeemed humanity all at once, but that of the growing group of his own followers as members of the Kingdom, that these principles of so-called 'non-resistance' had their positive counterpart in the power of love to overcome sin in others and did not reduce those who adopted them to helpless cyphers in the conflict against evil, but on the contrary made them more efficient units in that conflict. We saw too that the various pleas that have been put forward with a view to emancipating the Christian disciple from compliance with these principles —as, that they are meant to refer only to the inner disposition or spirit and not to the outward actions, or that they are counsels of perfection practicable only in a perfect world, or that they affect only the personal and private conduct of the disciple and not his duties as a member of society, or that they are an interim-ethic which is invalidated by the existence of historical conditions which Jesus did not foresee—all rest on various easily demonstrated misapprehensions.

The early Christians took Jesus at his word, and understood his inculcations of gentleness and non-resistance in their literal sense. They closely identified their religion with peace ; they strongly condemned war for the bloodshed which it involved ; they appropriated to themselves the Old Testament prophecy which foretold the transformation of the weapons of war into the implements of agriculture ; they declared that it was their policy to return good for evil and to conquer evil with good. With one or two possible exceptions no soldier joined the Church and remained a soldier until the time of Marcus Aurelius (161–180 A.D.). Even then, refusal to serve was known to to be the normal policy of the Christians—as the reproaches of Celsus (177–180 A.D.) testify. In the time of Tertullianus (say 200–210 A.D.), many soldiers had left the army on their conversion ; and his writings are the earliest record we possess of any Christians joining the army when already converted. While a general distrust of ambition and a horror of contamination by idolatry entered largely into the Christian aversion to military service, the sense of the utter contradiction between the work of imprisoning, torturing, wounding, and killing, on the one hand, and the Master's teaching on the other, constituted an equally fatal and conclusive objection. The Church-Order framed probably by

Hippolutos of Rome early in the third century and widely circulated in the East required magistrates and soldiers to abandon their calling before baptism, and excommunicated the Christian who insisted on joining the army. Origenes, the finest thinker the Church possessed for many generations, the man who was exempt from those crude eschatological notions which are generally represented as the context in which all early Christian utterances on social duty are to be read, took it for granted that Christians generally refused to serve in the army, and that they did so, not in fear of idolatrous contamination, which does not seem to have been a difficulty when he wrote (248 A.D.), but on the score of bloodshed ; and he defended them for doing so in a series of acute arguments that have never since been answered. Cyprianus, a highly influential and thoroughly loyal Churchman, appears to have held the same views on the matter as his 'master' Tertullianus. Arnobius almost certainly disapproved of Christians fighting, and his contemporary Lactantius (early fourth century) unequivocally pleaded for the same conclusion. No Church writer before Athanasios ventured to say that it was not only permissible, but praiseworthy, to kill enemies in war, without the qualification—expressed or implied—that he was speaking of pagans only.[1]

While the application of Jesus' teaching to the question of military service was in a way unmistakable, and was in fact generally made in the way that has just

---

[1] The words of Athanasios are quoted below, p. 257 n 1. His statement is perfectly general, and doubtless was meant to apply to Christians as well as pagans. It cannot therefore be put on the same level as Origenes' phrase "those who are righteously serving as soldiers" (see above, p. 135), which obviously applied only to the pagan soldiers of the Emperor.

been described, it is nevertheless true that the conditions in which the early Christians were placed did not in many localities call for any such application for a very long time. Jews and slaves were not enrolled at all in the Roman army. The Emperors (who were legally entitled to fill their legions by conscription)—not to mention the Herodian princes and the Jewish Temple-authorities—could normally get all the soldiers they wanted by means of voluntary enlistment; hence the chances of a Christian being pressed into military service against his will were practically nil. This position of affairs meant that for the vast bulk of Christians in the earliest times, the question as to the legitimacy or otherwise of their entering the army simply did not arise; the mind of the Church, while in full possession of the pertinent teaching of Jesus, had for a long time no occasion to make a definite application of it to this particular question or to lay down a definite ruling in regard to it. There was thus a certain unguardedness, a certain immaturity of reflection, which, besides accounting for the silence of early Christian authors on the point, helped to make room for various compromises and commitments.

For during this embryonic and quiescent stage of Christian ethical thought there were certain other factors at work, which militated against a clear pronouncement on the illegitimacy of the use of arms by Christians. To begin with, warfare stood on a different footing from other pagan customs which it was quite easy for the Church to condemn and reject without compromise. It was unlike adultery, in that it was esteemed and honoured by pagans, and not condemned: it was unlike idolatry, in that it concerned only a few, and not members of society in general. It was inseparably bound up with the police system by which law and order were maintained ; and the severity of the Christian judgment against it was thus mitigated by its association with that against which the Christian objection was not so easily felt or framed. Then again, there were various connections in which the Christians themselves thought of war without any admixture of repulsion or censure. They were fond of speaking of the Christian life itself as a warfare and of themselves as soldiers of Christ. Scripture taught them to think with reverence and esteem of the warriors of old as men acting with the approval and under the guidance of God. Many of them looked forward to a great military triumph of Christ over his enemies at the end of the age. In the meantime, they could think of war as a means of divine chastisement : they regarded the great victories of the Romans over the Jews in 67–71 A.D. as a divine punishment of the latter for their treatment of Christ. They were taught to think of the Emperor as appointed by God for the purpose of checking sin and maintaining order—tasks which they knew he could not fulfil without using soldiers. We have already examined in detail all these Christian aspects of war and seen that none of them, when rightly understood, contained anything inconsistent with the most rigid abstention of the Christians themselves from the use of arms. At the same time, it is easy to see that these lines of thought must have predisposed many Christians to miss the essential point when they came to consider the question of their own personal conduct. The various complications just enumerated and the absence of a unanimous or authoritative ruling on the point combined to render the issue far less clear to many than it would otherwise have been. This, of itself, meant that at any time after the inception of Christianity, the existence of Christian soldiers was at least a possibility.

Several other factors contributed to facilitate the actualization of this possibility. Not only was the question in some respects a complicated one ; but many members of the Christian Church were, as we know, of a very simple, unintellectual, and unreflective type of mind, and shunned on principle anything in the nature of clear dialectics. Such people were peculiarly liable, in that day as in this, to draw illogical conclusions touching their conduct as Christians from Old Testament wars or from Paul's use of military similes. As a matter of fact, we learn from Tertullianus, that the Christian soldiers of his time justified their position, not by any public-spirited appeals to the obvious needs of society,[1] but by references—often of an extremely puerile kind—to Old Testament precedents. They quoted not only the wars of Joshua and the Israelites, but Moses' rod, Aaron's buckle, and John the Baptist's leather belt, just as Christians who wished to attend the circus appealed to David's example in dancing before the ark and to Elijah as the charioteer of Israel.[2]

---

[1] Troeltsch represents the advocates of compromise in the third century as wiser than they really were, in speaking of " compromises and compositions," which recognize the necessity of these callings " (i.e. magistrates and soldiers) " for the social system, and-therefore enjoin here too continuance in the calling " (Troeltsch 124 : see above, p. 144 n 1).

[2] See above, pp. 109, 174 f. Hence Harnack's (*MC* 61) criticism of Tertullianus for refusing to treat his opponents' appeal to Scripture seriously, is only partially justified. Bigg says in another connection : " It was this . . . inability to grasp the idea of progress which led to the wholesale importation of ideas and practices from the Old Testament into the Christian Church " (*The Church's Task under the Roman Empire*, p. 27).

Another circumstance that operated in the same direction was the gradual and steady growth throughout the Church of a certain moral laxity, which engaged the serious and anxious attention of Christian leaders as early as the time of Hermas (140 A.D.) and had become an acute problem by the time of Pope Kallistos (216–222 A.D.) : this abatement of the primitive moral rigour would naturally assist the process of conformity to the ways of the world.[1]   The same too would be the effect of the gradual waning of the eschatological hope, which, while far from constituting the true ground of the Christian refusal of military service, was yet with many a main plea for their general aloofness from worldly life.[2]   And not only was the eschatological hope itself waning, but even in circumstances where it was still powerful, the Christian was reminded of the Apostolic counsel : " Let everyone remain in the calling wherein he was called "[3]—a ruling which had not yet received in any definite form the limitation which it obviously needed.   The converted soldier was the more willing to give himself the benefit of this ruling, inasmuch as his withdrawal from the army on the ground of his change of religion was a process attended with no little difficulty and danger.[4]   Finally, Christianity was characterized by several features, such as monotheism, absolutism, universalism, use of military language, wars in Scripture, and so on, which would naturally appeal to the military mind.[5]

There were therefore quite a large number of factors

---

[1] De Jong 26: "the increasing worldliness of Christendom had naturally resulted in an increased number of Christian soldiers."

[2] Harnack *ME* ii. 53 ; Troeltsch 111 n.

[3] Harnack *ME* ii. 52, *MC* 49 f.

[4] Bigelmair 177–179.   [5] Harnack *ME* ii. 53 n 1, *MC* 54 f.

at work, which combined to facilitate the conversion of
soldiers to Christianity and their continuance in military
life after their conversion, despite the fact that such a
state of affairs conflicted in reality with the ethical
demands made by the Church. The anomaly of their
position was easily overlooked by the men themselves,
who had become inured to their grim duties and had all
their lives regarded the profession of arms as honourable. Most of the considerations helping to justify their
position to themselves would also help to secure toleration for it in the eyes of their fellow-Christians; and the
inclination of these latter to disapprove would also be
further checked by yet other considerations, such as the
fewness of the cases involved, at any rate in early times,
joy at the erection of Christ's banner in the devil's
camp,[1] distance from the battlefield and easy blindness
to its horrors, and lastly, that charitable leniency which
naturally deters the Christian from objecting to a good
many acts of a co-religionist which he would not feel
justified in doing himself. It is thus that we are to
account for the omission of the Church to take a decided
line on this matter from the beginning. Apart from
the Church-Orders, the influence of which—though
probably extensive—we cannot exactly measure, we
have no extant record of any attempt being made to
compel soldier-converts to leave the army on baptism.

The admission of these few soldier-converts to the
Church sometime, let us say, in the second century,
perhaps not earlier than the reign of Marcus Aurelius,
proved to be the thin end of the wedge. It constituted
a precedent by which the judgment of the Church at
large was imperceptibly compromised. If a Christian

[1] Harnack *ME* ii. 53 n 2.

who was a soldier before conversion may remain so after it, then it follows that a Christian layman might become a soldier if he wished to. That this conclusion was drawn by the end of the second century we have already seen. If a few soldiers can be tolerated in the Church, then any number can be: if a few Christians may enlist, then any number may do so. Once the beginning has been made and allowed to pass muster, the obstacles in the way of a general reversion to a stricter standard become virtually insuperable.[1]

While all this is true, it is very easy to exaggerate and misrepresent the extent of the concession which the Church made to her soldier-members. For one thing, the absence of a definite ruling on the concrete point decades before circumstances had arisen calling for such a ruling, has been interpreted, quite erroneously, as if it implied a considered judgment, on the part of the whole Church, in the direction of conformity with the ways of the world. Thus Professor Bethune-Baker refers to the centurion of Capernaum, the soldiers baptized by John, Cornelius of Caesarea, Sergius Paulus, the soldiers who defended Paul, the command in 1 Tim to pray for kings, and the words of Paul in Rom xiii, as proving that war was sanctioned by the immediate disciples of Christ.[2] Like many others who have written on the subject, he not only makes no allowance

---

[1] " In the rapid expansion of relations and the haste of human affairs practices slide insensibly into existence and get a footing as usages, before any conscience has time to estimate them ; and when they have won the sanction of prescription, they soon shape consciences to suit them, and laugh at the moral critic as a simpleton, and hurry on to the crash ot social retribution " (Jas. Martineau, *Essays, Reviews, and Addresses*, v. 502).　　[2] B.-Baker *ICW* 16–18.

for the immaturity of Christian thought on this topic, but recognizes no distinction between what is sanctioned for the Christian and what is sanctioned for those who have not yet reached Christianity. If his argument is meant to show that the Christians of the first generation had come to the conclusion, after full consideration, that there was nothing in their Master's teaching which interfered with their own participation in war, then the double oversight just alluded to must be held to invalidate the argument. The attitude of laissez-faire, to which he alludes, was the attitude of those who had not yet realized that there was a problem to be solved : it is inadequate as an index even to the convictions and practice of the apostolic age, and still more so as a basis for modern Christian ethics. Bigelmair's account of the early Christian position embodies what may well have been the plea of some of the most unintellectual of the early Christian apologists for war. He regards the abolition of war as one of the ideals foreshadowed in the Sermon on the Mount, but as unattainable even in our own day and much more so in the time of the early Church. " Besides," he says, " in the struggle for it the individual is almost powerless." From this he concludes that the apostolic dictum " Let everyone remain in the condition in which he was called " was regarded as applying to soldiers, and that that is why we find Christian soldiers in the earliest times.[1] But if the fact that a certain calling cannot yet be abolished because the world is imperfect is sufficient to justify a Christian in pursuing it, then it is difficult to see why the sale of intoxicants, and prostitution, and even highway robbery, should not be regarded as permissible

[1] Bigelmair 164–166.

Christian vocations.[1] It is probable that there were in the early Church those who argued as Bigelmair does, but the argument is none the less radically unsound, and furthermore unrepresentative of the normal Christian habit of mind, both in regard to behaviour in general— for the early Church was very sensitive as to the rightfulness of the callings pursued by her members—and in regard to the particular question we are considering.

But apart from misinterpretations due to treating the silence or the laissez-faire attitude of the early Christians (which as we have seen arose largely from the immaturity of the problem and of the minds that had to solve it) as if it were the mature and deliberate judgment of men long familiar with the ins and outs of the question, we find even in the best modern authors a striking tendency to overestimate the degree of approval that was given by the Church to those of her members who took arms. Thus Bestmann, speaking of Origenes, says : " In regard to military service, his Church thought differently from her apologist."[2] Bethune-Baker: "The Christian society of the time found no cause of complaint in the fact of its members serving in the legions."[3] Bigelmair : Tertullianus " may very well have stood quite alone in his circle, somewhat as the soldier, who lays aside the crown, . . . is the only one of his many comrades."[4] Harnack : " As for the rigorous party, they hardly made anything of their prohibitions. . . . But these rigorists effected no change whatever in the actual situation "[5] :

---

[1] Cf Shakespeare, *King Henry IV*, Part I, I ii. 115:

> *Prince.* " I see a good amendment of life in thee; from praying to purse-taking."
> *Falstaff.* " Why, Hal, 'tis my vocation, Hal; 'tis no sin for a man to labour in his vocation."

[2] Bestmann ii. 295.　　　　　　　[3] B.-Baker *ICW* 25.
[4] Bigelmair 180.　　　　　　　　[5] Harnack *ME* ii. 53, 57.

" these injunctions of the moralists were by no means followed in the third century,"[1] Cunningham: "Military service was uncongenial to Christians, but was not regarded as in itself wrong." [2]   All this fits in well enough with one set of facts, but is flagrantly out of keeping with another set. It underrates, in the first place, the immense compromises to which the Christian soldier was committed by his position. Apart from all question of contact with idolatry and special temptations to which his place in the army exposed him, he had not only to take the lives of his fellow-men in the indiscriminate conflicts of the battle-field and to scourge and torture prisoners in the judgment-courts, but he was not even allowed to use his own discretion as to whether this severe treatment was justified in any given circumstances : for his military oath obliged him to inflict it, not when he felt it was needed, but whenever his superior officer—usually a pagan, and possibly a cruel and unjust man as well—thought fit to order him to do so. It is impossible to believe that the early Church swallowed this enormous compromise as easily as these modern authors would have us believe.

That as a matter of actual historical fact the Church did not do so, there is abundant evidence to prove— evidence to which the statements just quoted give far too little weight. The view usually taken is that the Church as a whole sided from the first with the soldiers, and that the authors who took a different line were individual extremists, mere voices crying in the wilderness, to whom nobody paid much attention. The reverse of this would be nearer the truth. The Christian soldiers of the time of Tertullianus were evidently under

[1] Harnack *MC* 73.　　　　　　[2] Cunningham 252.

the necessity of defending their position, and the way in which they seem to have done it does not enhance our respect for their clear-mindedness. No Christian author of our period undertook to show that Christians might be soldiers. The Church-Order of the third century forbade them to be so. Celsus, Tertullianus, Hippolutos, Origenes, Cyprianus, and Lactantius, all testify to the strength of the Christian objection to military service. If it is allowable to speak at all of a general position taken by the early Church in this matter, it will be that of the stricter rather than that of the laxer party to which we shall have to apply the term.

It is generally thought that, with the accession of Constantinus to power, the Church as a whole definitely gave up her anti-militarist leanings, abandoned all her scruples, finally adopted the imperial point of view, and treated the ethical problem involved as a closed question.[1] Allowing for a little exaggeration, this is broadly speaking true. The sign of the cross of Jesus was now an imperial military emblem, bringing good fortune and victory. The supposed nails of the cross, which the Emperor's mother found and sent to him, were made into bridle-bits and a helmet, which he used in his military expeditions.[2] In 314 A.D. the Synod of Arelate (Arles) enacted a canon which, if it did not, as many suppose, threaten with excommunication Christian soldiers who insisted on quitting the army, at least left military service perfectly free and open to Christians.[3] Athanasios, the 'father of orthodoxy,'

[1] Bigelmair 201 ; Harnack *MC* 44 f, 87 ff, 91 f ; De Jong 28.
[2] Sokrates, *Eccles Hist* i. 17.
[3] *Can Arel* 3 : De his qui arma projiciunt in pace, placuit abstineri eos a communione. Possible meanings are (1) the obvious one, excommuni-

declared that it was not only lawful, but praiseworthy, to kill enemies in war [1]; Ambrosius of Milan spoke similarly, if less baldly [2]; while Augustinus defended the same position with detailed arguments.[3] In 416 A.D. non-Christians were forbidden to serve in the army.[4]

Historians have not failed to notice, and in some cases to deplore, the immense compromise to which the Church was committed by her alliance with Constantinus. Thus Dean Milman says : " And so for the

cating those who lay down their arms in time of peace, those who do so in time of war being punished by the military and so not coming under the Church's jurisdiction at all (Dale 238 f, 281) ; (2) similar, but referring the peace to that now existing between Empire and Church (Harnack *MC* 87 ff) ; (3) taking arma projicere as = arma conjicere in alium, and referring the Canon to the gladiatorial games, as *Can* 4 deals with charioteers and *Can* 5 with actors (so Hefele 186 ; Bigelmair 182 ; and— fully and strongly De Jong 28 ff). Even on the last interpretation, the Canon implicitly permits Christians to use weapons in war-time. How far the decisions of this Synod were regarded as generally binding seems doubtful (Hefele 182 ; De Jong 28 n).

[1] *Letter to Ammonios* or *Amun* (Migne *PG* xxvi. 1173) : "We shall find in other things that happen in life differences of a certain kind existing. For instance, it is not lawful to kill ($\phi o \nu \varepsilon \dot{\upsilon} \varepsilon \iota \nu$) ; but to destroy opponents in war is lawful and worthy of praise. Thus those who distinguish themselves in war are counted worthy of great honours, and pillars are erected proclaiming their achievements. So that the same (act) in one respect and when unseasonable is not lawful, in another respect and when seasonable is permitted and allowed."

[2] *Exposition of S. Luke*, ii. 77 (Migne *PL* xv. 1580) : John the Baptist tells "soldiers not to make a false accusation, not to demand booty, teaching that pay has been assigned to the military for this purpose, lest, while subsistence is being sought for, a plunderer should be going about. But these and others are the precepts peculiar to the several duties (of life)," but all are required to be merciful. *De Officiis Ministrorum*, I xxvii. 129 (Migne *PL* xvi. 61) : "It will be clear that these and other virtues are related to one another. Thus for instance the bravery which guards the fatherland in war from the barbarians or defends the weak at home or (one's) allies from robbers, is full of justice," etc.

[3] Migne *PL* xxxiii. 186 f, 531 f, 854 f, xlii. 444 ff. I owe these quotations (notes 1–3) to De Jong (50–54) : cf also, for Augustinus, Gibb in *British Quarterly Review*, lxxiii. 83 ; Westermarck, *The Origin and Development of the Moral Ideas*, i. 347.

[4] *Codex Theodosianus* XVI x. 21.

first time the meek and peaceful Jesus became a God of battle, and the cross, the holy sign of Christian redemption, a banner of bloody strife.[1] This irreconcilable incongruity between the symbol of universal peace and the horrors of war, in my judgment, is conclusive against the miraculous or supernatural character of the transaction," viz. Constantinus' vision of the cross before the battle of the Milvian Bridge. Milman adds in a footnote : " I was agreeably surprised to find that Mosheim concurred in these sentiments, for which I will readily encounter the charge of Quakerism." Then follows a quotation from Mosheim. The text above continues : " Yet the admission of Christianity, not merely as a controlling power, and the most effective auxiliary of civil government (an office not unbecoming its divine origin), but as the animating principle of barbarous warfare, argues at once the commanding influence which it had obtained over the human mind, as well as its degeneracy from its pure and spiritual origin." [2] Lecky remarks : " When a cross was said to have appeared miraculously to Constantine, with an inscription announcing the victory of the Milvian bridge ; when the same holy sign, adorned with the sacred monogram, was carried in the forefront of the Roman armies ; when the nails of the cross . . . were converted by the emperor into a helmet, and into bits for his war-horse, it was evident that a great change was passing over the once pacific spirit of the Church."[3] Bigelmair observes : " It was a long way from the cross, at the foot of which Roman soldiers had once cast lots for the garment of the Jewish misleader of the people,

---

[1] H. H. Milman, *History of Christianity*, ii. 287.
[2] *op cit* 288.   [3] Lecky ii. 250.

to the cross which hovered at the head of the Roman legions as a military standard." [1]

But while the greatness and importance of this historic decision are unquestionable, we must be careful not to imagine that the capitulation of the Church to the demands of the State was more complete or decisive than was actually the case. An important piece of evidence in this connection is the existence of the various Church-Orders. Without repeating all that has already been said in regard to them, it may be observed that 'The Testament of our Lord,' which forbids a soldier to be baptized unless he leaves the service, and forbids a Christian to become a soldier on pain of excommunication, was compiled in Syria or south-eastern Asia Minor not earlier than the middle of the fourth century.[2] The Egyptian Church-Order, which lays down the same ruling, with the modification that, if a soldier has been received into membership and is commanded to kill, he is not to do it, and if he does he is to be rejected, is usually thought to belong to the first half of the fourth century.[3] The 'Hippolytean Canons,' in their present form, introduce further relaxations, but are of very uncertain, probably still later, date. The Apostolic Constitutions, in which the old stringency is really abandoned, are not earlier than the last quarter of the fourth century.[4] The existence of these Church-Orders is conclusive proof that in large sections of the Christian community, the decision taken by official Christendom, as seen for instance in the

---

[1] Bigelmair 8.   [2] Cooper and Maclean 41–45.
[3] See above, p. 120. Even if the Egyptian Church-Order be the work of Hippolutos himself, it was clearly regarded as authoritative long after his date.   [4] Maclean 146, 149.

Canons of the Synod of Arelate, was not accepted.[1]
Testimony is borne to the same effect from several
other quarters. 'The Disputation of Arkhelaos with
Manes,' a composition belonging probably to the second
quarter of the fourth century, opens with an episode,
one feature of which is the rejection of the military belt
by a large number of soldiers at Carchar in Meso-
potamia, on being converted to Christianity through
the generosity of a certain Marcellus, who ransomed a
crowd of captives from them.[2]　Then we have the
martyrdom of Theogenes in Phrygia, under Licinius,
for refusing—in the manner of Maximilianus—to allow
himself to be enrolled in the legions[3]; the sudden
decision of the revered St. Martinus of Tours to leave
the army the day before a battle (he met the taunt of
cowardice by offering to stand unarmed in front of the
ranks)[4]; the similar step taken later by his friend, St.
Victricius, afterwards archbishop of Rouen[5]; the letter

----

[1] Bigelmair says, à propos of the relaxation : "Time and circumstances
demanded their rights" (172) ; "No generally binding force belonged to
Church-Orders of this kind ; but they clearly exhibit the dispositions
which prevailed in wide circles" (173) : cf De Jong 39.

[2] The *Acta Archelai* are in Routh v. 36 ff (esp. pp. 37 f) ; ET in
ANCL xx. 272 ff.　For the date, cf Harnack *C* ii. 163 f : we need not
imagine that the story is necessarily true, but, as Harnack says, it is "yet
not without value" (*MC* 84 n, *ME* ii. 63 n 1).

[3] His Acta are quoted at length by De Jong 34–38.　Baronius
(*Martyrologium Romanorum*, Jan 2, note e, p. 8) records the martyrdom
of Marcellinus, a youth executed by Licinius, as Baronius says, "non odio
militiae . . . sed quod . . . Licinius suos milites litare praecepisset."
Whether that was the only reason in this case we do not know.　Licinius
did persecute his Christian soldiers.　Those who left his service permanently were treated with indulgence by Constantinus (Eus *Vit Const*
ii. 33) ; those who had left and then rejoined were penalized by the
Council of Nicaea as 'lapsi' (Hefele 417 ff ; Harnack *MC* 91).

[4] *DCB* iii. 839b ; De Jong 40–42.　De Jong also draws attention (48 f)
to the fact that the popularity of the Emperor Julianus (361–363 A.D.)
with the army and the support it gave him in his reversion to paganism
presuppose a comparatively small proportion of Christians in it.

[5] *DCB* iv. 1140b ("He . . . quitted military service for conscience'
sake, a desertion which entailed such maltreatment as nearly lost him his

of St. Paulinus of Nola (about 400 A.D.), persuading a friend to do the same[1]; the strictures passed by St. Gregorios of Nazianzus and by Khrusostomos (St. Chrysostom) on the military character[2]; and lastly the opinion of St. Basilios the Great that those who had shed blood in war should abstain from communion for three years.[3] It would carry us beyond the scope of our subject to go further in this direction; but enough has been said to show that the decision to which the leaders and the majority of the Church were committed by the patronage of Constantinus was very far from winning the immediate and unanimous assent of Christendom. It is evident that in many quarters the settlement was accepted only gradually and with an uneasy conscience.

It was in the nature of the case that this should be so. For the settlement was itself the result, not of any attempt to solve the ethical problem on its merits, but of a more or less fortuitous combination of circumstances. During the period when the conditions of life in Empire and Church relieved all but a very few of the need of making a personal decision, with the result that the problem in its different bearings dawned on the Christian mind only fragmentarily and by slow degrees —during that period, I say, the simplemindedness of some, the worldliness of others, and the charitable tolerance—not necessarily the approval—of the rest, were already silently determining what the result was to be. The consequence was that when the triumph of

---

life "); De Jong 42-46 (Victricius' motive, in part at least, was 'the aversion to bloodshed'—arma sanguinis abiecisti).

[1] Migne *PL* lxi. 300 ff; De Jong 47 f.
[2] Migne *PG* xxxv. 608 f, lviii. 590 f.   [3] Migne *PG* xxxii, 681.

Constantinus suddenly called upon the Church to come down definitely on one side of the fence or the other, she found that a free decision was no longer open to her. Her joy at the deliverance Constantinus had wrought for her was so great that it put her off her guard. She found herself compelled by the eagerness with which she had welcomed him, and by her own immaturity of thought and inconsistency of practice, to make his standards of righteousness in certain respects her own. Henceforth it was out of the question for her to insist on an ethical view and practice, on which her own mind was not completely made up, and which her great protector would inevitably regard as dangerous disloyalty to himself. Official Christianity was now committed to the sanction of war, so far as the practical conduct of Christian men as citizens was concerned, not only when they were convinced that the maintenance of righteousness demanded war—that in itself would have been a great and fundamental compromise—but in any cause, good, bad, or indifferent, for which the secular ruler might wish to fight. Further than that, the decision not only settled the practical question for the time being and doomed the dissentient voices, many and firm as they still were, to ultimate and ineffectual silence, but it tied up the freedom of Christian thought and made any unfettered discussion of the problem on its merits next to impossible for centuries to come.

The testimony of the early Church in regard to the participation of Christians in war will naturally vary very considerably in the strength of the appeal it makes to different types of Christians to-day. In view of all that we have just seen of pre-Constantinian times and in view of the subsequent history of Europe, it is difficult to resist the impression that the Church took a false step when she abandoned her earlier and more rigorous principles. How far the discovery of that mistake imposes upon Christians in these times the duty of correcting it—how far even the possibility of correcting it is still open to them—are questions on which opinion will be sharply divided. It is quite true that the Christian Church stands in a very different position from that in which she stood in the first three centuries of our era. But the question is, Is there anything in that difference, is there anything in our modern conditions, which really invalidates the testimony against war as the early Christians bore it, and as Origenes defended it? Not, we may answer, the passing away of the eschatological outlook, for the great apologia of Origenes is as independent of that outlook as any modern Christian could wish—not the development of national life and sentiment, for Christianity lifts the disciple of Christ above racial divisions and interests just as truly now, as it did then—not laws making military service compulsory, for the laws of States can never make right for the Christian what according to the higher law of the Kingdom of God is wrong for him —not his obligations to society, for these obligations he already renders in overflowing measure by the power and influence of his life and prayers as a Christian— not the breaking forth of high-handed aggression and tyranny and outrage, for these things were continually breaking forth in those early times, and the Christian now, as then, has his own appointed method of curing them, a method more radical and effectual than the use of arms and involving him in a full measure of suffering

and self-sacrifice—not admiration for, or indebtedness
to, fellow-citizens who have risked life and limb in the
struggle for righteousness on the field of battle, for the
right thing for a man to do has to be decided by reference to his own subjective conditions, and one can fully
esteem and honour the relative good in a sub-christian
course of conduct without being thereby bound to adopt
it oneself—not our inability to discover at once the full
meaning of Jesus' teaching for our complicated social
and economic institutions, for such discovery is a
lengthy process, in which one forward step at a time
has to be taken, and unless the step is taken on each
issue as it becomes clear, no further light is to be hoped
for on the issues that are next to it in order of obscurity
and complexity—not the unreadiness of the rest of the
world to become Christian, for the Christian's work now
as then is essentially one that has to be done by those
who constitute only a portion, for the present a very
small portion, of society—not the unreadiness of the
rest of the Church to become pacific, for the individual
Christian with a true message must never wait until the
whole Church agrees with him before he lives up to it and
declares it, otherwise all promise of spiritual progress
within the Church is gone—not, finally, the offence and
unpopularity which the message evokes or the vastness
of the obstacles that lie in its path, for the best service
Christians have ever done for the world has been done
under the shadow of the world's frown and in the teeth
of the world's opposition.   Men of very varied opinions
are in agreement to-day that the Church has failed :
but the Church, unlike other religious bodies, possesses
in the personal example and guidance of her Lord an
ever ready corrective to bring her back from her aberra-

tions. As Lecky (ii. 9) tells us : "Amid all the sins and failings, amid all the priestcraft and persecution and fanaticism that have defaced the Church, it has preserved, in the character and example of its Founder, an enduring principle of regeneration." We can in fact measure the value of all the great reformative movements of Christendom — Franciscan, Lutheran, Puritan, Methodist, and so on — by the extent to which they embodied attempts to bring human life and conduct into closer conformity to the spirit and teaching of Jesus ; and conversely, we can measure the unworthiness and harmfulness of the Church's failures, for instance, the tone of her many controversies, and the great stain of persecution, by the extent to which they involved departure from the same spirit and teaching. Of those who accuse the Church of failure many will none the less still keep their faith in her and their hope for her ; and of these again some will know clearly in which direction lies the way of amendment. It is for them to pass on to the world in its confusion and to the Church in her perplexity the knowledge that the true remedy for the most crying and scandalous evil of our time—an evil beneath which the whole human race is groaning and suffering—lies in a new and closer application to thought and life of the teaching of the Prince of Peace.

"LORD, TO WHOM SHALL WE GO ?
THOU HAST THE WORDS OF ETERNAL LIFE."

INDEX

OTHER RELATED BOOKS BY SEABURY

THE RISK OF THE CROSS: Christian Discipleship in the Nuclear Age by Christopher Grannis, Arthur Laffin and Elin Schade. Foreword by Henri J. M. Nouwen. "As the countdown begins on MX missiles and neutron bombs and the debate heats up, Seabury comes along with a perfectly timed workbook . . . for groups that want to discuss . . . peace."
—*The Christian Century*
Available in paperback.

DARKENING VALLEY: A Biblical Perspective on Nuclear War by Dale Aukerman. "The most powerful book on the nuclear arms race I have read."
—*Ronald J. Sider*
Available in paperback.

RUMORS OF WAR: A Moral and Theological Perspective on the Arms Race edited by C. A. Cesaretti and Joseph T. Vitale. An exploration of the economic, political and spiritual ramifications of the arms race.
Available in paperback.